♥ Dee, this novel is for you, with all my love ♥

During my early days as a teacher at Parkland Primary School, South Wigston, I was introduced to an exchange student from Wisconsin University, who would be joining us as part of her Education Degree. I was given the task of instructing her in the dark art of primary school teaching, and a lifelong friendship between Dee Paulsen (nee Hagman) and I, was born. Being young and a little crazy (!) we had a great summer term teaching my year six class and preparing them for high school. This was in the days before the National Curriculum - when teaching was still fun. After school was out, we met with other young teachers and friends, took trips together at the weekend and generally had a ball.

Sadly, the time came for Dee to head back to the States, but we vowed to keep in touch and meet up in Sturgeon Bay, one day. Years passed - Dee met Eric Paulsen, got married, had a son, Nels and then a daughter, Annika. Dee and Eric are now grandparents to Fritz and Gus and Mika the dawg - how did that happen? Keeping our promise, we finally made it over to Sturgeon Bay to stay with the Paulsens, met their friends the Jinkins, McCluskeys, and family members (including Auntie Bev and Uncle Elv).

During that five week vacation, Dee, Dave and I embarked upon The Great American Road Trip. We travelled from Washington DC, (via the Blue Ridge Mountains of Virginia), to Gatlinburg, Nashville, Memphis, Graceland, Madison, and finally Chicago and Sturgeon Bay. All in a car with no air conditioning. Proof, if proof were needed, that we come from good pioneering stock: English, Scottish and Swedish.

When it was time for us to catch our plane back to Heathrow, I promised I would write a romance set in Wisconsin. *Take Me, I'm Yours* is that romance. It might have taken a few years longer than anticipated, but here it finally is - with our love of America, the Paulsens, and our adventures running right through it - like a stick of seaside rock.

Chapter One

India painted the white picket fence with measured strokes, taking care not to touch the flowers behind it. Wisconsin sun beat down through the thin cloth of her baseball cap and she straightened, grimacing as sweat trickled between her breasts and down her spine. Squaring her shoulders, she dipped the brush into the tin of paint. Only two more staves, then she could have that cold beer she'd promised herself.

The sound of a motorcycle drew her attention towards the ribbon of track leading up from the bay. Shading her eyes as it sped towards her, churning up the dusty red earth, she frowned. And, for the first time since arriving in Door County, became aware of how isolated her house was. Giving no sign of how vulnerable she felt, she stooped and picked up a large monkey wrench from the toolbox at her feet. Slipping it into the deep pocket of her overalls she turned to meet her unexpected visitor, a fixed smile on her face, heart hammering like crazy.

'You India Buchanan?' the rider demanded, pulling up several feet in front of her.

'That rather depends on who wants to know.'

He gunned the machine menacingly and then killed the engine, rocking the motorcycle back on to its rest. Dismounting, he walked towards her with such purpose and determination that India took several steps backwards - and then stopped. No man, no matter how threatening, was going to get the better of her. She had her monkey wrench and was prepared to use it. Let him state his purpose, then get off her land.

Despite her brave words, it wouldn't do to let him know how frightened she felt. Looking up - he was very tall, she squinted against the sun and tried to gain the measure of him. His face was shaded by a baseball cap, eyes, hidden behind aviator sunglasses, gave no clue to his identity.

'Just answer the question, lady.' Walking over to the fence he stripped off his gloves, touched the still tacky paint and glanced at her over his shoulder. In that split second, India caught the suggestion of steel in the way he held himself, obstinacy in the line of his mouth. Here was a man used to having his own way, one not easily deflected from his chosen path.

'I - I . . .' India stammered, annoyed with herself for allowing him to intimidate her. She felt for the wrench to bolster her courage but it slid through fingers wet with perspiration, fell through the hole in her overalls and landed on the red earth with a dull thud. For a long moment neither spoke, looking instead at the potential murder weapon at their feet.

'Yours?' he asked. Bending, he picked it up and with a mocking little bow, handed it back, his mouth quirking in a humourless smile.

'Thanks.'

With commendable calm, India took the wrench and put it back in the rusty tool box, snapping it shut. She was glad her head was bent because she felt rather foolish. He didn't need to be psychic to work out that she'd been prepared to use the wrench against him. The idea was preposterous - she was of average height and slightly built, whereas he was tall and looked capable of anything.

She guessed it would take more than an inexpertly wielded wrench to deflect him from his purpose. Whatever that was.

The twist to his lips showed that he thought so, too. Hooking sunglasses over the handle bars of the motorcycle, he gave India a more searching glance. As though his initial impression of her had been wrong and he was thinking on his feet. In spite of the heat, she shivered; no man had ever looked at her with such calculation. She knew men found her attractive but being regarded with such open hostility was a new experience.

Determined not to be browbeaten, she returned his calculating regard with a scornful stare. One which made plain that no man, no matter how threatening, was going to break her spirit. Unconsciously, she brought up her chin and sent him an unruffled look.

'One hundred and ten percent Buchanan, aren't you?'

He made it sound like a bad thing as he pulled the peak of his baseball cap lower to shield his eyes from the noon day sun and, she hoped, from her cool regard. 'Would you mind telling me what the hell you're doing here, lady?'

'I would have thought that was obvious.' She indicated the paint can with the toe of her trainer. Instantly, she regretted her snarky tone because he closed the distance between them in two easy strides. He was so close that she could smell the dust on his clothes, catch a hint of expensive aftershave undercut by bike oil, and see a small crescent shaped scar above his lip.

'Want to know what's obvious?'

'No. But I somehow think you're going to tell me,' India maintained her composure despite the anger pulsing from him. She wondered what she could have done to earn the wrath of this formidable stranger but had no time to give it further thought. He shook his head as though her defiant stance had made him lose his train of thought. From his expression, it seemed as if it would give him the greatest pleasure to take her by the shoulders and shake every last ounce of defiance out of her. Then the moment was gone and, taking a couple of steps back, he rubbed his hand across his eyes as if waking from a dream.

Gaining mastery over his emotions he continued. 'You're smart Mizz Buchanan, I'll give you that. You've an edge that living in New York gives a woman.'

'How did you know I . . .'

'Lived in New York? Oh, I made it my business to find out all about you.'

10

'Really? Now, look, Mr-Whoever-You-Are, I really don't have time for this, so if you wouldn't mind?' Glancing at her watch, she reminded herself he wasn't the first man who'd tried to unnerve her with a show of machismo. She'd squared up to them in the boardroom and stood her ground in the weekly team meetings at the art auction house where she worked. This man might not be wearing a suit, but he was no different.

'You don't get it, do you, even though the answer's staring you in the face?'

'Get what?'

Thrusting her hands into the pockets of her overalls she faced him down with the streetwise stare she'd perfected within one month of moving from England to New York. It got her home safe at night through the downtown areas and gave her the nerve to take the last ride on the subway.

'You've got something I want. Something I want real bad . . . and intend to have.' He glanced towards the house basking serenely in the noon day sun, then back towards her. *Now* she knew who he was . . . now it all made sense.

'And, do you always get what you want?'

'I guess I do,' he drawled, implying that she was a fool to doubt it. This time his smile was calculated to charm, win her over; but he'd left it too late. She knew who he was and hell would freeze over before she let him holler down her rain barrel!

'That much is obvious.'

To make plain that his high opinion of himself was unwarranted, she half-turned away. Nevertheless, she was

11

aware of his eyes narrowing as he treated her to a slow, scorching once over. The insulting kind which made no attempt to disguise the fact that he was assessing her qualities as a woman and sexual partner, as much as any adversary. The glance was intimate, reducing her to the level of a commodity that could be bought and sold . . . like all the other women he'd ever encountered, his cynical expression informed her.

'You could have saved yourself a visit. I've no intention of selling my family's home. Especially not to a MacFarlane,' she retorted, angered by his measured appraisal. 'Now I'll thank you to get off my land. You're a lawyer, aren't you? I'm sure I don't need to remind you of the laws of trespass. Or that possession is nine tenths of the law.'

'Oh, I'm going.' He swung his leg over the motorbike. Now it was her turn for a second look, from the taut rear in bike leathers to legs which seemed almost too long for a motorbike. She stopped short, reminding herself that he was a MacFarlane, her family's sworn enemy. This 'meeting' was merely an opening skirmish. The battle proper lay ahead and it was bound to be a long and bitter campaign. MacFarlane seemed determined to have the last word and leave her with food for thought. 'I suggest that you get yourself a good attorney Mizz Buchanan. You're going to need one.'

With that he turned the key in the ignition, rocked the bike back onto its wheels, and with a mocking little salute roared down the track towards the bay, leaving a cloud of pale red dust in his wake. It settled on India's skin and adhered itself to the newly painted picket fence.

'Damn.'

Feeling as if her legs were about to give way, India found strength enough to rush into the house. Heading for her bedroom, she looked down over the long drive which led towards the bay. He was still there, as she knew he would be, his motorcycle turned sideways on to her property as he gave it one last covetous look. Seemingly guessing that she wouldn't be able to resist watching, he mimicked his earlier mocking salute and then drove off. India waited until he headed down the coast towards Sturgeon Bay and the powerful throb of the vintage Triumph died away.

You're a Buchanan all right.

His tone had been derogatory, his look disparaging. The visit had been designed to unsettle her and let her know - should she be in any doubt - that he would be a formidable adversary. His behaviour, in spite of all the many kindnesses she'd received since moving to MacFarlane's Landing, shocked and unnerved her. It reminded her that the feud between their two families, which had festered on for the last hundred and fifty years, was still alive and kicking.

Now it was down to them - the last of the Buchanans and MacFarlanes to carry the feud forward. To end it. Clearly, MacFarlane wanted a fight and was prepared to bring it to her door. But he'd reckoned without her grit, determination and sense of family honour.

'Look all you like, MacFarlane,' she called out even though she knew he couldn't hear. 'This house will never be yours.'

Chapter Two

Logan MacFarlane rode the Triumph up his grandfather's drive and into the triple garage with practised ease. He killed the engine and revelled in the silence for a few minutes, his mind filled with the image of India Jane Buchanan squaring up to him with a monkey wrench. Like she was Barbara Stanwyck in one of those old horse operas his grandfather watched on DVD.

He gave a humourless snort. Just who did she think she was? Acting like some lady from out East and him some farmhand she hadn't quite gotten round to dismissing. She was deliberately provocative, cussed and - he searched for the English phrase - yes, hoity-toity. Grim-faced, he left baseball cap and sunglasses on the bike's seat and went into the house in search of his grandfather. He found him on the deck overlooking the lake, sitting so still that a heron, perched on the post at the end of the jetty was preening itself unperturbed. Fear gripped Logan's heart and his blood ran cold because he knew that one day he would find his grandfather sitting exactly like this - in his favourite seat, with all life gone from him.

This novel is dedicated to our 'American Family'

- the Paulsens of Sturgeon Bay, Wisconsin -

Dee, Eric, Nels, Kat, Fritz, Gus, Annika, Bobby and Mika

He shook himself. That day wasn't today and there was business to discuss.

Walking over, Logan touched his grandfather lightly on the shoulder. Without opening his eyes, his grandfather reached up and covered Logan's hand with his own. The movement sent the heron flapping across the lake, its long legs trailing in the water, like some prehistoric bird. As if it knew that Logan was the bearer of bad news and didn't want to hang around to see the old man's reaction.

'Well?' his grandfather prompted.

'Not well,' was the terse reply. He tightened his grip on the old man's bony shoulders and his heart twisted with love and concern at how fast those muscles were atrophying, leaving nothing but skin and bone. Another six months and . . . he put the thought firmly from his mind.

'Didn't think it would be,' his grandfather harrumphed with a degree of satisfaction, turning to give him an I-told-you-so look. 'Her great-aunt Elspeth will have taught her well - you can be sure of that. Buchanan women are mule-headed. And ornery,' he added, making Logan laugh at the old-fashioned word. 'Didn't manage to charm her then? Unlike those females you bring round here once to show them off - and never invite back.'

Logan ignored the comment. He knew his grandfather wanted him to get married, settle down and produce mini MacFarlanes. There was plenty of time for that - he was only thirty-three for God's sake, he had his whole life ahead of him. Didn't he? Pulling up a chair, he joined his grandfather on the deck to look out over Lake Michigan, eyes narrowing thoughtfully.

'Didn't think that charm was required in this case. I figured I could ride over, offer her a generous settlement for her great-aunt's house and bring the papers round next week for the old lady to sign. Then she could return to whatever it is she does in New York and we could finally get our inheritance back. Instead of which,' he paused, not sure if he was amused or angered by what had passed between them earlier.

'Instead of which?' his grandfather prompted, turning sideways to look at him.

'Instead of which, she threatened me with a monkey wrench.' He shrugged and his grandfather gave a dry bark of laughter.

'A monkey wrench, huh? Now that I would've paid good money to see. Little Miss Buchanan facing down Logan MacFarlane, soon-to-be Assistant District Attorney? As I said, her great-aunt will have taught her well. I take it,' he asked in a gruff voice, 'that you acted like a gentleman. At all times?'

Logan had the grace to look away, avoiding his grandfather's hawk-like scrutiny. He shrugged, 'Maybe I could have handled it better. She was . . . she was . . .' he struggled to find the words.

His grandfather cut to the chase. 'Have we a fight on our hands?' He gestured for Logan to help him out of the chair.

'I'd say so.' Logan frowned as he guided his grandfather back towards the house for his afternoon nap. Both at his grandfather's unsteadiness and how badly he'd handled his meeting with India Buchanan. He suspected he hadn't quite acted 'like a gentleman' and that his grandfather would disapprove of his method and manners. 'She was wearing coveralls and a paint-streaked baseball cap but she had a certain air about her.' He wondered what colour her hair was under that baseball cap. Recalling the fierce, challenging look in her blue eyes he was betting it was . . .

'That'd be her fancy education,' his grandfather broke in. 'Spent most of her life in some top-notch boarding school in England while her parents were posted round the world as part of the diplomatic corps, from what I've heard. Then four years at Vassar gaining a high opinion of herself and a low opinion of everyone else. You know what those damned Ivy League colleges are like?' He grabbed onto the handrail by the back door and hauled himself over the step and into the large kitchen, Logan's hand resting lightly on his back.

'Considering you paid to send me to one of the best, guess I do,' he grinned at the old man's back. 'Maybe I could've been more diplomatic. I'll do better next time.'

At that the old man span round as fast as arthritic bones would allow.

'So, there's going to be a next time?' He regarded his grandson sharply. His green eyes might be rheumy with age, but he missed nothing.

'Of course, you don't think I'm gonna let some uppity little Miss from back East tell a MacFarlane what to do, do ya?' He mimicked John Wayne, his grandfather's favourite actor, and they laughed, before each became lost in their own thoughts.

Logan imagined standing once more in front of the Buchanan residence which had one of Door County's famous lighthouses built almost in its back yard, towering over it. With its wrap round veranda and views overlooking MacFarlane's Landing and the Bay it was prime real estate. But it was more than that. It was his family's home and he wanted it back. Not for himself - his future lay in Washington, or for his parents who'd moved away years ago - but for his grandfather, for whom the feud was alive and kicking, even after all these years.

Sometimes, it seemed like the only thing which kept him going.

He watched his grandfather edge his way carefully round the kitchen, holding onto the countertop for support, making it appear that his legs were as strong as they had been fifty years ago when he'd captained the soccer team. But, in truth, John MacFarlane was fading before his grandson's eyes, although they both pretended otherwise.

Who knew how long he had left . . .

That's why Logan had made it his business to get the house back into MacFarlane hands - when his mind should have been focused on the coveted post in Washington that his grandfather had mentioned.

'Uppity little Miss from back east, huh? Logan, my boy, you've spent too many hours watching horse operas with me when you should've been out having fun. You're beginning to sound like John Wayne, know that?' Having had the same thoughts only moments earlier Logan laughed and his grandfather joined in. And, for a few seconds, he

18

was once more the strapping figure that Logan remembered from childhood. John MacFarlane - County Court Judge, famous for presiding over cases wearing thousand-dollar silver-tipped Western boots beneath his black robes. And for striding round Ephraim in a Stetson like he was the sheriff of Dry Gulch.

Everyone knew John MacFarlane and trusted him. Everyone except Elspeth Buchanan, India's great-aunt.

'Oh, I've had my share of fun, believe me.' Logan's white smile was a testament to his expensive orthodontist and memories he couldn't share, not even with his grandfather.

'I don't doubt that for a second,' John said, giving him a shrewd look. 'You're a MacFarlane, and MacFarlane men know how to live life to the full.'

'Is there any other way?' Logan parried.

'What happens in Chicago - stays in Chicago, that it?'

'You've got it in one. Now,' Logan moved the conversation along. 'I believe it's my pick tonight. How about watching Pride and Prejudice, Notting Hill or those old Bridget Jones movies you love so much?' He pulled a comical face, knowing the opposite was true. 'Something to give us some pointers on how the English think and behave? Research you might say.' His expression darkened and John - ever perceptive, picked up on it.

'You're right, son. Never leave a Buchanan believing they've had the last laugh.' He said the last with such vehemence that it triggered a bout of coughing. Logan was immediately at his grandfather's side but the hacking cough had alerted his nurse who marched into the kitchen and started fussing over the old man. John swatted her away as if she was a bothersome fly.

'Leave me alone, woman, I'm not ready to die. At least, not this afternoon. Not while a Buchanan's living in my house.' The thought seemed to anger him further and Logan, fearing for his grandfather's wellbeing, sought to distract him.

'What say we watch a movie together while your nurse prepares your medication?'

'One where the English get their asses whupped by some honest pioneers - or, even the Indians?' John asked, in a clear attempt to show his grandson that he might be old, but he still had some fire left in him. 'Set you up for round two.'

Logan groaned inwardly, knowing that meant another viewing of Mel Gibson in The Patriot - a film whose historical inaccuracies and biased coverage of the revolutionary wars made him wince every time they watched it.

But he could deny the old man nothing.

'Sure. Popcorn and soda?'

'You're kidding, boy, right? Salted nuts and Bourbon - oh, stop looking at me like that, woman,' he said to his nurse, who had tutted disapprovingly. 'The diet that goddam quack's put me on won't make me live any longer - it'll just make it seem like I am.'

'Time for your medication and your nap, Judge,' the nurse said. 'You can watch your movie later?' She looked at Logan for his support and he was quick to give it.

'Okay. Catch you later?' Logan laughed and gave his grandfather a gentle hug.

'Not if I catch you first,' the old man retorted, reaching for his hated walking frame and following the nurse to his bedroom.

After checking his watch, Logan turned on his heel and headed for the jetty, his heavy biker boots making the wooden timbers creak. Sitting down, he stripped off the boots and rolled down his leather trousers to reveal board shorts underneath. Slipping on the deck shoes he'd discarded earlier he glanced back at the house. While his grandfather slept, there was just enough time for him to take his boat onto Green Bay. Maybe get the image of India Buchanan standing on MacFarlane land with the monkey wrench in her hand out of his head. Allowing himself another grim smile, he tossed his boots and leathers to the back of his boat and leapt on board. Instinct told him that it would take all his skills as a lawyer and personal qualities as a man to plan a successful campaign against the Buchanan women.

Sailing helped him to relax, it allowed the left side of his brain the freedom to supply solutions to whatever problem was dogging him. India Buchanan definitely fell into that category - *problems to be dealt with*. MacFarlane's Landing would be back in his grandfather's possession by the end of the year, if it was the last thing he did. Time was against him so he'd better bring forward his plan to give Miss Buchanan a life lesson into the bargain - nobody messes with the MacFarlanes and gets away with it.

The feud wasn't over, it was simply entering a different phase.

Chapter Three

Later that same day, while MacFarlane was sailing his skiff across Green Bay, India sat on the swing seat on the porch rocking herself into a calmer frame of mind. MacFarlane's visit had unsettled her and she wondered if she'd bitten off more than she could chew. She'd promised her great-aunt that she'd fetch her home from hospital in Chicago, nurse her back to health - with professional help, naturally - and restore this old house to its former glory.

And, as everyone who knew her could attest - whatever India Jane Buchanan set her mind to, she usually achieved. Whether it was to study at an Ivy League University, gain a position in a top New York art auction house, or resist all attempts by her parents to make her move with them to Paris when they took up their next post.

The encounter with MacFarlane had left her feeling angry and upset, and, for once, questioning her belief in herself. Would she really be able to carry out her promise to her aunt? Pursing her lips, she stared across the lake and into the middle distance, sighing at the complexity of the task ahead. A cloud of red dust rising up from her drive brought her out of her dreams. Surely, she thought, mouth dry and heart hammering, MacFarlane wouldn't have the gall to come calling twice in one day? Then she gave herself a shake - of course he would? That's who he was. That's how the MacFarlanes operated, if her aunt's stories were to be believed. Having no useful weapon to hand, she used her hand to shield her eyes against a sky so blue it was in danger of burning her retinas. Recognising the battered old estate car bumping its way along the uneven track to the front door, she exhaled a relieved breath.

And, as the car pulled up outside her front gate, settling another coat of dust on the still tacky picket fence, she wondered if it was worth the effort required to sand down the fence in a couple of days' time and start all over again? Hmm - probably not. Mind you, it would be one way of showing a certain resident of MacFarlane's Landing that she meant business . . .

'Indy! Hi!' the doors of the wagon opened and a heavily pregnant woman got out, followed by three children. 'Okay if we use your pool, Hun? Our filter's bust and they can't fix it until tomorrow. In this heat wave - for crying out loud.'

'Of course. Go ahead, children, it's all yours.' India waved to the children as they whooped and raced round to the back of the house. Their mother, Lotte Erikson, India's near neighbour, joined her on the swing seat. It rocked alarmingly as she lowered her third-trimester weight onto its ancient rockers and got down to the real reason for her visit.

23

'I was talking to Marge. Said she saw MacFarlane riding that old motorcycle of his off your land this morning, looking madder than Hell. Although, how she knew what his expression was when he was driving at his usual breakneck speed, is beyond me. Earlier, I saw him going into his grandfather's law office in Sturgeon Bay with a box file under his arm. Didn't even bother to answer when I said good morning. He might be a fancy pants lawyer in Chicago, but this ain't Chicago and being polite to folk matters round here.' Getting off the swing seat she waddled over to the ancient cream fridge on the shady side of the porch and helped herself to a diet soda. Turning, she gave India a searching once over. 'You look kinda upset. Has he been pestering you over the house, honey?'

'Let's just say he paid me a less than neighbourly visit, and leave it at that, shall we?' India got up and guided her visitor into the kitchen where it was slightly cooler. And from where they could keep an eye on the children splashing about in the pool. India smiled to herself, Aunt Elspeth had installed the pool for the long vacations when school or university were in recess. A subtle bribe to make her stay longer in Door County, not that she needed one. She loved her great-aunt, she loved the old ramshackle house on the edge of the lake and -

'Indy, you know my opinion of him, don't you?' Lotte broke into her thoughts, struggling to find the right words to describe MacFarlane. Failing she snorted with laughter. 'Guess I can never decide whether I'm relieved that an old married lady like me is beneath his notice, or piqued because he's never given me a second glance. Or any of the other women in MacFarlane's Landing. He's very careful to keep that *side of things* well away from prying eyes and noses. But, my, he really is a hot tamale, ain't he? Not,' she gave her swelling stomach a proprietary pat, 'that a gal in my condition should be having such thoughts. Mind you, with the way my hormones are raging at the moment . . . no man's safe!'

India laughed. Lotte was so down to earth that, for the moment, she was able to forget her worries. Letting out a relieved breath, she remembered the day, over a month ago, when Lotte had arrived on the doorstep of her great-aunt's house with a bag of cherry muffins under her arm, and a brood of kids under her feet to welcome her to MacFarlane's Landing. Since then, they'd become close, and India regarded Lotte as a friend, confidante and sometime sounding board.

'Should you be out driving, Lotte? I don't want that bumpy drive to encourage Junior's early appearance. You know my phone's on the blink. And the cell phone signal's intermittent at the best of times.' India tried to change the subject; she knew Lotte was dying to find out what MacFarlane wanted. And, having found out, would relate it to half the neighbourhood - that's how the bush telegraph worked in the little community of MacFarlane's Landing. But India also knew that if she swore Lotte to secrecy she'd take any secret to the grave.

That's the kind of woman she was.

'You ought to get the house phone fixed, Indy. How're

people supposed to get in touch with you. In an emergency, say?' Lotte raised her heavy knot of blond hair off the nape of her neck and blew out her cheeks. India moved the ancient electric fan on its rusty pole closer to her pregnant friend, admiring the white-blonde hair and blue eyes which marked out her Swedish ancestry.

'I've managed all right without one so far, haven't I?' She was in no hurry to have the phone fixed, preferring to remain incommunicado and to keep her parents and everything she'd left behind in New York at bay. If she wanted to make a phone call she only had to drive into Ephraim or onto the highway where her mobile phone picked up a signal. Deftly, she changed the subject. 'Come on let's go and watch the children play and paddle in the shallow end to cool down.'

They walked through the open plan house and onto to the raised cedar wood deck at the rear which overlooked the lake. Steps from the deck led down to the swimming pool, gloriously cool in the scorching summer heat. Even the chemical smell of the chlorine was inviting and the water reflected the cloudless sky, making India feel she was in Tuscany or somewhere more exotic than Door County, Wisconsin.

At the back of the property a lighthouse cast its long shadow over the pool and dominated the shoreline. Door County was famous for its many historic lighthouses and this one, joined to her aunt's ramshackle Victorian house like a Siamese twin, was one of the oldest. Its shaft acted like the gnomon on a sundial, marking the hours on different parts of India's great-aunt's property as the sun wheeled across the sky. India was becoming expert at guessing the time from where the shadow fell at different times of day, and that pleased her. It made her feel part of the place, as if she truly belonged, and that there was more to her than simply being an intern in a fancy-schmancy New York art auction house.

'Do you and the children want to stay for tea?' India asked, shrugging off her introspection and suddenly in the mood for uncomplicated company; something to distract her from thoughts of MacFarlane, and her great-aunt's illness.

Lotte laughed. 'I love the way you say that. TEA. It's so British. TEA.' She pronounced, imitating India's accent. 'Like the Queen.'

'Know her well, do you? And I love the way you say British and not Brit-ish.'

'Just *adorable*,' they chimed together, India mimicking Lotte's Wisconsin accent.

'Well, do you wanna?' India asked. She'd never considered herself exotic - just ordinary. A girl with an American father and an English mother, someone who'd graduated summa cum laude in History of Art at Vassar. Her English accent had gone unremarked upon in cosmopolitan New York, but fascinated the inhabitants of this narrow peninsula jutting out into Lake Michigan. It marked her out, made her seem different from the rest.

Lotte glanced at her watch and sighed.

'Better not. After their swim, the kids'll want to watch their favourite shows. And I don't wanna be the one to tell them you haven't got a TV. Time you got one, by the way, then I could stay longer. For tea - and other such quaint English customs. Scones and - crumpets?' She tried the words, experimentally and they both laughed. 'We've got a spare TV in the den, I'll get Gerry to bring it over after work some night. Honest to God I don't know how you survive without a television, dishwasher or air conditioning, Indy.'

'There speaks a pioneer woman. I suppose you wouldn't have embarked on the Oregon Trail without finding out if cable had made it to the west coast ahead of your wagon train.' India laughed and fetched towels from the cupboard for the children to dry themselves.

'Sassy,' Lotte remarked, tapping India's cheek good-naturedly before retrieving a dog-eared handbill from the pocket of her maternity shorts. 'Damned hormones - nearly made me forget. There's a picnic at the Laurenson's Saturday week in aid of the Children's Hospice. It could be my last public appearance before Junior's debut so I hope you'll come. All the ladies have to dress up a picnic basket to be auctioned off to raise funds for the Hospice.'

India pulled a face. She knew that by the weekend MacFarlane's visit would be the talk of the neighbourhood and she wasn't in the mood for jokes made at her expense. No matter how good humoured. Everyone knew chapter and verse of the feud between the two families and were, metaphorically speaking, queuing up to buy ringside seats to watch them slug it out while they took sides.

'Honestly Lotte, can't I just make a donation? I might

be brilliant at auctioning million dollar works of art, but I'm hopeless at that sort of thing. Besides, I may be travelling down to Chicago to visit great-aunt Elspeth in the nursing home that weekend.'

'How is your great-aunt?' Lotte asked, easily side-tracked.

'In the words of the doctor: as well as can be expected in the circumstances. She's had a very serious bout of pneumonia and, although a plucky old lady, I don't think she should spend another winter alone in this house without some form of nursing help. Not to mention, central heating. I don't relish being the one to tell her, though.' She pulled a wry face, Lotte nodded and then laughed.

'Old Mizz Buchanan is a tough old lady. She used to chase us off the jetty out there by the lake when we were kids. We loved to sneak down there and use it as a diving board although we all had pools of our own. Nothing like the lure of the forbidden, is there? Then she'd call us over to the porch and instead of a scolding, give us cold lemonade from that old fridge out there. I remember, one time . . .' India zoned out as Lotte chattered away.

The image of great-aunt Elspeth lying in the hospital bed like a tiny, injured bird upset her. Her great-aunt, who had always seemed so strong and indomitable now appeared to be fading away, bit by bit; like an old photograph left too long in sunlight. It broke India's heart to see Elspeth so diminished, and she knew that the only ones who could make her whole again were the medical team in Chicago. Once she was well enough, she'd bring her home. She closed her mind to the possibility that Elspeth might never be well enough to return home. That the house would have to be sold - doubtless to the MacFarlanes, to pay for her medical bills and aftercare.

She was determined that, whatever happened with her aunt, she'd rather burn the house to the ground than sell it to them. Especially after Logan MacFarlane's unneighbourly visit earlier.

'You okay, Hun? You look very - fierce. Maybe Logan MacFarlane's visit has upset you more than you know?' Ever perceptive, Lotte had hit the nail on the head. India started as Lotte's hand touched her freezing cold skin, scorching her. 'Sorry, Hun, hormones; I'm hotter than a tick in hell at the moment.'

India laughed. 'I'm fine,' she lied and gave her new friend a reassuring smile.' Just fine.'

'Oh-kay,' Lotte pronounced, unconvinced. 'If you say so.'

'I do. This old house needs time and money spent on it to drag it into the twenty-first century,' she said. 'And the lighthouse needs serious renovation. Even I wouldn't dare to climb to the top without a risk assessment form, completed in triplicate.' They glanced around at the kitchen's peeling wallpaper, heavy furniture, ancient plumbing and ad hoc sanitary arrangements.

'Couldn't your parents . . .'

'Help out? Of course they could, and wouldn't even miss it. But Father wants the feud to end when Elspeth passes on,' her voice was gruff and tears blurred her eyes. 'Father would

30

sell the house from under her, if he could; he has no feeling for the past, for family. Maybe that's why Grandmother left it to Elspeth instead of him. How can they be so cold? So unfeeling?'

'Maybe the decision will be made for you,' ever-practical, Lotte opined. 'I can't see any doctor allowing her to spend another Wisconsin winter alone in this house. The temperature drops way below zero and she's beyond lugging logs down to the cellar to feed the stove.'

'You're right. Father and I have some difficult decisions to make, after all Elspeth's his aunt, too - and he has a duty to care for her. As for Mother, she wants nothing to do with it. Compared to the acres of rich farmland her family owns in Berkshire, Aunt Elspeth's little patch of dirt is precisely that - a patch of red, Wisconsin earth where nothing will grow.'

India glanced out towards the lake and the cloudless sky once more. Today, winter seemed a long way off . . . and, for the moment, time felt on her side. Her false air of serenity was shattered when Lotte touched on a more pressing problem.

'Have you told her about the MacFarlanes' offer?'

The mention of the MacFarlanes made India shiver, in spite of the heat. MacFarlane was an unwanted complication. She'd never come across such an arrogant, loathsome man, and she thought she'd come across every subspecies of the genre in Washington where her family lived and New York where she worked. It seemed incredible that MacFarlane seemingly had enough professional and interpersonal skills to warrant him being appointed assistant DA and had his sights set on Washington - if what she'd learned from Lotte was true.

By all accounts his rise had been meteoric. Clearly, having good ol' John MacFarlane as his grandfather had done him no harm.

A case of the grandson also rises?

And yet - there was something wild and untamed about him, an unpredictability that she wasn't used to. The men in New York and Washington were just as determined in their own way, but more urbane and polished, hiding naked ambition behind a veneer of sophistication and good manners. Not something Logan MacFarlane could be accused of! If his grandfather was anything like him . . . small wonder the feud was alive and kicking.

The thought of MacFarlane boldly riding across her property brought angry colour to her cheeks. In retrospect, she knew she'd handled their encounter badly. Instead of being all English and icily polite, she should have said: 'Git off my land you varmint or I'll set the dogs on ya,' like a pioneer woman defending her homestead. Then he would have got the message loud and clear.

No way was she selling her great-aunt's house to the MacFarlanes.

Not now.

Not ever.

'Indy - have you told her yet?' Lotte persisted, when India didn't answer.

'No. I haven't.' Another sigh and then she changed the

subject. 'Lotte, will you come back tomorrow and help with this wretched picnic basket? I've no idea what's expected of me. I might be able to recognise a fake Jackson Pollock at five paces but that's as far as my artistic abilities stretch. No one in their right mind would bid for one of my disasters.'

'Sure. And then, after the auction, they -' Lotte pulled herself up short, her expression suggesting that India had enough to think about. 'Hey kids! Get back in the car,' she shouted at her brood. Turning she addressed India in the same tone. 'Now you make sure you lock your door tonight, honey. The MacFarlanes are top dog round here and used to getting their own way. We don't want Logan MacFarlane prowling round your porch and baying at the moon for what he can't have.'

'Don't worry. He won't be allowed to set foot in this house unless invited. And that will never happen. Even if I have to sleep in the kitchen in Aunt Elspeth's rocker with a shotgun across my knees.'

Although, where she'd find one of those she had no idea!

'Atta girl,' Lotte laughed, raising a quizzical eyebrow at the image and the vehemence with which it was stated. Lotte wasn't the first to speculate that there was more to Miss India Buchanan than met the eye. And, judging by her expression, she'd like to be there when MacFarlane found that out for himself.

*****

33

That evening, India sat in the bay window of her bedroom, keeping her toes and knees warm beneath one of Elspeth's faded comforters, watching the sun setting over the bay. As the evening closed in around the jetty, the beam from the lighthouse grew brighter and cast its benevolent light over the water as it had for the last one hundred and forty-six years.

The Friends of Door County's Lighthouses did their best to keep it in working order but soon it would reach a point where time and money (not to mention health and safety considerations) would make push come to shove, if it was to survive. She frowned; there was more chance of the feud continuing than the lighthouse casting its welcoming beam across the bay for another hundred years or so. And when time, money and energy ran out, the MacFarlane's would be poised, ready to move in for the kill.

The Buchanans and the MacFarlanes . . .

She'd been brought up on stories of the feud and had thought of it as nothing more than a whimsical legacy from the past. But now, with her great-aunt in hospital recovering from pneumonia, the MacFarlanes about to move in and contest ownership of the house, and her parents pressurising her to return to New York, it didn't seem so quaint.

It must have made Logan MacFarlane's blood boil to see her painting the newly mended fence, she thought with grim satisfaction. Clearly, he'd thought it was a simple matter of persuading a frail old lady to sign a few papers, drawn up by his grandfather's law firm - natch, and accept his family's generous offer for house, lighthouse, land and outbuildings. Then everyone would be happy - the house would be back in MacFarlane hands and Elspeth Buchanan could live out her days in comfort and security.

Except . . . except Elspeth Buchanan had no intention of selling, least of all to the MacFarlanes, and her great niece was there to make sure no one forced her hand. However, MacFarlane didn't hold all the cards, India thought with quiet satisfaction as she watched the sun sink below the horizon. He didn't know about the ace up her sleeve, her plans for the regeneration of the old house.

Glancing around the shuttered bedroom with its faded drapes and threadbare carpet, she felt a real sense of ownership and awareness of what she could do to the old house. She recalled the blazing row she'd had with her parents when she'd informed them of her intention to leave New York, resign from her coveted post at the art auction house and walk away from a relationship they were keen to encourage - to a man she considered stuffy and controlling. Just because he had the right name; the right lineage.

In their eyes, if she was married, settled down, she'd soon forget all about the lighthouse, MacFarlane's Landing and acting nurse to her elderly great-aunt.

'But India darling, it will be more trouble than it's worth,' her mother had said, with the weariness of one who had witnessed years of litigation between the two families. 'Old Judge MacFarlane will make sure you never get permission to trade from the house and his grandson will tie you up in red tape at every turn. James, *you* tell your pig-headed daughter that I'm right.'

'Listen to your mother, India Jane,' her father had advised, glancing up from the Washington Post over breakfast.

'The shame of it, a Buchanan, running a bed and breakfast . . .'

'A Boutique Bed and Breakfast,' India had corrected. 'And there's nothing shaming about setting up in business.'

'Your grandparents will die of shame when they hear about it.' India always knew she was winning an argument when her mother referred to her family back in England. 'Trade,' she sniffed, looking every inch the daughter of a family who could trace their roots back to William the Conqueror.

'As a matter of fact, Granny Meredith not only told me to 'go for it,' she's given me a loan to cover the renovations and to tide me over until I see a profit . . .'

'Which could be never,' her mother had cut in. 'Mummy *would* do that. And what about Tom Harvey and your forthcoming engagement? What will his parents say?'

'I've told you many times, Mother, I have no intention of marrying Tom Harvey and that the engagement, only exists in your - and possibly his mother's, imaginations.'

At that point her mother had thrown up her hands and looked out of the window and down the street in George Town, Washington, with the air of one who'd lost everything she held dear: name, status, and control over her errant daughter.

'Hm?' James Buchanan had looked up from his newspaper, clearly having lost interest in the mother/ daughter wrangle and now looked panicked because he knew something was required of him. India smiled at the memory, loving him for his vagueness and knowing that if her ambitious mother disowned her, however temporarily, it was a sign she'd won the argument.

'Please, say something to dissuade your daughter from throwing away her chances,' her mother had pleaded.

'You know, I've never really liked Tom Harvey.' Then, suddenly gaining a handle on what was expected of him, James Buchanan had stepped up to the plate. 'India Jane, listen to your mother.'

'You see?' her mother had spun round, 'your father agrees with me.'

'I do?' Frowning, he tried to recall the moment when that had happened.

'Absolutely,' India's mother had replied.

'My mind's made up,' India had said, crossing her arms across her chest and bringing the discussion to an end.

'You see, darling, her mind's made up. Futile trying to dissuade her. You know what a pig-headed lot the Buchanans are.' He said it as if it was a trait he was proud of and reminded Mrs James Buchanan, nee Winthrop, that he was just as proud of his lineage and family history. The Buchanans had found their way out of the slums of Glasgow and made enough money - perhaps best not to inquire too closely how they'd done that - to pay for their passage over to the New World. That determination, fighting spirit, mule-headedness was in his blood and his daughter's. However, at heart, he was a kind man and hated dissent and so tried to find common ground between the two women he loved. 'India, darling, if you want to start your own business why not try somewhere more . . .'

'Civilised?' her mother had finished for him.

'Conducive,' he'd amended, diplomatically. 'Washington. George Town for example? We'll be moving out in a few months for our next posting - Paris,' his eyes had lit up at the mention of the capital city. 'You could live here rent free, cut costs, make it work. But, MacFarlane's Landing? Madness, my love.'

Nodding in unison, they'd turned towards her and India had sighed. They always presented a united front when the chips were down.

'Why,' her mother had added what she plainly considered to be the clincher, 'you could even move to Paris with us. Study for another degree, a PhD in art history from the Sorbonne would be a real feather in your cap. Spend time wandering the art galleries, seeing all the paintings you love in real life instead of via the internet.'

It all sounded very plausible and part of her would have liked to pursue that dream. But she knew the deal came with Tom Harvey, or another suitable man of her parents choosing, in tow.

'Aunt Elspeth agrees with me. And Granny Meredith . . .'

'Elspeth would. No surprises there. And Mother will do anything to vex me,' Daphne Buchanan had said, aware this was one argument she wasn't going to win. 'Just don't blame me when you've sunk all of your money - and Granny's - into a business doomed to failure. Why, guest houses are two a penny in Door County.'

'Not *just* a guest house. A Boutique English-style Bed and Breakfast,' India had muttered under her breath.

'You'll probably end up having to sell to the MacFarlanes in order to pay off your creditors.'

'I would never do that,' India remembered the vehemence with which she'd delivered that statement, and her mother's last comment -

'This is one time your father and I won't bail you out.'

That comment rankled with India. She couldn't remember any occasion in her adult life when she hadn't stood on her own two feet. Her parents had paid a pretty penny for her education, true. But that had been to suit themselves as they'd moved from one diplomatic post to another.

Now, wandering over to the dressing table, she picked up a silver-framed photograph of her parents. Foreign Service Officer James Buchanan and the Hon. Mrs James Buchanan, cultured, fluent in European languages, aware of the nuances of etiquette and precedence. Career diplomats - always packing and moving on to another post, each one a step closer to achieving the Holy Grail, a posting in Paris or London. Absent parents who'd delegated her upbringing to a boarding school in Berkshire, England, holidays spent with Aunt Elspeth in MacFarlane's Landing or her maternal grandparents and tribe of cousins.

Perhaps, now, her parents would realise that their

being distant parents had made her the independent and resourceful young woman she was; not easily pushed around and manipulated by anyone, and certainly not by Logan MacFarlane. Maybe they did have her best interests at heart. Or believed that, if she was safely married off, or at the very least engaged to Tom Harvey, they could pack up and move to Paris with a clear conscience and not worry about her.

As had always been the case.

It was time, India reflected as she replaced the photo on the dressing table, to put down roots and end her peripatetic lifestyle. She'd chosen this sublime spot, with its ancient lighthouse sending a beacon of light out across Green Bay, as steady and regular as a heartbeat, to do just that.

And if her parents and the MacFarlanes thought they could talk her out of it, they had *seriously* underestimated her.

Chapter Four

Logan turned his motorcycle off the Egg Harbor Road and headed towards MacFarlane's Landing via White Cliff Road. Sun glancing off the surface of Green Bay, just visible through the trees, made his heart soar and he soon forgot all about Washington, his ailing grandfather, the disputed ownership of MacFarlane's Landing and Miss India Buchanan. The road ahead was deserted so it was easy for him to become his alter-ego as the bike picked up speed. No longer Logan MacFarlane, Assistant District Attorney, fast-tracked for the Supreme Court, but Steve McQueen riding his 1961 Triumph motorcycle at the perimeter fence of Stalag Luft III and sailing over everyone's head as machine gun bullets whined past his ear.

'Yeah, baby.' Gripping the Triumph more tightly with his knees, he grinned. This was the life: the freedom of the open road - miles away from his office in Chicago where work would be stacking up, waiting for his return, along with his uber efficient P.A. who tutted and left him feeling that he'd turned up in class without his homework. Despite worries over his grandfather's failing health he was full of joie de vivre. Riding his beloved Triumph always made him feel energised. Besides, he had the added fillip of heading for the picnic auction where he would make it plain to Mizz India Jane Buchanan that *she* was the outsider and he was the homeboy.

He slowed down. It wouldn't look good if he added yet another citation to the many speeding tickets he kept in the glove compartment of his sports car. He wasn't going to make the Supreme Court that way. But the morning was just too perfect to spend worrying about what might be, and the lure of the open road hard to resist. Grinning, he waited until he'd passed the pull-in where state troopers lay in wait to catch unwary motorists daring to break the speed limit and gunned the motorcycle forward. He'd been riding these roads since he was a boy and he knew that the section of road beyond the pull in would be free of speed traps, so he let his bike have its head and sped towards MacFarlane's Landing.

Today, Mizz India Buchanan was going to get her comeuppance.

*****

India settled her picnic basket on the passenger seat of her aunt's '51 Buick, wedging it in place with her sweatshirt. The old Buick was well known, and as India drove along in stately procession, she was greeted by discreet honks and toots from other drivers and waved back. She really was beginning to feel part of this community. Light-hearted, she rolled down the window and let the wind ruffle her red-gold hair, styled today in a French plait with loose tendrils curling over her ears. At least she could enjoy herself, secure in the knowledge that MacFarlane wouldn't be seen dead at anything so un-cool as the basket auction. Lotte had promised her as much and that had been a factor in deciding to attend.

Not that she was *afraid* of him, she was afraid of no man. It was simply that she wanted their next meeting to be managed by her, and on her terms. He'd stolen the march on her last time and that wasn't going to happen again.

Glancing down briefly at her rather pathetic looking picnic basket nestled on the seat beside her, she temporarily lost concentration and didn't see the powerful motorcycle overtaking on her left-hand side. For several seconds she forgot where she was and braked hard as if she had just been undertaken on a country lane in Berkshire, England. Trying to stop the heavy old car was like trying to turn round a cruise liner on the high seas. She overshot the Laurenson's drive by several feet, narrowly missing the line of cars parked there. Heart pounding, she glanced in the rear view mirror and saw MacFarlane rocking the Triumph back on its rest. Then he swung a firm muscled leg off the bike and dismounted Western style, as if he'd just tethered his horse outside the saloon.

Ambling over, he gave the dusty old vehicle a thorough once over before speaking.

'Morning Mizz Buchanan. I take it that you are aware

that, in this country, we drive on the right-hand side of the road? It's an easy thing for a visitor to forget.' His saccharine sweet smile and intimation that she was a bird of passage made India lose her temper and react more furiously than was wise.

'What the bloody hell do you think you're doing, driving around like a maniac? And for your information Mr MacFarlane, I hold an American passport and driving licence and am as familiar with these roads as you are.'

'Such language from a lady,' he tutted, shaking his head. The mocking twist to his lips showed that he thought her a fraud - pretending to be as American as Mom's Apple Pie when they both knew her to be as British as fish and chips. India felt as if she'd presented her visa at a foreign embassy and it'd been rejected out of hand and she'd been sent to stand in line with other undesirable aliens.

'Why, you -'

He didn't give her time to finish her sentence. Instead, he extended his hand to help her out of the Buick and opened the car door with a great show of old-world courtesy. India wasn't taken in and swatted his hand away to demonstrate that she recognised cheap showmanship when she saw it. However, in spite of her best efforts to ignore him, her foot became trapped between the seat and the door and she fell out of the car, landing at his feet in an ungainly heap. Getting up, she dusted herself off and tried to regain her composure, but the seat belt had wound itself round her ankle and she was forced to endure MacFarlane's ironic grin as he helped to unwind it. She caught the amused, patronising look he directed towards guests standing on the Laurenson's drive watching them, too.

Women. What are they like?

Their good-natured smiles and MacFarlane's comic sideways nod as she brushed herself down and straightened her skimpy top, made India feel an interloper, a city-creature unsuited to rural life. Fuming, she realised that MacFarlane had stage managed her first public appearance with aplomb. Leaving her feeling that she was the ingénue in the opening act of a summer season comedy by the Peninsula Players in Sister Bay: *Fish Out of Water.*

Grim faced, India retrieved the picnic basket from the foot well of Elspeth's Buick.

She could feel, rather than see, his interested gaze on her derriere as she reached over for the basket and was glad she'd worn Capri pants this morning and not shorts. She had no intention of revealing more of herself to MacFarlane - physically or in any other fashion, than was strictly necessary.

When she straightened and turned back ready to deliver a sarcastic jibe which would leave him in no doubt exactly *who* he was dealing with, he'd disappeared. Piqued by this casual dismissal and annoyed with herself for caring, India gave herself a severe mental talking to. She didn't have time to do more than that, as Mary Laurenson - a statuesque woman in her early sixties wearing the summer uniform of the Bay, shorts and an open-necked shirt, approached her.

'India honey, so glad you could make it. Give me your basket, the auction's about to start.' Mary threaded her arm through India's, handing the basket over to her husband who was auctioneer for the day. 'Start with India, Al, she's taking Elspeth's place today.' There was a murmur of sympathy as everyone knew Elspeth Buchanan wouldn't have missed this annual event if she could have helped it.

Al Laurenson did as commanded, keeping his features diplomatically neutral as he glanced at the jumble of goods crowded together under the cellophane protecting the basket. India's rushed attempt at assembling a basket had been made ten times worse by her sudden braking and it ending upside down in the passenger well. No one in their right mind, his expression told her, would bid more than fifty dollars for her creation - no matter how worthy the cause.

'Can I remind you good people that we are trying to raise enough money to extend the wing of the Children's Hospice today? And count on your generosity? This pretty basket has been donated by Miss India Jane Buchanan. Elspeth Buchanan's great-niece for those of you who don't know.' Was it India's imagination or had MacFarlane given a snort of derision at Al's introduction? There was no time to speculate, however, because the auction was off to a flying start. 'Who's going to start the bidding?' Al Laurenson asked the crowd, smiling encouragingly at India.

'Two hundred dollars.'

There was a ripple of excitement as heads turned towards whoever had made the opening bid. India scanned the crowd, but it was her neighbour who informed her,

'It's Judge MacFarlane's boy. He doesn't normally come to these events, just gets his secretary to make a donation on the MacFarlanes' behalf. He must be pretty taken with your handiwork, India to bid so generously.'

Or trying to humiliate me. She flushed as curious glances were directed towards her. There could be no one in the Bay area or MacFarlane's Landing who didn't know chapter and verse of the feud between the MacFarlanes and the Buchanans.

MacFarlane's opening gambit generated some good-natured bidding from the other men who relished the opportunity to compete. 'Three hundred dollars,' one man offered, egged on by his neighbours.

'One *thousand* dollars,' was MacFarlane's drawled response. There was a collective intake of breath and India wished the ground would open and swallow up either her or MacFarlane - preferably MacFarlane - and put an end to this embarrassing charade. Instead, she was forced to bear more good-humoured glances as Al, relishing both his role as auctioneer and the drama of the moment, spun out the proceedings.

'One thousand dollars once; one thousand dollars twice; for the third and final time of asking, one thousand dollars. Miss India Buchanan. Sold to Mr Logan MacFarlane.' He brought his gavel down and there was an appreciative round of applause. India was relieved that her ordeal was over, but furious with MacFarlane for his interference which she knew stemmed as much from a desire to humiliate her as from any wish to boost the Hospice fund.

Even more gallingly, it felt as if MacFarlane had bought not only the basket, but *her!* Like this was some kind of undignified slave auction. Was she the only one who'd picked up on the nuances of his game playing? The only one who got it?

Al auctioned off the next basket and so spared India the sight of MacFarlane's undoubtedly smug expression as the other men gathered round to slap him on the back in congratulatory fashion. If she could get through the afternoon without having to talk to him she could just about live with the humiliation of being 'bought' by him.

The other baskets were sold and then Mary Laurenson returned India's basket to her. 'I don't understand . . . didn't M-MacFarlane buy this?' It stuck in her throat even to say his name. It occurred to her that maybe he'd bought it, seen it and rejected it all in one fell swoop to teach her a lesson. But exactly what that lesson might be she wasn't exactly certain. All she knew for sure was that it was all part of MacFarlane's plan to make their relative positions in the Door County hierarchy plain to all.

'Sure did. But you've got to deliver it, India. That's the tradition. Such a pretty effort, too, with the flowers and all.' Her gentle voice broke through India's wild thoughts. India was brought back to the present when Lotte piped up at her side.

'In the old days, bachelors would come from the secluded farms and bid for the baskets, that way they could get to meet the unmarried girls of the settlements. Dance with them for the day. It was a kind of matchmaking I guess.'

MacFarlane knew that, damn him! No wonder he'd kept grinning at her in such a knowing fashion. What's more everyone else in the community knew it, too, India raged inwardly, face burning. She was about to snatch the basket back from Mary when good manners prevailed and she managed a gracious smile instead. God, but the man was hateful; now she would have to see this farce through to its conclusion.

'I'll deliver it,' she said through gritted teeth. 'It will be my pleasure. And as for you,' she turned towards an unrepentant Lotte, who was grinning broadly at her side. 'I'll deal with you later, Missy.'

India's heightened imagination as she made her way towards MacFarlane, made it seem as if the crowd parted before them like the Red Sea. And there, standing at the end of a long tunnel with the sun behind him was MacFarlane. She was dazzled momentarily as a shaft of sunlight danced off the lake and touched the auburn lowlights in his dark hair, casting his face in shadow.

She was not so dazzled, however, that she missed the sardonic twist to his lips as she ran the gauntlet of their neighbours and progressed towards him. A second later, MacFarlane's expression altered and became a welcoming smile, innocent of all malice. India was acutely aware of the undercurrent of antipathy simmering just below the surface of the polite smiles they exchanged and wondered if anyone else in the gathering felt it. She'd give anything to wipe that patronising smile off his handsome face and make it clear that he might have bought the basket, but that buying her aunt's house would be an entirely different matter.

Chapter Five

'Mizz Buchanan,' Logan greeted India, in that moment the undisputed king of all he surveyed. How easily he'd outmanoeuvred her. Persuading her to part with her aunt's house in return for a substantial sum would be a piece of cake! His grandfather would be celebrating Thanksgiving there, if they hurried things along. It was achievable, he was sure of it. Hell, didn't they have a whole legal team at their command?

India made her way towards him in unhurried fashion as the community waited for the next scene to unfold.

'MacFarlane.' She acted as though she was a princess and he, a pauper. That, instead of being wrong-footed, she'd come out on top once more.

Plainly, she wasn't going to be tricked into making a fool of herself in front of all these people. The light of battle in her violet eyes and stubborn set to her mouth reminded him that she was a hard-edged city girl, tough as nails and not easily manipulated. Handing him the basket, she looked down at his long-fingered hands with their clean unbroken nails and gave an imperceptible sniff. These, her look implied, were the hands of a lawyer, not a son of the soil and she was unimpressed by them, and him. Logan was used to fending off women attracted by his money and family name. To meet someone unimpressed by either was a new, rather discomforting experience.

Feeling outgunned, he decided to assert his position as alpha-male as he had done so easily that morning when he'd found her painting the fence. He looked down at his thousand-dollar basket of fruit and flowers and gave it, and then her, a long look - making plain his disdain. Two could play *that* game. The basket was a rushed job and he'd got a poor bargain. However, this was about so much more than a basket of fruit. And they both knew it.

'Did this all by yourself?' He turned the basket in his hands, feigning admiration. He was about to exact his pound of flesh, ounce by painful ounce and she'd better take her medicine like a good girl. 'Guess four years studying History of Art at Vassar has given you an advantage over the other ladies.'

Warm colour sweeping India's cheeks was the only outward sign that she'd registered the put-down. When she curled her hands into fists and gave him another of her scornful looks, Logan knew his dart had hit home. He suspected that she'd give anything to snatch the basket back, give in to the urge to slap him hard and walk away, head held high. Such a princess! It was written all over her face, though she tried to conceal it. He'd rattled her and that pleased him. Round one to the MacFarlanes.

She glanced up at him, violet eyes vivid in her pale face, two spots of colour high on her cheekbones. He'd bet that she never applied anything less than Factor 50 sunscreen to protect that pale, Celtic skin. Then he frowned - where had *that* come from? He had to stop reading GQ when he was in the barbers! He couldn't afford to let this become personal, couldn't allow himself to see her as anything other than an adversary who stood in the way of his grandfather's wishes.

'Two thousand dollars. Or the equivalent in pounds or euros.' Her tone made it plain that the money was of no importance to her, family honour was what counted.

'Two thousand dollars? Oh, I get it. You want to buy the basket back?'

'Anything other than spend another second in your company,' she replied, dropping all pretence at civility.

'Ouch!' He put his hand over his heart, feigning injury.

'You'd have to grow a sensitive skin before anything I could say would hurt you, MacFarlane.'

'Really?'

'Really.'

He gave her one of his 'looks'. The type that quashed many an uppity intern in the family law firm who thought Daddy's money was a substitute for hard work and determination. He used the same hard, cold stare to good effect when summing up at a trial, hammering home a point of law to an opposing councillor. Most quelled before it. But she stood firm and would not drop her gaze. Instead, resting one slim hand on her hip, she matched his cool regard with a steadfast one of her own.

There was money and breeding in that stare and Logan remembered hearing somewhere that her maternal grandmother came from very old, English landed gentry.

Plainly, over one hundred and fifty years of improving themselves had benefited the Buchanans as much as it had the MacFarlanes. Rough edges had been rubbed away, sow's ears had been turned into silk purses, and no trace of humble origins could be detected. Yet, somehow this slip of a girl from out east had the edge over him and he didn't like it.

Raising her hand, she brushed away the tendril of red-gold hair that the hot wind off the Bay had teased free of her plait and blown across her face. The gesture made something tighten in his loins and his breath constrict as an inconsequential thought struck him - at least he knew what colour her hair was. He told himself to get a grip, to stop thinking of her in *that* regard. India Buchanan was one woman he couldn't afford to get wrong, or underestimate. Then he became aware of her making an inventory of *him* - eyes sliding over the scar on his lip, measuring him from top to toe. He read curiosity in her faintly raised eyebrow and almost fell into the trap of raising his fingers to touch the scar, an old habit left over from childhood. He was shocked by the realisation that she was as intent on finding out as much as she could about *him*, compiling a dossier for the forthcoming battle over the house and land.

He deflected her interest with a subtle put-down. He guessed that she was a twenty first century feminist, and luckily he knew exactly which buttons to press to provoke a reaction.

'I'm being very selfish,' he began.

'You are?' she asked, instantly on her guard.

'Of course - monopolising you when you must be itching

to join the other ladies at the quilting bee. They're making a quilt to commemorate the founding of MacFarlane's Landing one hundred and fifty years ago, by my ancestor Sean MacFarlane. '

'I would be interested to help, of course,' she smiled sweetly and glanced over at the ladies sitting in the shade of the Laurenson's veranda, stitching away. 'Provided that space could be found to incorporate the initials of my ancestor Jim Buchanan into the quilt. My family has always considered that the part Jim played in opening up this frontier has never received the prominence it deserves.' She addressed her last remarks to the group of interested people who had sidled up and were, quite shamelessly, listening to their conversation. 'He was one of the first Europeans to find the bay and trade furs with the Native Americans.' She addressed her remarks to them, establishing her credentials, in case anyone doubted her pedigree.

It seemed that she was not above using the opportunity to score points off him. 'Are you casting doubts on the facts recorded in the county archives, Mizz Buchanan?'

Their conversation would be talked over in coffee houses and in the local supermarkets for weeks to come. Everyone knew of the feud, it was local folklore and better than any soap opera. He needed to gain the upper hand over it, and her.

'Indeed, no. I just think that, perhaps, they would benefit from closer scrutiny. Who knows,' she smiled innocently, 'It could be . . . if I studied the old records, that this part of Door County should more aptly be named, Buchanan's Landing.'

There was a sharp intake of breath as folk waited for his reply. Fixing a polite smile on his face, Logan couldn't stop a tiny pulse at the corner of his mouth, next to his scar, giving away his agitation. He rubbed at it with his forefinger and took a long breath before replying. He hadn't become the youngest Assistant DA in living memory without learning that a good advocate knew how to wait for the best moment to deliver his riposte.

'That's an interesting theory Mizz Buchanan. However,' he drew the interest of the group away from her and back to him. 'I believe the accepted wisdom is that history is written by the winners?' Implicit in his statement was that the MacFarlanes were winners, and the Buchanans losers.

Sore losers at that!

His wolfish grin implied he'd turned the tables and she'd do well to appreciate what a formidable counsellor he was; skilled, articulate and capable of marshalling his arguments. She would soon find out she was punching above her weight in taking on a MacFarlane. After all, what was she? An intern at some swanky art auction house in the Big Apple? Pu-leeze - there was no contest. Bowing, he held out his hand and she regarded it quizzically as though she suspected he was about to pull the rug from under her.

'The band's about to strike up, Mizz Buchanan. I'll put this precious trophy out of harm's way and then we can dance.'

'Dance?' It was plain that he was the last person on earth

she would dance with. Logan was only too happy to explain the tradition and notch up another hit in the process.

'It's a quaint little custom, one we wouldn't expect a visitor to know about.' His subtle use of *we* and his condescending look drew the other Door County residents together, like they were co-conspirators. It excluded her, the foreigner. 'The gentleman who buys the basket claims first dance with the lady who made it.' He gave India a bland look, hiding the sting behind his words. 'I know you British are fond of tradition, so I'm sure you'll approve.'

He put just enough emphasis on *British* to underline her nationality. Her reaction was swift. 'I'm not some bird of passage, MacFarlane. I'm here to stay. You'd better get used to the idea, no matter how unpalatable you find it.' Ha. Now the gloves were off, he considered it time to move in and deliver the coup de grace.

He placed the basket carefully on one of the trestle tables set out for the barbecue. The sun beat down on them and, tiring of their battle of words, the crowd drifted away. Making the most of the opportunity of their being alone, Logan dropped all pretence of politeness.

'I wouldn't advise you to make any long term plans, Mizz Buchanan. Come the fall you'll be lo-ng go-ne.' He drawled out the last two words. 'I've met women like you and, as the saying goes: when the going gets tough . . .'

'The tough hire a good attorney? Isn't that what you advised a few days ago?'

'You're right, I did,' He took a step towards her and she flinched, so he took a couple of steps away from her.

Maybe he was coming on a bit too strong? He wanted to make plain his intentions, not scare her with a show of false machismo, although she didn't look as if she scared easily. His grandfather's words came to mind: *I take it that you acted like a gentleman. At all times?* Time to rein it in a little. 'Relax, Mizz Buchanan. Although murder may be on my mind, and I believe that you could drive a man to doing something he'd later regret, I only want to dance with you.' He held out his hand but she made no move to take it. That made him take stock. Usually, he had to make excuses to extricate himself from unwanted relationships, fending off women who saw themselves as the next Mrs Logan MacFarlane and were already choosing place settings at Bloomindales.

'I'd as soon dance with a grizzly, MacFarlane.'

'My sentiments exactly.'

'Then why bother?' she flung back.

'Why *bother*? Because of tradition. Because two hundred pairs of eyes are watching us. And, because I want to know why you - and your great-aunt, have seen fit to ignore the letters my grandfather's lawyers have sent you.'

'I don't want to dance with you, MacFarlane, because I don't care for *you*, your grandfather or the bully boy tactics you've employed with an old lady. And I - *we*, haven't answered your letters because it's not our intention, now, or at any time in the future to sell MacFarlane's Landing. Is that plain enough for you?'

'I -' The five-piece band, shaded from the sun under an awning, struck a chord.

'Ladies and gentlemen, take your partners please.'

'You *can* dance I take it?' he asked, smarting from her use of *bully boy tactics*.

'Of course I can,' she snapped back. 'You don't spend most of your adult life attending embassy parties and not learn to dance.'

He took her by the elbow, steering her towards the band. 'I didn't mean the Viennese Waltz, I meant country dances. Boy, you're certainly a product of your country and your class, Mizz Buchanan.'

'Meaning you're not, Mr Hot Shot Assistant District Attorney? I'll take that as a compliment, although judging by your expression it wasn't meant as one.' Shaking her elbow free of his grasp, she started to walk away. Quickly, he blocked her path, making it crystal clear that she wasn't going to refuse to dance with him and make him the laughing stock of the county.

'Has anyone ever told you that you have a bad attitude Mizz Buchanan? You're haughty and arrogant. And you've looked down your aristocratic nose at me once too often this afternoon.'

'Arrogant!' India spluttered out. 'I'm arrogant? Pot and kettle, MacFarlane. Pot and kettle.' He wasn't exactly sure what that meant, but guessed it wasn't a compliment.

'Exactly.' Before she had time to protest further, he took her hand in a firm grasp and bent his head solicitously towards her. To all outward appearances they looked like an attractive, well-matched couple enjoying each other's company on one of the best days Door County had seen that summer.

'Let go of my hand, MacFarlane. This farce has gone on long enough,' India snarled through gritted teeth, trying to free her hand without attracting attention.

Part of him enjoyed seeing her struggle. When it came to a war of words they were evenly matched, but when it came down to a show of strength, he was a man and she was a woman. With a cavalier disregard for her feelings, he rested one hand on the curve of her waist and held her right hand captive. 'You seem a little agitated, is it the heat?' Plainly, his mock-concern was more than she could stand.

'You . . .' Anger robbed her of words. That pleased him, she was at her most formidable when she was icy cold and in command of her temper. A temper which matched her red-gold hair. 'Damn you, MacFarlane,' she hissed, making her right hand into a fist.

Effortlessly, but gently, he prized her hand open and laced his fingers through hers, making it impossible for her to escape. She looked up at him helplessly, acknowledging she would have to do as he asked; for now. Her reluctant capitulation touched him in an unexpected way, warming him to the core and making his blood beat thickly through his veins. He found this new awareness of her an unwelcome distraction and, as her body radiated heat, and her perfume assaulted his senses, he was aware of only one thought.

This wouldn't do. It wouldn't do at all.

*****

Despite the antipathy she felt towards him, India found the light touch of his hand on her waist was not unpleasant. And that the lacing together of their fingers was disturbingly erotic. She became aware of him not simply as an adversary, but as an undeniably sexy male. Gazing up into his confident, arrogant face took every inch of her courage and grit, but she managed it, registering the faint freckling of his skin, testimony to his Celtic ancestry. Eyelashes which were unfairly long, wintery green eyes beneath straight eyebrows and thick hair brushed back off his forehead.

What? Was she crazy?

This man wanted to take her home away and destroy her dreams for the future. He was a barracuda and she was looking up at him like a simpering virgin. She'd better snap out of it if she wanted to come out ahead. Giving him her most glacial stare earned more mocking advice.

'Smile, Mizz Buchanan. You wouldn't want to give the good folk of MacFarlane's Landing the impression you weren't enjoying yourself. Now, would you?' India fixed a wide, very false smile on her face and as they danced her eyes never left MacFarlane's face. The message in them left him in no doubt as to her low opinion of him.

They danced in silence, India holding herself stiffly in MacFarlane's arms, and putting as much space between them as possible. MacFarlane maintained a firm grip on her hand, as though he suspected she might renege on the deal and make a run for it before the dance ended.

'Would you mind releasing my fingers, MacFarlane?' she

demanded through gritted teeth, the smile still fixed on her face. 'I swear that you've stopped my circulation.'

MacFarlane pretended to consider her request at some length.

'Actually, I would mind very much,' he drawled, but he did slacken his hold. Some of the feeling returned to India's fingers. 'Better?' he asked solicitously.

She shot him a venomous look, hiding her relief that righteous anger had the power to dissipate the feelings of sexual attraction experienced earlier. She shouldn't underestimate Logan MacFarlane, he was an advocate and used to dealing with people. Once he had discovered the chink in her armour he would exploit it to his advantage. It was imperative that she put distance between them.

'Can I go now?' she asked when the band finished playing.

But, evidently, MacFarlane hadn't finished with her.

'You know, lady. I paid a thousand dollars for the privilege of dancing with you.'

'And?' India asked, anticipating the next jibe.

'And instead of a flesh and blood woman I get the Ice Maiden.'

'Let's put the record straight, shall we? You paid a thousand dollars to humiliate me. To make the point that Mr-God-Almighty-MacFarlane can buy anything he wants.'

That didn't please MacFarlane, his face coloured and then he shrugged. 'You know, I think I prefer Mr-Hot-Shot-Assistant-District-Attorney to Mr-God-Almighty-MacFarlane.'

'You don't get a choice.'

'Is that right?'

'It is.'

'So, what choices am I allowed?' His eyes narrowed and his slow, considering look scorched a trail of fire across her skin, making her aware that other, more dangerous ideas were going through his mind.

'None where I am concerned.'

'Think you're pretty damned cute, don't you Mizz Buchanan. No doubt you're used to getting your own way. I'm betting you only date men you can wrap round your little finger. Any man who stood up to you wouldn't get a second glance, let alone a second date. Correct me if I'm wrong.'

That assessment was too close for comfort as, unbidden, Tom Harvey's aggrieved face swam before her. And standing right behind him, like a guard of honour were her disappointed parents.

'Only a second-rate lawyer like you MacFarlane would stoop so low as to speculate on the personal life of . . .'

MacFarlane didn't give her the chance to finish her sentence, he caught hold of her hand and pulled her towards him. The movement was so unexpected that she lost her balance and teetered on her heels.

'There's nothing second rate about me, Mizz Buchanan. As a lawyer; or as a man. And I've never had to buy what has always been given freely. Want me to demonstrate?'

With deliberate calculation he slid his hands down the length of her body, caught her by the hips and pulled her into his pelvis. The rough movement was intended to shock and punish. In spite of her earlier resolution, India gave a responsive shiver. MacFarlane caught the slight frisson. The angry spark in his eyes died, replaced by something warmer, smokier. In that instant their animosity was forgotten, supplanted by a sexual attraction so potent that it took them both by surprise.

MacFarlane pulled India closer into his body and she burned with a heat that owed nothing to the fierce afternoon sun, but everything to the way his firmly muscled body seemed to fit naturally into her softer, feminine curves. One of his hands fanned out across the dip in her back above her buttocks; the other touched the sensitive hollow between her shoulder blades.

The music changed from the waltz to a smoochy ballad and they moved in time to it. It would, India thought dazedly, have been the most natural thing in the world for her to lay her head on his shoulder. To surrender to the feeling of floating dreamlike in his arms. To link her arms around his neck and curl her fingers into his thick, dark hair. But sixth sense warned her that she couldn't afford to drop her guard for one second. MacFarlane was at his most dangerous when he was being charming. She simply couldn't afford to take the risk.

Sighing, India glanced up at him through her lashes. What was he feeling? What was he thinking?

Her hands were pressed flat on his chest, as though keeping him at bay, and she could feel the rise and fall of his rib cage. His swift, shallow breathing showed that he, too,

63

was sexually aroused. She looked up and caught his glance; he gave her a look that made her mouth go dry and her heart beat faster.

For one terrible, delicious, light headed moment India thought that he was going to kiss her.

Then the music stopped and people were applauding the band. They remained in each other's arms, like lovers. India became aware of people staring, grinning; she broke free and agitatedly smoothed down her sun top and Capri pants. MacFarlane ran his fingers through his hair. For several dazed seconds they looked at each other, thunderstruck, and then MacFarlane broke the mood.

'Your ordeal is over. Mizz Buchanan. I won't keep you. Doubtless there will be other men eager to dance with you.' India did not care for the dismissive way he dropped her hand, or the way he released her . . . as though the contact had contaminated him.

'Don't think that you can get what you want just by being nice, MacFarlane,' she said sarcastically as he moved away. Turning he gave her a long look and then grinned in genuine amusement. The smile was full of charm, hinting at a MacFarlane she would never know; a MacFarlane who wasn't her enemy.

Unaccountably, the thought depressed her.

'I don't need to be nice, Mizz Buchanan, I have the law on my side.'

India's reply was forestalled as Lotte and brood claimed her attention. Lotte's face was alive with inquisitiveness and India knew she would have to do some deft fielding of questions this afternoon. When she next glanced at MacFarlane he was standing with a group of his own friends.

Twice MacFarlane had had the last word. She'd make sure it didn't happen again.

*****

The sun set over the bay trailing red fire across the water as India took her leave of the picnic. Driving the Buick back to MacFarlane's Landing she tried to make sense of the day's events - picnic auction, coruscating conversation with MacFarlane, *the dance*, the kindness and generosity of everyone. What was real and what was imagined? Reaching the house, she parked and then walked into the old fashioned kitchen and poured herself a glass of white wine. Pausing on her way back to the porch, she slotted her iPod onto its sound dock and cranked the volume up a couple of notches. On the swing seat she cradled her wine glass and listened to Pavarotti singing Nessun Dorma. Unlike her apartment block in New York there was no one here to bang on the wall and tell her to turn down the 'god-damn racket'. Closing her eyes, she let the music wash over her, soothing, releasing tension.

The aria took her back to the opening ceremony of the Torino Olympic Winter Games in February 2006 which she'd attended with her parents. Best seats in the house, of course. When Pavarotti had sung *Nessun Dorma* she'd been moved to tears and hadn't wanted the evening to end. Afterwards, they'd bought her the CD and next day had taken her skiing, like a normal family. It hadn't lasted of course, she'd been sent back to boarding school and her parents had moved on to their next posting - Rome.

Sitting watching the sun set over Lake Michigan, that weekend seemed light years away. The aria now reached its crescendo then died away, becoming part of the sultry night air, heavy with moisture and the chirping of crickets. In the darkness the buoy at the end of the jetty flashed rhythmically, reminding her of the story her great-aunt told of how Jim Buchanan almost died of hypothermia during his first Wisconsin winter, struggling to build the jetty and establish the light which would guide trappers to the safety of the bay.

This was real. This was her inheritance. And she knew, with sudden clarity, that she'd never let MacFarlane take it away from her.

It was then that she heard it, the unmistakable sound of a motorcycle turning off the main road. Alert, she sat up. Now she could see the single headlight and hear the throaty purr of the big machine as it stopped short in the darkness.

She knew it was MacFarlane's Triumph, of course she did. *Now* what did he want? She'd had enough hassle from him over the last couple of days to last a lifetime and wasn't in the mood for playing games. Getting to her feet she went back inside the house and, for the first time since moving to MacFarlane's Landing, locked the door behind her and slid the bolts home.

Chapter Six

Bright morning sun streamed through the shutters and woke India from a troubled sleep. Her heart was beating wildly, breath came in gasps and her nightdress - soaked in perspiration, had twisted round. Lying still, she let the slanting buttermilk light banish strange fragments of a half-remembered dream.

MacFarlane . . .

His motorcycle slowly edging her along the jetty . . . slipping into the silent waters . . . reaching out to him . . . MacFarlane astride his powerful bike, laughing down at her as dark waters closed over her head.

'*Now* will you dance Miss Buchanan?'

Reliving the dream made her break out in goose bumps in spite of the heat and the old mahogany ceiling fan turning with slow precision above her bed. The steady beat of the paddles stirred the yellowing muslin drapes, helping to slow down her racing pulse and return her breathing to normal.

After a few moments, she swung her legs out of bed and staggered over to the window, half-drunk with sleep.

Pushing it open, she breathed great lungfuls of fresh air and looked past the bright borders of the front garden where the waters of the bay danced in the sunlight. Was it a product of her overactive imagination, or could she really make out tyre tracks in the soft red earth? Last night she'd sat in the darkened house, not daring to switch on the lights until he'd revved his bike down the drive and faded into the night.

'Damn you MacFarlane. Get out of my head.' Groaning, she turned away from the window. But, even as she tried to exorcise him, she recalled a conversation with Lotte a few days earlier as they'd been assembling the now-infamous picnic basket.

'What can I tell you about MacFarlane? His family is the nearest thing we've got to royalty in these parts. Kinda like the Kennedys - but without the scandals,' Lotte had laughed at her own joke. 'His grandfather is a high court judge, and his father could've been one too. But he settled for making mega bucks as a divorce lawyer to the rich and famous.'

'Is there a Mrs MacFarlane?' India asked, believing there was good advice in the adage: know your enemy. Leaning confidentially over the coffee cups Lotte had filled in the gaps.

'The old judge is a widower. But there's MacFarlane's mom - what a gal! When she wasn't giving Logan's father the runaround, she was in Chicago on a shopping binge, trying to melt her Platinum card.' Then an insight into the darker side of MacFarlane's psyche. 'Poor Logan. Guess we all felt sorry for him when he was a kid. The way his Mom would breeze in and out of his life. Pick him up, smother him with love and presents and then dump him when she got restless. Or when the next guy came along.'

'Poor little rich kid?' India heard an echo of her own childhood in the MacFarlane's.

The upheaval of last-minute diplomatic postings. Being sent to stay with her English cousins for the summer when term finished at her boarding school in Berkshire. Interminable Christmases spent with her father's distant relations in Williamsburg, being given everything and anything she wanted. Except the one thing she couldn't have - her parents' undivided attention and love. The chance to put down roots; to stop travelling between two continents every time a school holiday loomed.

Oh yes, she understood exactly what it meant to be a poor little rich kid . . . She stifled the surge of empathy and reminded herself that they were enemies. She'd be a fool to forget it, even for a second.

'Sure. He'd got the money. The name. The ritzy parents,' Lotte had continued. 'But that kinda set him apart from the neighbourhood kids, you know? He was a loner; he'd go off for days on his own - to God knows where. When the MacFarlanes realised that he was running wild they had him shipped to some fancy school back East. Never saw much of him after that.'

'What does the community think of him, now?' India wondered if the local people would support her scheme which would bring employment to the area. Or if they would side with this Yankee 'lord of the manor'.

'They like him, I guess. He takes his position in the community seriously, although he lives in Chicago. If he can't attend charity events he always sends a generous donation. Folks appreciate that kind of commitment from a high flyer like MacFarlane. And of course, he makes it his business to look after Judge John. If he makes DA we'll be real proud of him. A Door County boy, up in Washington, draining The Swamp.'

The answer was not to India's liking. MacFarlane had taken great pains to remind her that she was a 'foreigner', a summer visitor, like the migratory birds on the lake. He was MacFarlane of MacFarlane's Landing, and around here that counted for something. She was going to have to fight for what she wanted.

'Is there a special woman in his life?' she asked off-handedly, assuring herself that her interest was purely academic. Lotte gave her an oblique look over the top of her coffee cup.

'Women; plural. Smart professional ladies; all cute, slim and expensive looking. All hoping to become Mrs Logan MacFarlane. Sometimes he brings them down for the sailing or the winter skiing. But never the same woman twice, just in case they got ideas. Talk is: his taste runs to women with long legs and brains.'

'No surprises there, then,' India remarked, her feminist hackles rising even as she measured herself against MacFarlane's ideal woman. 'And I suppose the gentleman prefers blondes, too?'

Lotte shook her head, shooting another sideways,

teasing glance. 'Nope. Brunettes. Guess that puts us outta the running on all three accounts, India honey.'

'Bloody glad to hear it,' India stated, just a little too emphatically and Lotte raised that inquiring eyebrow again, blue eyes full of mischief. Dismissing Lotte's sudden interest with an impatient wave of her hand, India changed the subject.

Now, staring at the empty road, she remembered the second part to her dream. The part she wanted to forget; the part where she'd been standing on her porch alongside MacFarlane watching the sun setting over the lake. His arms were warm and strong around her and one hand had curled possessively over her breast. She was ashamed to admit that, in her dream, she didn't fight him. Instead, she'd relaxed back against the hard musculature of his chest and put her hand over his. Pressing it closer to her breast, holding it there to prolong the feeling. It mortified her to admit that, in that dreamlike state, she'd never felt safer or more secure.

Or more aroused!

Then the dream had fast forwarded and he'd spun her round, his lips on her breast. And then . . . Flushing, she raised her hand and pushed her hair off her hot face and tried to forget *that* part of the dream. How she'd felt. How every inch of her had wanted him to lower her on the decking and make love to her. Instead, she forced herself to remember the haunting image of him leaving her to drown in the lake.

Now will you dance, Mizz Buchanan?

That was the real MacFarlane.

'Damn him.' She cursed the dreams which left her troubled and filled with a nameless longing. Turning away from the window she set about getting dressed and going downstairs to make breakfast.

The sun streamed into the kitchen and heat rose to greet her. Another scorching hot day. She was glad that she'd finished painting the fence and porch rails, she'd have melted in this heat. Besides, it was time she started to tackle the interior of the house, to put her plans into effect.

It was seven o'clock, earlier than she'd thought, thanks to her troubled night. But she resolved to make the most of the early start. Fetching a glass of fresh orange juice from the fridge she made breakfast, showered, put on some old shorts and tee shirt and then spread her things out on the Victorian pedestal table in Elspeth's dining room.

She worked for an hour with swatches of material, sketching, choosing colours from a wand of samples, and making notes. Fetching the measuring tape, she changed the track on her iPod and continued with her work. Engrossed, kneeling among the swatches spread out on the floor, she didn't notice the front door opening until a shadow fell across her.

Glancing up, she was startled to find that the shadow belonged to MacFarlane. Unbidden memories of last night's erotic dream returned and she blushed. Oblivious to her consternation MacFarlane had a good look around the room and then swung his attention back to India, crouched at his feet, as if in supplication.

'I did knock, Mizz Buchanan,' he said above the music. Without waiting for her permission, he walked further into the room, as if staking his claim merely by standing on the floorboards of her great-aunt's house. 'But you didn't hear.'

Putting down her swatches, India reached up and switched off the music and tried to buy time to compose herself. Her heart was thumping and hands were shaking. Seconds earlier she'd been thinking about MacFarlane. To look up and find him standing there, it was just as if she'd conjured up his presence.

Get a grip, India, she chastised herself, catching MacFarlane's amused glance. No doubt he was used to the unsettling effect he had on women. Frowning, India armoured herself against that charming, too-knowing, smile.

'Have I called at an inconvenient moment?' he asked, knowing only too well that he had. Holding out a hand he gallantly helped India to her feet. She dusted off her shorts, disadvantaged by that cool, scrutinizing gaze. Unaccountably, she wished she'd taken more care with her appearance. The old cut off shorts and shrunken t-shirt made her look about eighteen, not the professional businesswoman she purported to be.

Long legs and brains.

India was aware of the bramble scratches on her legs. The bruises on her shin from dragging her great-aunt's heavy furniture around. The tangled mass of newly washed hair held off her makeup-free face by a knotted bandana. She hadn't given her appearance a second thought before

MacFarlane had walked into the house. Now she was acting like a gauche teenager and that troubled her. Consequently, when she asked: 'Have you been there all night, MacFarlane?' the tension was apparent in her voice.

He had the grace to look shame faced and rubbed the bridge of his nose with a long, brown finger. A habit she was starting to realise covered inner agitation and uncertainty.

'Yeah . . . that.' A rueful smile lit his face, making him appear disarmingly boyish. 'My intention was to apologise for my behaviour at the picnic. Then I saw you sitting on the porch listening to Turandot.'

'And?' If this was an apology then she wanted the full works.

'And then I remembered that very serviceable wrench you carry around on your person and had second thoughts.' He looked at her poker face, as though trying to read her expression. India laughed at the thought of his being frightened by her monkey wrench. Then she sobered. She didn't want to seem too friendly or to give the impression that she was falling for his charm as Lotte had intimated most women did. She was still smarting from his behaviour towards her yesterday.

'Really?' Wandering away, she closed her sketch pad and note books. She didn't want him to see her plans for the renovation of the house and Boutique B&B.

'You say that like you don't believe me.'

'I don't.' Her reply was sharp, she had the distinct feeling that MacFarlane's charm offensive was part of his design to wrest this property from her. By fair means or foul. She suspected him of putting into practice the old saying about catching more flies with honey than vinegar.

'Scout's honour.'

Facing him, India experienced a gamut of conflicting emotions. Anger, that he should think she could change her opinion just because he came over all 'Mr Nice Guy' and flashed that winning smile. Relief, that she wasn't going to have to cross swords with him today. And, more startlingly, the realisation that for some contrary reason she was actually glad to see him.

Figure that one out. Maybe she was lonely, maybe she should get herself a dog. A big dog that would keep him and every other unwelcome male off her property.

'I'd put even money on you never having been a Boy Scout, MacFarlane.' The cool reply hid her inner turmoil. MacFarlane laughed, but didn't bother to confirm or deny it. Instead, he wandered around the dim, shuttered room touching her great-aunt's collection of Victoriana.

Like India, he'd made no special effort with his appearance that morning, even though he'd come to her house, uninvited, to mend broken fences. He'd dressed with the casual assurance of a man who knew that he looked good in jeans or a suit, and looked fit and athletic in long cargo shorts and deck shoes. His hair was ruffled from the motorcycle ride and his cheeks were glowing with healthy colour.

Under other circumstances, India might have found him

attractive. But a large shadow loomed over them - the house, her dream, the family feud.

'Okay, MacFarlane. Let's get serious for a moment. I don't believe you've come here to apologise. I think that everything you said yesterday, you meant; and now you're having second thoughts. You're thinking, 'I've put her back up. Now she'll never consider my offer'. You've come here today to see if I can be won over by charm where down right rudeness failed. Correct me if I'm wrong.'

India walked through into the kitchen and he followed her.

After filling the coffee filter from the tap, she turned and saw the kitchen through his eyes. The ancient cooking range, stained enamel sink, faulty wiring, peeling wallpaper and the damp patch over by the door where the rain had come in last winter. However, India was also aware that, like her, he would see potential in the old house. All the original features were intact, as if waiting for a loving hand to bring them back to life. She had every intention of ensuring that the loving hand would be hers, not MacFarlane's.

'You haven't answered my question, MacFarlane.' She switched on the coffee machine, then stood with her back to the sink waiting for his answer.

Pulling up a chair, MacFarlane turned it around and straddled it like the simple country boy he pretended to be. He sat with his arms folded across the back of it, like they were old friends, and he called by every day at this time for coffee and cookies.

'Guilty as charged M'lud.' He spoke with a passable English accent and India grimaced as she got cups and saucers down off the peeling shelf. Sobering, he continued. 'Look, I know I played it wrong yesterday. I've played it wrong since day one; I should have listened to my grandfather.'

'Why, what did he say?'

'He said that Buchanan women were ornery, that's when they weren't being downright stubborn.' India raised an eyebrow at the unflattering description. MacFarlane evidently thought that, even for him, the description was a step too far. Looking unsure of himself he sent her a frank look. 'We are in the business of being honest, aren't we?'

'Certainly. Cards on the table.'

'He also told me that your aunt would burn the house down before she let a MacFarlane set foot in it.' For a few seconds neither of them spoke, sharing instead the realisation that he was the first MacFarlane to set foot in the house for over fifty years.

'She said that?' India gasped, finding it hard to imagine her mild tempered aunt being so vehement about the house. Although she'd always wondered why her aunt had let it fall into disrepair when she'd had the money and the means to restore it. It was as if her heart wasn't in it, as if she regarded it as a burden, nothing more than an empty space in which to end her days.

MacFarlane broke into her thoughts.

'There's bad feeling between my grandfather and her, over and above the house business - do you have any idea what that could be?' India shook her head. 'Two things I do know: your great-aunt has granted you power of attorney over her estate while she's ill. And you're the last of the Buchanans.'

'As you are the last of the MacFarlanes,' India cut in, appealing to him directly. 'I suppose, to you and your grandfather it would make a neat ending if I sold the house, lighthouse and landing to you and went back to New York? Put everything right. If you were me, would you sell?'

MacFarlane looked straight into her eyes for several long seconds but didn't answer. Then shaking himself free of dark thoughts, he looked past her to an old photograph hanging on the wall.

'May I?' he asked.

'Go ahead.' She fussed with milk and sugar, keeping her eye on him as he took down the sepia photograph. Stuck inside the frame alongside the photograph was a scrap of paper, signed and witnessed.

'The deeds to the house and the landing.' Reverently, he turned the old photograph over and read the date. 'I'd heard that you'd got this but I didn't believe it. I thought you'd have had it locked up in a bank vault.'

'Well if it went missing I'd know where to look, wouldn't I?' He winced at her tart reply, but soon bounced back, uncrushable as ever.

'It must have been some poker game when Sean MacFarlane put the house and MacFarlane's Landing up as an IOU, and Jim Buchanan won both on the turn of a card. They say that spades were trumps the night he lost everything.'

India nodded. 'Great-aunt Elspeth can remember her

father telling her about it when she was a child.' She didn't add that it'd been drilled into Elspeth that the house was theirs - fair and square and would only pass back to the MacFarlanes *when hell froze over and the camels came skating home.* 'I believe that Sean MacFarlane eventually came up with the money - but Jim Buchanan refused to let him redeem the IOU. Said he'd reneged on the deal; taken too long and that the house was his.'

MacFarlane scratched his nose thoughtfully.

'It's a delicate point of law. A gentlemen's agreement that went wrong.'

India raised an eyebrow. 'I don't think either of our ancestors could be described as gentlemen. Pioneers perhaps; Jack-the-Lads certainly. Two immigrants escaping the deprivation of the Glasgow slums and a Scottish mining town . . . with an eye to the main chance. A couple of rogues might be a more accurate description.' She pushed milk and sugar towards him.

Taking the photograph from him she looked at the two canny Scots. She wondered if she resembled Jim Buchanan, with his hungry eyes and thin face. She glanced at MacFarlane and decided that he didn't favour his forefather. The old photograph gave Sean MacFarlane a consumptive pallor, accentuated the typical Celtic colouring and hinted at sandy hair and pale blue eyes.

'What are you thinking?' MacFarlane asked and India realised that she'd had been staring at him.

'I --- I was just wondering if we resembled our ancestors,'

she stumbled over the words. Feeling suddenly awkward, she moved over to the sink in the pretence of watering her great-aunt's geraniums. MacFarlane followed her there, regarding his reflection in the old spotted mirror to the left of the sink. India was about to make a cutting remark about him being vain when he forestalled her.

'Come here.' When she hesitated, he took her hand and pulled her in front of the mirror and then stood behind her, looking over her head at their reflection. He held the framed photograph in his left hand, his right hand resting lightly on her shoulder. Their bodies touched briefly and MacFarlane glanced at her through the mirror.

'You have Buchanan's chin, and his mouth. Stubborn and determined. Your nose . . . let's see.' Now he turned her to face him, mischief in his eyes. 'Hm, too aristocratic by far. Probably got that from your mother's illustrious ancestors. Very haughty; very English.' He traced a line from her nose to her top lip with his finger. After last night's erotic dream, which he must *never* learn about, India felt the intimate touch was too much. But she couldn't back away because she was trapped between MacFarlane and the sink.

As though unmoved by the closeness of their bodies, MacFarlane continued.

'Eyes?' Tilting her head, he consulted the photograph, regarding her with an almost detached air. But his hands were warm against her skin as he held her chin in his hands and his voice was deep and husky. 'His are narrow and rather shifty; but yours are wide spaced and blue; the blue of Scottish harebells.'

'MacFarlane you're full of blarney. Are you sure you haven't got Irish blood running through your veins, too?" India knocked his hand away to break the dangerous mood settling upon them. Electricity crackled in the super charged atmosphere as she remembered being in his arms yesterday at the dance. His hand on her breast in her dream. Today they were alone in her kitchen with no one to interrupt them; who knew where this foolery would lead?

The thought made her nervous.

Ignoring her, MacFarlane continued as though she hadn't spoken.

'Hair? Hard to say.' He put the photograph down and ran his fingers lightly through her naturally wavy hair. The delicate nerves at the nape of her neck curled in on themselves as his fingers lightly grazed her skin. Warm colour stole across her cheeks and India cursed herself, knowing he would interpret the bloom of colour as a reaction to his touch.

'You're full of it, aren't you?' she asked, knocking his hand away.

Plainly unaffected by her froideur, he ignored the reprimand and didn't step away but consulted the photograph again, as though reading an important brief before a trial. 'Perhaps his hair was dark brown or had an auburn tinge to it. Not copper, like yours. Now, lips,' he continued matter of factly.

'Stop it MacFarlane. You've gone far enough.'

'But I haven't mentioned the lips, or the ears or . . .'

'Enough MacFarlane, you hear?'

'Lips. Well, his are thin and mean looking. While yours,

81

Miss Buchanan are generous; as you no doubt know. And could drive a man crazy at the thought of kissing them.'

MacFarlane's voice took on a rough edge as though he'd been haunted by the thought. His eyes had narrowed and were now focused on her lips and India knew she'd been wrong to think him unaffected by this dangerous game playing. She was faint with longing and anticipation, but desperate to hide it. She wanted him to end this teasing. Wanted him to stop; or to kiss her hard until her lips were bruised and her body cried out for more.

'Are you listening to me, MacFarlane?' In reply MacFarlane ran his thumb across her lips, which had parted unconsciously to receive his kiss. Then he cupped her face in his hands.

'Relax Miss Buchanan. This is, after all, purely in the spirit of scientific enquiry. Think of it as cementing the *Special Relationship* between our two great countries.'

'Mac. . . mphm.'

India's protest was smothered even before it was uttered when his mouth descended on hers. The kiss was sweet and all the better for being wanted. India couldn't be certain whose hands had curled round whose neck first, but it didn't matter. None of it mattered. She was as willing as MacFarlane to prolong the kiss. It wasn't until she felt the exploratory kiss change into something more passionate and dangerous that she knew she had to call a halt.

'End of experiment.' Pushing him away from her, she walked over to the coffee machine. 'Legend has it that they raised the money for their --- their passage to America by selling everything they possessed and putting it on the nose of a horse at Lanark races. I have a feeling they acquired the money in a less honourable manner. Stole it, even?' She was amazed how cool and collected she sounded considering the opposite was true. Pouring out the coffee, she put the cup and saucer onto the table with a shaky hand, spilling some of it. If she didn't look at him, regaining her self-control would be that much easier. MacFarlane drank his black and unsweetened, taking a biscuit from the battered tin on the table and acting as though they were old friends and had simply been discussing the weather.

'The MacFarlanes and Buchanans have come a long way since then,' he observed. 'Your family in the diplomatic corps; mine in the law courts. I wonder what Jim and Sean would think of it all?' To put distance between them and the dangerous moment over by the sink, India placed the framed photograph with its precious deeds back on the wall. Then she sat back at the table and drank her coffee with MacFarlane, all ladylike and poised.

'He wouldn't want me to sell,' she said, once more in control.

'And Sean wouldn't want me to give up trying to get MacFarlane land back.'

'A Mexican standoff, then. An impasse,' she observed as they looked at each other challengingly.

But, evidently, he couldn't let it rest there. He gave it one more shot. 'Okay, I'll admit that legally you are under no obligation to consider our offer. Possession being nine tenths of the law, as you said. Morally, however, I think you owe it to my grandfather to at least consider the price we would be willing to pay for the house.' He leaned across the table to her, all pretence gone. He became MacFarlane the attorney as he pressed his case. 'Let's face it Mizz Buchanan, your great-aunt won't be well enough to live here alone when she comes out of the nursing home. What will she do with the house when you return to New York and the money for her care runs out?'

'Who says I'm returning to New York?' The words were out before India could stop them.

MacFarlane's head jerked up and he drummed his fingers on the table, the only outward sign of his agitation. Then he had himself under control and continued.

'You're used to living in a big city. In England, too, where the climate is milder. You'd hate it here in the winter - snow and ice - everything closes down once the tourist season is over. No theatres, only a couple of good restaurants.'

'You forgot to mention the wild animals foraging in the dustbins and having to chip ice of the water before having a wash in the morning.' Giving him an old-fashioned look, India continued. 'You think New York is any different? The crowded, overheated subways, the frozen sidewalks. Why, sometimes, a girl can't even get a taxi to take her to Bloomingdale's,' she responded in a mock New York accent. It was obvious that he didn't take kindly to her mocking tone.

'Frankly,' he continued harshly, 'I don't see you making it through to Groundhog Day.'

'I'll have to prove you wrong then, won't I?' India snapped, angered that he thought her a lightweight who would pack her bags and leave at the first snowflake. 'I come from good pioneer stock, too.'

MacFarlane's smile was wide and wolfish. 'On your father's side maybe. But your mother's an 'honourable' isn't she? Her father's a viscount, typical English gentry. When the women hereabouts were hacking their way through virgin forest with their bare hands, her ancestors were embroidering dainty handkerchiefs and making dynastic marriages to men with impeccable pedigrees and blood lines.'

The accuracy of his statement made hot colour return to India's cheeks, but for a different reason this time. How dare he diss her family?

'You seem to know a great deal about me, MacFarlane.'

'I've made it my business to find out.'

Raising her head, India gave him a searching look. He was harder and more determined than she'd given him credit for. No doubt he'd Googled her and her family, consulted Debretts, even. He probably knew her credit rating and what loans she could raise. He'd know how to do such things quietly and without a fuss.

Time to be more guarded and circumspect. Certainly no more kisses by the sink!

'You know, MacFarlane, for someone who's supposed to be mending fences, you've done a lousy job. In case you're wondering, you've managed to put my back up good and proper.'

'*Good and propah.*' He laughed, a wry twist to his lips.

'You know, Mizz Buchanan, just when I think I've got you all figured out, you surprise me. I guess I expect you to think and react like an American, but lady - you're British through and through. '

'I shan't ask you if that's an insult or a compliment. I might not get the answer I want,' India replied with all the hauteur of her aristocratic forebears.

MacFarlane looked as though he was about to make an observation, then he changed his mind. He smiled and led the conversation in another direction. 'So, what does India Buchanan do when she's not painting fences and attending picnic auctions?' He took a long swallow of his coffee. At the mention of *picnic auction* India sent him another sharp look.

'As you've been kind enough to remind me, I live in New York.'

She could hardly believe that he had the gall to sit at her kitchen table and help himself to another biscuit when she'd made it plain that the lady was not for turning. Clearly, MacFarlane was in no hurry to leave. He was playing a long game. A game he expected to win.

'Doing what?'

'I work for an Art Auction House. Most of my time is spent in front of a computer scouring the internet for estate sales, getting in quick when an unknown Master is about to come on the market for the first time. Persuading the owner's heirs to sell through us rather than a rival auction house, pipping them to the post often as not. The Impressionists are my field of expertise, but I'm happy to work with any art work.'

'Well paid?'

'I'm on commission, so yes, very well paid.'

India was rewarded by another assessing glance as MacFarlane took on board that she wouldn't sell the house for love nor money. Especially not money. Plainly, he wouldn't be able to buy her off, if that's what he had in mind. Draining his coffee MacFarlane placed the cup back on the saucer.

'A competitive field.'

'I've always been a competitor.'

'I can well believe it. Most men would find that characteristic - in a woman - undesirable.' He drew out the sentence as though considering the implications of it.

'Most men do,' was India's swift rejoinder. 'But that's their problem. So,' this time she changed the topic, 'are you a hot shot attorney, MacFarlane? What do you specialise in? Criminal law, I'd guess.' She gave him a shrewd look, trying to see beyond the casual clothes and imagine him in a dark suit, delivering his speech, presenting his evidence. Or, more improbably, gowned and bewigged like an English barrister.

'Don't like talking about yourself, do you?' he asked India as she picked up their cups and saucers and carried them over to the sink.

'I get the nasty feeling that anything I say will be written down and used in evidence against me . . . isn't that how it goes? Or can I plead Fifth Amendment?'

MacFarlane deftly avoided answering her question.

'Tell me, are all the women in New York like you?' he asked, as if he'd never travelled further than Sturgeon Bay. The homespun, country boy act didn't fool India and she remembered what Lotte had said about him liking women with long legs and brains. Something told her that he'd never suffered from a shortage of professional, city women.

'Oh no; only the ones of - how did you put it - of my country and my class,' she replied, eyes deceptively wide and innocent.

MacFarlane opened his mouth as if to say something then smiled a tight little smile. Sending her a long, hard look it was obvious that he was reminding himself that he'd come here specifically to make amends. India gained the impression that she was pushing him harder than he liked or was used to. That pleased her.

'You have a good memory, Mizz Buchanan, so let's leave it there. I hope you never decide to leave the auction house and become a lawyer. The legal profession isn't ready for you.' Was that a compliment India wondered as he glanced at his watch and stood up. 'I've taken up enough of your time.'

India walked him to the back door and onto the porch.

However, MacFarlane couldn't resist one last dig. When he turned to face her, his eyes had lost their wariness and antagonism and were bright with mischief. 'Maybe, before you go back to New York, you'll show me round the old place.'

India followed him down the steps and onto the path

where his motorcycle was waiting. "I'm not going to rise to the bait this time MacFarlane. As for a conducted tour, you can buy a ticket and look round the old lighthouse like other folk do. It's Open Day next month and I hope Aunt Elspeth will be well enough to attend. There will be cake,' she added by way of a clincher.

'Homemade? By you, Mizz Buchanan? Like the one in your picnic basket?' Obviously, he couldn't resist one last jibe, even if it was delivered with a smile.

'Of course. A secret family recipe. Why don't you bring your grandfather along?' The words: *secret* and *grandfather* made him bring up his head and give her a sharp look. Then, swinging his leg over the Triumph, retrieved the baseball cap and Ray Bans hooked over the handlebars. He made a play of putting them on before inserting the key in the ignition, as if to show he would leave in his own good time, not when she ushered him off her property.

'Thanks for the coffee.' He fired up the powerful machine and then turned off the ignition. 'Do you like the theatre?'

India was taken by surprise.

'Why?' It was an uncharitable and suspicious response to his question. And predictable too, the twist to MacFarlane's lips told her. She changed it to: 'Yes. Yes I do.'

'I thought - as a tourist - you might like to visit the Peninsula Players one night.' There was heavy irony behind *tourist*.

'As a *citizen* of Door County, I'll think about it.'

They stood looking at each other, neither seemingly

wanting to take the leave of the other. The mood was broken as a vehicle came bumping up the long drive.

'You've got a visitor. Male by the looks of it.' MacFarlane's tone implied that she was working her way through the male population of MacFarlane's Landing and that no man was safe. Much to her irritation, MacFarlane showed no signs of leaving. She folded her arms and waited to see who the caller might be. No doubt he'd construe that as being neighbourly, she thought it a damned impertinence and another timely reminder not to trust him.

The car drew up in a cloud of red dust and an elderly man got out.

'Hello Doctor Voss,' MacFarlane greeted the driver.

'Hi there Logan, what're you doing here?'

'Paying Mizz Buchanan a friendly visit,' MacFarlane replied.

Dr Voss looked between India and MacFarlane, evidently sensing the atmosphere. Then he turned to India. 'The nursing home's been trying to raise you all morning. Elspeth's had another fall. She's being transferred to hospital in Chicago where they're considering a hip operation. She's an old lady and not as robust as she thinks, India. In my professional opinion, you should get over there, just as soon as you can.'

Chapter Seven

India's heart stalled and the sun seemed to drill a hole through her skull. She swayed on her feet, black dots floating before her eyes and ears filled with a hollow rushing sound. Instinctively she reached out for MacFarlane who swung his leg off the motorcycle and was at her side in seconds, curling a strong arm around her waist. Her legs buckled and from a distance she heard Dr Voss: 'Take her indoors Logan, out of the sun.'

Somehow, she found herself back in the kitchen drinking a glass of water MacFarlane had put in her hand.

'I . . . I'm all right, really,' she protested, thoroughly embarrassed by the attention. 'It was - I'm simply worried about Aunt Elspeth - another fall? At this rate they'll never let her come home.' Tears filled her eyes and she brushed them away with the back of her hand, angry at having shown weakness in front of MacFarlane. He thought her a tough, dyed-in-the-wool city girl and here she was swooning in the sun like some Jane Austen heroine. Glancing down, she was relieved to see her bosom wasn't heaving in the prescribed manner and there was no danger of having to be cut out of her stays.

Doctor Voss insisted on taking her pulse. 'Have you ever fainted before, India?' Releasing her wrist, he went on. 'You look quite pale, my dear.'

'No. No, of course not. I'm not the fainting type.' She shot MacFarlane a challenging look in case he thought kissing him earlier had reduced her to a quivering wreck. He was looking at her with concern though, rather than calculation. Pulling herself together, she continued in a steady voice revealing none of her inner turmoil. 'I'm fine. Really.'

But Doctor Voss wasn't satisfied. 'Have you been overdoing things? Working too hard?' he probed in a kindly professional manner. Then, looking at MacFarlane, 'Has she, Logan?'

India was annoyed that Doctor Voss should presume MacFarlane had the right to answer for her. Time she put the record straight, or by this evening the story would have grown in the telling. From a simple faint it would be recounted how India Buchanan had collapsed dramatically in MacFarlane's arms, pregnant with twins for all anyone knew!

'I'm fine. Just fine.' Getting to her feet she walked over to the sink to empty her glass, glad her back was turned towards them, otherwise they would have seen her hands shaking. 'I'm sure you both have better things to do than discuss whether or not I've been overworking.' There was a touch of asperity in her voice which Doctor Voss picked up.

He turned to MacFarlane, talking over India's head, as though she was invisible.

'Logan?'

'Well,' MacFarlane said, straight-faced, 'she *has* had a great deal of excitement recently.'

India spun round. Really, the man was insufferable! Did he think one stolen kiss was enough to make her go weak at the knees?

'That's better,' the doctor said. 'The colour's returning to your cheeks, India. I'm an old fool for breaking the news to you like that. A good thing Logan was there to catch you.'

'Isn't it, though?' India's bright reply hid her annoyance. But MacFarlane caught the intonation in her voice, and the wry smile that she was learning to recognise pulled at the corner of his mouth. 'Can we forget about me and get back to my great-aunt?'

'Of course,' the doctor pulled out his notebook.' It appears Elspeth fell getting out of bed this morning. Luckily, she managed to reach her panic switch and a nurse came right away. She's in good hands but bound to feel a little confused and disorientated. I think you should go over there, India, just to reassure her. *And* to find out the full extent of her injuries. She's an old lady and you're about all the family she's got.' He closed his notebook with a snap.

India bit her lip. Of course she'd go. There was no question. But how would she get to Chicago? It was a five-hour drive in a decent car. Her great-aunt's old Buick would never get there.

'Could you drive me to Green Bay Airport, Doctor Voss? I could catch the shuttle to Chicago and get there before dark. Or, I could hire a car; it isn't safe to venture further than MacFarlane's Landing in Elspeth's Buick.' Already her mind was racing ahead, thinking of packing, ringing her parents to tell them of the accident.

'I wish I could, honey. But I've got evening surgery and my partner's out of town on a fishing trip.'

'No need to worry Doctor Voss, I'll take India to Chicago.' MacFarlane took command of the situation with an air of authority which seemed natural.

It was the first time he'd ever used her Christian name. His slow, Mid-Western drawl wrapped itself easily around the syllables - *Indie - ahr*. Icy fingers played an arpeggio down her spine and she shivered. Swiftly suppressing the sensation, she hoped MacFarlane hadn't noticed that the skin on her arms had developed goosebumps. His use of her Christian name set a dangerous and unwanted precedent. She found his presence disturbing and unsettling enough and had no intention of letting their relationship become more intimate.

Full of guilt, she reminded herself that while she had been kissing MacFarlane her great-aunt had been lying on a nursing home floor. Not that MacFarlane was to blame for that, but both incidents were linked in her mind. She'd been an idiot to let him kiss her. It had put her in an impossible position and would make litigation over the house all the more difficult.

Had that been MacFarlane's intention from the outset? To compromise her?

Gah! Letting out a huff of annoyance, she removed the bandana holding her hair off her face. It had tightened like a vice and the slow, dragging beat of an impending headache made her feel sick. Twining the bandana round her wrist, she shook out her hair and, running her fingers through the tangled copper once more, was glad to lean back against the sink for support. Glancing over at MacFarlane she caught his frown. It seemed that freeing her hair and raking her fingers through her curls had somehow offended him.

Now it was her turn to quirk her mouth up at the corner, suspecting he would take great pleasure in seeing a scarlet letter embroidered on her shirt, warning that she was a danger to any man fool enough to get close. What would her great-aunt say if she knew India had been 'consorting with the devil'? *Her* opinion of the MacFarlanes was unequivocal.

'That's settled then,' Doctor Voss rushed on, missing the exchanged glances and taking her silence for acquiescence. 'I'll phone the hospital for an update in an hour or so. I'll see myself out. You and Logan have things to arrange.'

You and Logan.

India found the coupling of their names disturbing. As though in some indefinable way they were now an item. She dismissed the preposterous thought immediately. If MacFarlane had intended to unsettle her with outrageous talk and stolen kisses, he'd succeeded. But she'd be damned if she'd give him the satisfaction of knowing it.

The door closed and then they were in the kitchen. Alone.

'I believe the phrase is: caught between a rock and a hard place?' MacFarlane broke the silence, guessing the feelings she imagined she'd been clever enough to hide. She gave him a stare. He seemed very much at home sitting on the corner of the kitchen table, casually swinging his leg back and forth. India looked into cool green eyes and tried to forget about the kiss.

But it was *out there* and couldn't be called back.

Time to redraw the boundaries.

'Naturally, it is very kind of you to offer to help me,' she began stiffly, sounding priggish and, worst of all, exactly like her mother. How often had she heard her dismiss some unwanted attention, refuse an unsuitable invitation with that English upper-class reserve and hauteur?

MacFarlane gave a sardonic laugh. 'Lady, you think no such thing. It's written all over your face. You want a lift to Green Bay but you're damned if you'll let me be the one to take you there.' He shrugged. 'Go ahead, put your pride before your great-aunt's welfare. Your choice.'

Standing, he made his way towards the kitchen door.

'MacFarlane. Wait.' She swallowed hard. 'I'd very much like a lift to the airport, if it wouldn't inconvenience you too much.' There! She'd said it. Now, let him make capital out of that and she'd scream.

Straight faced, MacFarlane turned and tipped her a salute. 'Why it'll be my pleasure Ma'am.' A glance at his wrist watch. 'An hour long enough for you to throw some things into an overnight bag? I'll phone the airport, make the reservations.'

India wondered if she'd heard right.

'*Reservations?*' she stressed the plural.

'Sure. You don't think I'd let a country girl go down to the Windy City on her own.'

'Knock it off, MacFarlane. Chicago's a one-horse town compared to New York,' India snapped. MacFarlane laughed at her furious expression and then levelled with her.

'Relax and put your suspicious mind at rest, I was planning to go to Chicago for a few days anyhow. There are some things I need to sort out at my law practice.' India wondered if her claim to the house was among them. Seemingly misinterpreting her frown, MacFarlane went on. 'Don't worry, you won't be inconveniencing me at all. Who knows? You might be glad of a friend in Chicago; even if it's me.' He challenged her to deny that he'd be the last person on earth she'd call on in time of trouble. Swallowing hard, India decided that saying nothing was the best course. MacFarlane's mouth pulled back in a sardonic smile, as though he could read her mind. 'One hour. Make sure you're ready.'

With that he left, closing the kitchen door behind him and India stood rooted to the spot until she heard his motorcycle rev up. Then she ran to the kitchen window and watched as he drove down the dusty drive and onto the highway. Only when the dust had settled and the roar of the Triumph died away did she breathe a sigh of relief.

Turning from the sink, she looked at the photograph of their ancestors accusingly, then ran upstairs to pack.

*****

The journey from Green Bay Airport to O'Hare International Chicago was a brief one. Ordinarily India enjoyed flying, but she was now too tense to relax. She still suspected MacFarlane of having an ulterior motive in helping her. Fortunately, the shuttle was so crowded that they were allotted seats across the aisle from each other. That suited India just fine. At least she wouldn't be forced to make polite conversation and could concentrate on what she was going to do about her great-aunt's future care. *And*, where she was going to get the money if MacFarlane decided to initiate legal proceedings over the house. All *her* money was earmarked for renovating the property and, as far as she was aware, her aunt had little of her own. Her parents might be prepared to help meet her aunt's hospital bills but they'd made it quite clear at their last meeting that they weren't prepared to help India realise her dream of opening a Boutique Bed and Breakfast establishment.

'Pardon me, Miss.' The elderly man on India's left hand side attracted her attention.

She groaned inwardly. The last thing she wanted was to spend the journey exchanging small talk with a total stranger.

'Yes?' she began tentatively, turning towards him. He leaned across her, then spoke to MacFarlane who was seated across the aisle from them.

'Would you and your young lady like to sit together? I don't mind moving.' India was just about to protest that not only was she most definitely *not* his young lady, but that she was perfectly happy with the seating arrangements.

MacFarlane, however, had already risen to his feet and given their fellow passenger one of his charming smiles. Of course, India thought furiously, he would welcome the opportunity to sit next to her and wind her up throughout the flight.

'I'd appreciate that,' he said, and India was forced to accept the situation with good grace. She stood up as the business man and MacFarlane exchanged seats, her body poker stiff when MacFarlane brushed past and settled himself on her left hand side by the window.

'Thank you, sir,' MacFarlane leaned across India to shake hands with their new-found friend. As he did so, his shoulder grazed the tender flesh of India's breast and an electric current of awareness jolted through her, as if she'd been branded. After that, she tried to make herself as small as possible to avoid it happening again. Seemingly, the contact had no visible effect on MacFarlane. Giving India one of his trademark, mocking smiles, he retrieved a legal magazine from his leather messenger bag and proceeded to read it.

Sitting stiffly in her seat she waited for him to tire of his magazine. Waited for him to engage in another acrimonious discussion about the house.

Waited for him to pay her some attention!

The very idea! Angry with herself, she drew a small breath. MacFarlane heard the sound and glanced her way, briefly, before returning to his magazine. What was the *matter* with her? Wasn't he the last man on earth she wanted to share an intimate space with? Become involved with? What was happening to her?

Cool, calm India Jane Buchanan was fast becoming an emotional wreck.

Predictably the throb of her headache returned and she laid her head back against the seat, closing her eyes. After some time she opened them, caught the flight attendant's attention and asked for a glass of water so she could take an aspirin. Swallowing the painkiller, India acknowledged that her relationship with MacFarlane had undergone a sea change. From the moment they had danced together there'd been a heightening of awareness. An unspoken acknowledgement that, though they might be adversaries, they were also sexually attracted to each other.

It was obvious in the way they avoided body contact in the confined space of the cabin. In the way that MacFarlane, despite his outward show of sangfroid, had been reading the same page of his magazine for the last fifteen minutes. Upside down?

India let out another sigh. This was an unforeseen and unwelcome complication.

Closing her eyes again she tried to catnap, shutting out MacFarlane's provocative image. After some time she jolted awake, aware of the flight attendants making their way along the aisle dispensing coffee and pre-wrapped biscuits.

'Coffee Ma'am?'

'What? Yes, black please, no sugar.'

'Sweet enough, huh?' MacFarlane asked, all innocence. The female flight attendant turned her attention to MacFarlane, giving him a hundred-watt smile as she performed the mundane task of handing him his drink.

That irked India.

Small wonder he had such an inflated idea of his own importance. Every female over the age of consent apparently melted before his engaging smile. Small wonder, too, that he found it so hard to deal with her. From the start of their stormy relationship she'd made it clear that it would take more than a smile to win her over.

She might be willing to acknowledge the potency of his appeal. But that's as far as it went. He wasn't her type, and she didn't care who knew it. It would do him no harm to discover that she was immune to him. In fact, it would also do *her* a great deal of good. She'd never come across a man who so pushed her to the limits of patience and endurance!

Looking towards him, she was about to ask how long before they landed. He was staring out over Lake Michigan though, lost in his own thoughts. Did those thoughts include her? Perhaps he'd had enough of *her* and the undercurrent below the surface of their most innocuous conversation. Despite her confident assertion that he was not her type, she was dismayed to discover that his diffidence affected her more than she cared to admit.

Now *that* was the kind of feminine logic she'd always taken pains to deny. No man was going to shake her faith in herself, rattle her confidence - least of all Logan MacFarlane. What was it about him, she frowned, which provoked such a violent reaction in her?

She glanced at MacFarlane again. His head was cast into relief against the bright cold blue of the sky. The sun burnished his hair, finding threads of auburn and chestnut among the dark brown. It touched the fine lines radiating from his eyes, and down past his long straight nose. His skin was lightly sunburned and drew attention to those eyes which were a pure, clear green. And, most annoying of all, he had thick, long lashes - the sort most women would die for. Quite a package and almost too attractive for a man . . .

'Aspirin working yet?' He spoke without looking at her, as if sensing she'd had enough of him for one day.

'Yes,' India nodded. Her headache was no better, but it seemed the safest thing to say.

MacFarlane put some papers back in his messenger bag. As he did so, the flight tickets fell out of the front pocket and onto the floor. India retrieved them, glancing at them as she returned them to MacFarlane. The price of the round trip to Chicago reminded her of the overinflated price MacFarlane had paid for the picnic basket and her humiliation at his hands that day. Apparently, she was in his debt once more and it didn't sit easily.

'Will you take a cheque for the tickets, MacFarlane?' she inquired stiffly, keeping her features neutral. 'I want to hold onto my cash until I get a chance to go to the hole in the wall, tomorrow.'

'I don't recall asking you for any money, Mizz Buchanan.' The ice in his voice matched her own clipped tones.

'I can't allow you to pay my fare,' India protested.

'Can't, or won't?'

'Look, don't make a big deal out of this. I'm used to paying my own way in New York.'

'In case it's slipped your attention, this isn't New York,'

MacFarlane cut in, adding, 'I daresay you're one of those women who insists on looking at the check on a dinner date and then paying her share?'

The description was too close for India's comfort.

'And I suppose you're one of those men who orders from the menu without consulting the woman he's with.' Raising her hand to her temple, she massaged it. Thanks to MacFarlane, her headache showed no signs of abating.

'And tell me, Mizz Buchanan, do the men you date object to you *paying your way*?' He made the term sound insulting and degrading.

'No. They do not.'

'How very . . . thrifty of them.'

'It has nothing to do with economy as you well know, MacFarlane!' Just as this argument had nothing to do with her insistence on paying for the ticket. Another pain stabbed at her temple. 'Oh, for goodness sake, drink your coffee and leave me alone!'

MacFarlane looked as if he wanted to say more but returned to his coffee and the view of Lake Michigan thousands of feet below. Closing her eyes, India arched her neck and tried to massage away the headache by kneading the knotted muscles there. That helped; as did shutting out MacFarlane's aggravating image.

He didn't need to know that she *always* insisted on paying her way because she didn't want to be beholden to any man who asked her out to dinner. Neither did she 'invite them up for coffee', having learned all too quickly what *that* meant.

And if such behaviour had earned her the label *Ice Queen*, so what? That was preferable to having her name bandied around the water cooler as her date discussed with the other men what had happened back at her apartment. She worked in a male dominated field and, although things were changing, she needed to protect herself and her reputation.

*****

The plane touched down and MacFarlane found a cab to drive them to the hospital. Despite her early assertion that she was fine, he thought India looked drawn and anxious. He was beginning to learn what made her tick and suspected that she wanted him out of her hair. *Now*. However, he had no intention of leaving her alone, good manners dictated that he should be on hand if she needed any help, somewhere to stay for the night. And, much to his surprise, he found that he liked being in her company, although she lived up to his grandad's assessment that Buchanan women were ornery and wrongheaded.

Now that he knew her better, he guessed it would kill her to admit that she needed a helping hand. His least of all. Added to which, he couldn't get that kiss at the kitchen sink out of his head. It was all he'd thought about on the plane while she'd huffed and puffed and shifted about in the seat next to him. When she'd closed her eyes, briefly, he'd made the most of the opportunity to study her face and he liked what he saw, family feud or no family feud. When she'd shown signs of waking up, he'd glanced at the journal in his hand in order to look busy. It was then that he'd discovered that it was upside down.

India Buchanan was smart, she must have noticed, too.

He felt like kicking himself.

Instead, he waited until she was in the cab and then slid over beside her, directing the driver to the hospital. Unusually, India was slow on the uptake and it took her a few seconds to realise that he was coming with her. Her reaction was only too predictable.

'Wait,' she said to the cab driver. Then, turned: 'MacFarlane, get out of the taxi, your responsibility towards me is over. There's no need to accompany me to the hospital.' Her expression, and the way she was biting her lip, suggested that she was wondering how to explain his presence to her aunt.

'There's every need. Go ahead,' he instructed the driver who shrugged in resigned fashion. It gave MacFarlane a degree of satisfaction to note that the driver followed *his* instructions over India's. When they reached the hospital, India was at boiling point and didn't bother to hide it. Watching a range of conflicting emotions flicker across her face, MacFarlane wondered why he derived such pleasure from arguing with her.

'You really *don't* have to come in with me,' she said, as he paid off the taxi driver. 'In fact, I'm telling you categorically - do *not* come in with me.'

'Categorically? Telling? Wouldn't it be more polite to *ask* me not to come in with you, Mizz Buchanan?' It amused and annoyed him in equal measure that she couldn't get rid of him fast enough. A new experience. He was more used to explaining, politely but firmly, to the women he dated that he wasn't interested in a long-term relationship. Most accepted it with good grace but one or two had clung on, limpet-like, hoping to make him change his mind.

'Look, I'm fine. I'll visit my great-aunt, then take a taxi to the nearest Best Western and check in.' India let out a heavy sigh, indicating she'd reached the end of her tether. 'Please. Just *go*.'

Dropping their luggage on the floor, MacFarlane paid the taxi driver and put his wallet back in his pocket. 'Any one would think you were trying to get rid of me, Mizz Buchanan.' His tone was dry and he was pleased to see her blush. He had, after all, gone out of his way to help. She could be a little more grateful.

'Yes, of course. I'm sorry. Thank you very much.' The niceties having been observed, she started to walk away from him.

Something akin to anxiety made MacFarlane's heart tighten. He didn't want her to walk off. He didn't want her to be alone in Chicago staying in a Best Western when he had room back at his place on Lake Shore Drive. The only way he could think of stopping her in her tracks was by aiming a well-chosen dart.

'Judging by the looks your cute little outfit has attracted ever since we left Green Bay, you need a bodyguard to keep you out of trouble.'

Turning, she looked at him as if she didn't quite believe what he'd just said. 'Excuse me? *Cute little outfit?*'

'Cute - and provocative,' Picking up their luggage, Logan walked briskly towards Reception and India had to run in order to keep pace with him. There was something about the way she was forced to trot alongside in order to keep up with his long strides that he found most gratifying. However, he hid it well as the automatic doors of the hospital whooshed open and they entered. India glanced at her reflection in the stainless-steel doors of the lifts, as if trying to work out what was so outrageous about her 'cute little outfit.'

He guessed the suit had cost a small fortune and doubtless had a designer label inside the jacket. Not that he was the least interested in what women wore. But he couldn't ignore the looks men had directed towards India while they'd been in the airport queue, and the corresponding looks they'd shot him, as if to say: *You lucky son of a bitch*. The suit was so different to the paint-stained overalls she usually wore and, something about the very rightness of it, made him take a deep breath and . . .

'Can I help you?' The clerk at the reception desk repeated the question when neither MacFarlane nor India appeared to hear her.

'We're here to see Miss Elspeth Buchanan . . .'

India elbowed him out of the way with subtle but definite force. 'I'm here to see my aunt, Elspeth Buchanan. My - my *friend* is just about to leave.' The interested, openly flirtatious look the clerk gave him morphed into something else in response to India's tone. Sniffing, she consulted the computer, located Elspeth Buchanan's name and gave the floor and room number to MacFarlane, ignoring India. Leaning forward, she indicated the lifts, giving MacFarlane an unrivalled view of her cleavage.

Sensing India's anger at being side-lined by the clerk, he thought it diplomatic to break the mood. 'I'll wait here for you.'

'There's no need.'

'There's every need. Go see your great-aunt.' He sat down, picked a magazine off the table and, ensuring it was the right way up, flicked it open. He could tell that she was far from pleased, but short of calling security to have him forcefully removed, there was little she could do.

India was still smarting from his high-handed treatment when she walked into the florist's shop in the foyer. She bought flowers and a helium balloon in the shape of a rabbit bearing the message: GET WELL SOON. Then she made her way to the tenth floor and room 16. The last she saw of MacFarlane before the lift doors slid together was him walking over to the coffee machine by the front door and the clerk at the desk checking him out while his back was turned.

*****

Elspeth Buchanan was lying tucked up in bed with the cot sides raised for safety. She had a black eye and severe bruising on her nose and cheek bone. There was no sign of her being in traction or plaster casts and India was grateful. Perhaps

Doctor Voss had exaggerated the extent of her injuries? Entering the room, she closed the door quietly behind her. Clearly, her great-aunt was sleeping; she would leave the flowers and a message with the nurse and would come back tomorrow to talk things over with the doctors.

Looking down at her great-aunt, India was touched by her frailty. Her eyes smarted with unshed tears. She looked like a child lying there - so small in the large bed, her shallow breathing hardly making the covers rise and fall, and India was suddenly afraid. Her aunt had always been so tough, so indomitable, her champion against the world, including India's father, her own nephew, when the chips were down.

Elspeth had supported her after her parents insisted that she exploit her natural talent for languages by reading Modern European Languages and Politics at University. They saw that as the first step towards her becoming the wife of a career diplomat. They couldn't understand her penchant for the world of art. When her parents united against her they usually got their own way. Without Aunt Elspeth's support, she would have ended up in some dull university, bored out of her mind. Instead, she'd got her way and had studied Art History.

Now, however, Elspeth seemed to have shrunk in size, her once copper-red hair finally faded to grey, her spirit drained from her, lying in the bed like an injured bird. Fragile and insubstantial, a shadow of her former self. India bit her lip and tears blurred her eyes as love for her great-aunt overwhelmed her. She had always loved Elspeth, now she wanted her to wake so that she could tell her. But her great-aunt slept on and India didn't disturb her. She'd visit again tomorrow.

Softly closing the room door behind her, she walked down the corridor and found a nurse at a desk. Leaving a message for her great-aunt she then made an appointment to see the consultant. Next, she got back into the lift to join MacFarlane in the reception area. As the lift descended, she fetched a small mirror from her bag and applied powder to the delicate skin below her eyes. She didn't want MacFarlane to know she'd been crying.

He was right, of course, she needed a friend, someone she could rely on. In spite of the animosity between their families, India was suddenly grateful that MacFarlane had insisted on coming to the hospital. But she'd walk across hot coals before admitting it. She knew she'd behaved appallingly since getting on the plane in Green Bay and resolved to mend her ways. She'd be firm, yes - and keep him at arm's length, but not react to his barbed comments.

The lift came to rest on the ground floor and the doors opened quietly. MacFarlane was exactly where she'd left him. Even though his head was bent over his magazine, and he had zoned out from his surroundings, an aura of sexuality and power emanated from him. India felt it, just as the clerk had. The difference was, she knew how dangerous it would be to become entangled with him.

He raised his head as India walked towards him, his green eyes catching her scrutiny before she had time to lower her gaze. Dropping the magazine onto the table, he stood to greet her. In spite of her attempt with the face powder, he could probably tell she'd been crying.

'Bad news?' he asked, laying a gentle hand on her shoulder.

'No. She was asleep. I'm coming back to see her tomorrow and to talk to the consultant,' her voice trailed away.

'But -' he prompted, sensing there was more.

'She looked so frail lying there and I suddenly realised how much I loved her.' India felt the tears threaten again and brought the conversation to a close. Turning, she picked up her overnight bag and got out her mobile to call for a taxi.

Gently, MacFarlane removed the phone from her hand.

'It's taken care of.'

'Then I need to find the nearest Best Western and -'

'That's taken care of, too.'

'It is?'

'You need somewhere to stay. I know a couch you can crash on. If you don't mind roughing it.'

'No, I don't mind,' was India's dull response. The trauma of the day was taking its toll. She was bone weary, too tired to argue or to care where she slept. The frown creasing MacFarlane's forehead suggested that he viewed her uncharacteristic docility with suspicion. But he said no more as they got into the taxi and made their way towards Chicago, just as city lights were coming on.

They followed the main highway that swept along the

shore line of Lake Michigan, past the famous Buckingham Fountain where jets of water shot high into the air, illuminated by bright coloured lights. MacFarlane pointed out Sears Tower and the Hancock Building, their windows burnished gold by the setting sun. Clearly sensing that she was exhausted, he didn't make one remark about her being a tourist and this being his home town. Plainly, he knew when enough was enough.

The taxi swept along Lake Shore Drive where yachts and pleasure cruisers moored alongside jetties were strung with lanterns. All very different to how India had imagined it. She was touched by the magic of it and her tired spirits revived. MacFarlane caught her expression as she gazed at the landmarks he pointed out.

'Not quite the one-horse town you imagined, is it?' he grinned, proud of his city.

'It's so pretty! Small wonder Sinatra called it "My Kind of Town". I take it all back.'

'You're forgiven,' MacFarlane said, sitting back and watching her as they headed towards exclusive condominiums built on the lake shore.

At last the taxi stopped.

'We're here.'

A uniformed doorman opened the taxi door and helped India. MacFarlane paid the driver, picked up their bags and guided her into the large atrium entrance to the condominium. India took in the discreet decor, marble floors, glass and chrome, the fountain and lush green plants. MacFarlane put a key into the lock on the elevator, called the lift and they were whisked silently up towards the penthouse.

The doors opened with a 'ping' and he indicated that India should head down a thickly carpeted corridor ahead of him. They stopped in front of a door which was ornately carved to disguise the fact that it was a security door. Two sets of keys unlocked the fortress and India went in ahead of him. Disarming the burglar alarm by punching in his personal combination, MacFarlane flicked a switch and low lights came on at strategic points around the room. He gestured at a white leather couch, over the back of which was spread an Amish quilt. Depositing their bags to one side of the sofa, he tossed his keys into a carved wooden bowl on a console table.

The atmosphere of trust and friendship that had built up during the taxi ride, vanished as the truth dawned on India. How could she have been so stupid?

'This is *your* apartment.'

'Is that a problem?' MacFarlane asked, seemingly sensing the sudden drop in temperature. 'I promised you a couch for the night. You're sitting on it. But should you prefer, there's a serviceable bedroom through that door.'

India felt herself blush hotly at the suggestion. Did he really expect her to sleep with him? To her dismay, although her brain told her the idea was outrageous, her body whispered something different. Sudden heat suffused her, trailing prickly fingers the length of her body, her lips parted unconsciously and for one crazy moment she allowed herself to wonder what it would feel like to make love with MacFarlane.

Swiftly, she lowered her head. MacFarlane was developing a knack for reading her like an open book. It had to stop.

'Relax lady,' he drawled. 'You have the look of a lamb being driven to slaughter. My tastes run to something rarer than prim and proper Englishwomen, who no doubt at the moment of ecstasy lie back and - what's the saying - think of the Empire.'

'God, you're an arrogant bastard, MacFarlane!' India brought up her chin, spitting out the words. 'For your information, the Empire is long gone; but men like *you* have somehow survived into the twenty-first century.'

'Men like me, huh?' He sent her a derisory look. 'You're priceless, India. Know that? One minute you're outraged because you think I've lured you here to take you against your will. The next you're piqued because I haven't. You're one mixed up lady.' Giving a bitter laugh, he walked over to a large, mirrored drinks cabinet and poured himself a Scotch. He offered her one, but she shook her head. 'Poor India. You can't tell the difference between the Good Samaritan and the Big Bad Wolf. I have no ulterior motive in bringing you here tonight, other than a desire to help out a friend in a crisis.'

A friend? That was stretching incredulity a bit, wasn't it?

'And if I don't believe you?' she asked, clinging to her defensive position and not liking the patronising *Poor India*.

'That's your problem.'

'I see.'

MacFarlane broke the mood with some brisk talking.

'Okay, let's establish some ground rules. I've no intentions of jumping your bones after plying you with strong liquor. Got that? There's a guest bedroom in there complete with its own bathroom and all the usual stuff. You'll find linen in the closet and a robe in the bathroom.' He drank his whisky and then poured himself another, diluting it with bottled water. 'The kitchen's through there,' he gestured with his glass. 'There's a phone in your bedroom; use it to phone your parents and tell them about your great-aunt's fall. In fact, do whatever you want. You can even have 911 on fast dial in case you're worried that I can't contain my animal lust.'

'Thanks, MacFarlane. I'm -' But he didn't give her a chance to explain or apologise.

'One more thing . . .'

'Yes?'

'I won't knock on your door in the middle of the night if you promise not to knock on mine. Deal?' The whisky had apparently restored his sense of humour and he now found her posturing more amusing than insulting.

Damn him! He always ended up with the final word and the last laugh. She was about to explain that it was anxiety over her aunt's condition which had made her overreact, but then changed her mind. Enough said. Picking up her weekend bag, she headed for the guest room.

'Good night MacFarlane,' she called over her shoulder, not trusting herself to look back at him. If he was laughing at her, so help her, she'd do him an injury!

'Good night Mizz Buchanan, sweet dreams.'

India closed the door behind her and stood still in the silent room. She remembered the previous night's dream, the one she'd woken up from thinking of MacFarlane and wondering how it would feel to make love to him. Now, here she was in his apartment, just the one layer of bricks separating their bedrooms. Shaking free from the mood she showered, made the bed, and tried to settle down for the night. She was dog tired, too tired even to sleep. She could hear a police siren wail in the streets below. She looked out into the never-quite-dark night sky of the city. She could almost have been in New York . . .

But, in New York there was no man who disturbed her dreams and waking hours like MacFarlane.

That was India's last thought as tired, chastened and very confused, she fell into a deep dreamless sleep.

Chapter Eight

Next morning, MacFarlane knocked on India's bedroom door and waited for a response. When none came, he pushed the door open and entered, bearing a cup of Earl Grey tea. Standing at the foot of the bed he called out softly, 'India. You awake?'

India stretched out starfish-like in the large double bed, reaching down with her toes to find the coolest spot and gave a sigh of contentment. Unlike her aunt's house, MacFarlane's apartment had air conditioning, comfortable beds and 500 thread count bed linen. All of which had contributed to the best night's sleep she'd had in months.

'Tom?' she murmured.

'Not Tom,' MacFarlane's tone dispersed the last vestiges of sleep.

Without further preamble he pulled back the heavy drapes, letting the morning sun stream across the bedroom. It touched India where she lay face down on the bed, naked. She didn't scramble to pick up the sheet which had fallen onto the floor, because she knew that's what he expected.

117

Instead, she lay motionless, pointedly waiting for him to leave the room. Taking his time, he allowed himself a measured appraisal of her nakedness, from tousled hair, past graceful curve of spine and buttocks, to the long, slender bones of her feet. There was nothing furtive or surreptitious about his scrutiny; his regard was admiring and mouth was drawn back in an appreciative, if slightly ironic, smile.

During those long, drawn-out seconds the air thickened and, in spite of air conditioning, the room became overheated. A heavy silence descended and India's skin prickled with awareness, every sinew in her body tightening in anticipation of . . . of what, she wasn't sure. Turning her head sideways she caught their reflection in the tall mirror to one side of the wardrobe.

MacFarlane looked back at her, then after a moment or two, spoke and broke the spell.

'Your tea, Ma'am. I'll set it down there, shall I?'

Clearly, MacFarlane wasn't cut out to be a butler! India glared at his reflection as he set cup and saucer down on the bedside cabinet, knowing he was enjoying every minute of this role playing. Question was, how could she sit up in bed and drink her tea without revealing more of herself than was modest or seemly?

A gentleman, she fumed, wouldn't stand there gawping, he'd cough and retire discreetly. However, she reminded herself that when it came to the dispute over the house and land, Logan MacFarlane was no gentleman. Demonstrating an uncanny ability to second guess her, he continued in the same faux English accent.

'Before you ask, I did knock, m'lady, but you were snoring so loudly you didn't hear.' Although openly enjoying her discomfiture he did look away while she reached down and picked up the sheet. Drawing it across herself, she flipped over onto her back and fought the instinct to pull the sheet right up to her chin and shield herself from his too interested glance. Recalling his mocking words last night - *I won't knock on your door in the middle of the night if you promise not to knock on mine* - she allowed the sheet to billow around her and acted as though having a man in her bedroom at this hour was nothing out of the ordinary.

'You make a rotten butler, MacFarlane, know that?' Her voice croaky, she rubbed the last traces of sleep from her eyes with her knuckles. Inexplicably, that gesture made MacFarlane's face darken as though she'd done something to displease him. Now what? God - she'd never understand what made him tick, so gave up and drank her Earl Grey instead. After a few sips she eyed him over the rim, wondering what would happen next.

'I dare say more training's required,' he admitted. 'I'm not used to bringing early morning tea to ladies in the guest room.' India quickly picked up on his use of *guest room*, it suggested that any woman staying over was more likely to spend the night in his bed. 'I take it that the Earl Grey is to your satisfaction, Madam?'

India was surprised to find that it was. 'And in a china cup, too,' she observed, unable to resist the little dig.

'What did you expect? A chipped mug? A tin cup left

over from the days the MacFarlanes went prospecting for gold up in *tham thur hills*? Maybe I should have brought you a cup of moonshine, would that have been more to your taste and confirm your low opinion of me?' If he expected India to contradict him, he was disappointed.

'Funny, ain't ya?' she replied using a similar tone, placing the china cup back on the bedside table.

'If you must know,' he went on, 'Granny MacFarlane gave me her best china when I moved to Chicago. Perhaps she thought it'd have a civilising influence on me, as well as reminding me of home in Door County.'

Home. His emphasis on the word brought them back to the dispute over MacFarlane's Landing, the elephant in the room. She was sure that he was playing it down, a ploy to get her to lower her guard and then he'd be in like Flynn. Perhaps he envisaged Granny's tea set in pride of place in *her* aunt's dining room.

Stretching her arms above her head she gave a sensuous yawn, drawing on all her skills as an actress to wipe that cocky smile off his face. Her body language suggested that it was an everyday occurrence for her to wake up with a man in her bed. MacFarlane's smile vanished and was replaced by that frown once more. As though the same thought had occurred to him and he found it unpalatable.

For several heartbeats they looked at each other, as the sun touched the thin sheet and cast into relief the shadowy contours of her body - breasts, angle of her hips, the faint, dark triangle of body hair.

'Who's Tom?' It seemed to pain him to ask the question.

'Just a *man* I know.' A careless shrug and she paused on the word long enough to imply that she knew many men, and Tom was just one of them.

'Is that so?'

'It is.'

Now he was wondering if she was as prim and proper as she made out. Wondering, too, judging by his expression, how it would feel to lie beside her in a bed warmed by her body and scented by her skin. However, just as India was rejoicing that she was points ahead of him in this game-playing, her traitorous body played a trick on her, sending hormones scudding through her veins and causing an involuntary flush to sweep over her. Now it was her turn to wonder how it would feel to have MacFarlane's face buried in her breasts, his long, lean leg parting her thighs, his weight pressing down upon her.

Something unspoken hovered in the air and they both acknowledged it: a wish, a primitive longing as old as time. India forced herself to act more sensibly, she was entering dangerous territory and she'd best have a care. MacFarlane wasn't like the men she was used to in New York, he was dangerous and more resourceful. She'd do well not to push him too far, or too hard.

Sitting straight up in bed to demonstrate that she was mistress of the situation, she arched an eyebrow. 'Is there something else, MacFarlane? Other than waking me at this god forsaken hour?'

Giving himself a mental and physical shake he walked over to the wardrobe. 'I've left breakfast for you in the kitchen. Here's a robe . . .' Opening the wardrobe door, he pulled a dressing gown off a padded hanger and laid it across the foot of the bed. 'See you in the sitting room in five, I need to tell you how the alarm works in case you want to go visit your aunt.' He walked over to the bed and India shrank back against the pillows, unsure of what he was about to do. 'Relax, Mizz Buchanan, I'm only interested in retrieving Granny's precious tea cup.' *Not you.* 'It's vintage,' he added, with all the camp feyness of a New York designer. India caught the subtle hint of his aftershave as he bent to retrieve the cup and shivered spontaneously. 'In case you wondered, I'm heading for the office.'

Realising that a snarky tone served best to remind her of the contentious nature of their relationship, India came back with, 'Yes, yes; I can see that. You don't need to draw me a diagram.' But she gave him a second look, nonetheless.

In a summer-weight business suit, just the correct shade of ivory white, the delicate jade stripes of his cotton shirt and silk tie emphasising his green eyes, MacFarlane seemed light years away from the man who'd sported a disreputable pair of shorts and rode a Triumph. *Clothes maketh the man*, India thought, observing this smoother, more sophisticated MacFarlane. He exuded power and wealth, and she didn't doubt for one moment that he would use both against her. Chicago was MacFarlane's city, she was the stranger and would have to be doubly careful here. Further acquaintance had shown her that, just when she thought she'd got him all figured out, he had a way of turning the tables on her.

'I've written instructions on how to set the alarm on this piece of paper.' MacFarlane bent towards her, placing the paper in the hollow created by her uplifted knee. He dropped a spare set of keys on top of the paper. The weight of them made the sheet slip and exposed India's breasts. *As he'd meant it to?* Blushing a furious, flustered pink, she made a grab for the sheet now at waist level.

'Allow me, m'lady.' Reaching for the sheet his hand inadvertently grazed her nipple. The sound which escaped India's lips was a beguiling mixture of outrage and delight. Dramatically the mood of playfulness vanished and the simmering awareness they'd been at pains to deny flared between them.

Looking up into MacFarlane's face, India saw mirrored there the conflict raging within herself. He wanted her. He wanted her so badly that, momentarily, he was prepared to let it blind him to everything else. For a brief second, she gained a tantalising glimpse of how it would feel to be MacFarlane's woman. To know for certain that this burning regard was reserved for her alone. To recognise that he would only have to walk into a room and look at her in *that* way for her body to quiver in response. An inkling of it must have shown in her face because, without apology, he stretched out his hand and touched the gentle swell of her breast.

There was nothing threatening in the gesture; his touch was inquisitive, exploratory, reverential almost. India's breath quickened as he bent his head towards her and she closed her eyes, anticipating the warm touch of his mouth on her nipple. Then the alarm on MacFarlane's watch bleeped the hour, reminding them of time and place and the reality of their situation. India opened her eyes. MacFarlane glanced at his watch.

The dangerous moment passed.

'Seven o'clock,' he said with enviable control. 'Traffic'll be gridlocked on the intersection. Time I was outta here.' He pulled the cuff over his watch, as though impatient to be gone.

'Of course.' India acted as if nothing more innocuous than a 'good morning' had passed between them.

'Do you think you'll be able to work the alarm?' he asked in a business-like tone.

'I - I'll do my best,' India assured him, sinking lower in the bed and pulling the troublesome sheet up to her chin - decorum overcoming her earlier pretence of sophistication, of being totally relaxed about having a man in her room at this hour.

Strike that - not just any man, MacFarlane. Her enemy.

Why didn't he just bloody well go?

'I get in at about six. You gonna be okay, on your own?'

I'll be fine, she wanted to scream. *Just as soon as you leave the room.*

'I'll try and stay out of trouble,' she assured with a nonchalance she was far from feeling. MacFarlane flashed an unexpected, heart-stopping grin.

'Lady, that I very much doubt. Just in case you need a good attorney here's my card.' He handed her a printed card with the name of his law practice: MacFarlane, MacFarlane and Levison.

'Two MacFarlanes for the price of one?'

This time, he didn't rise to the bait. 'Have a nice day.' The inflection in his voice parodied the clichéd greeting. Then, closing the door softly behind him, he left her alone.

India lay still until she heard the front door close. Then, letting out a long breath, she pushed off the sheet and walked over to the window where she stretched out, hands above her head, and let the sun stream in on her. Turning, she caught sight of herself in the long mirror. Her skin was glowing; her lips had a full, bruised look, as though MacFarlane had kissed them. Her eyes were luminous, enlarged pupils betraying her sexual arousal. No man had ever brought her to this state of almost delirious sensuality by a mere touch.

No man.

And certainly not Tom Harvey or others like him who hadn't been allowed to kiss her goodnight after a night at the theatre, in case it gave them ideas.

She ran her hands over her heated skin, feeling the touch of MacFarlane's long fingers where they had cradled her breast. She shivered at the memory and the realisation that she wanted MacFarlane as much as he wanted her. Groaning, she covered her face with her hands. How would she manage to spend another night with a man she at once hated and found devastatingly attractive? Abruptly she turned from the mirror, entered the bathroom and ran a cold shower which, contrary to everything she'd read, did nothing to dampen the wild imaginings of her overwrought senses.

*****

Later that morning, India walked into her great-aunt's hospital room and was assailed by the sweet scent of lilies and gardenias. Every available surface was covered with flowers from well-wishers. Elspeth Buchanan was sitting up in bed, nursing a black eye and bruised cheek, reading the Door County Advocate. India was relieved to find that she was looking much more like her old self.

'It looks like a botanic garden in here, Aunt. I feel rather redundant,' India joked as she placed her own small bunch of flowers in the sink, filling it with water. Then she faced her great-aunt. 'You look much better than when I peeped in on you yesterday. Don't you dare frighten me like that again!' she admonished.

'The nurse told me you looked in. Why they didn't wake me I can't imagine. Now, don't fuss India Jane, I'm a tough old bird, ask anyone who knows me. Don't stand there like a stranger, child. Come, give me a hug.' India complied and Elspeth held her close for a few moments, rubbing her back affectionately. 'You smell real good, India. What are you wearing?'

'Chanel 19.' India kissed her great-aunt's cheek before straightening.

'My, and you look real good, too,' her aunt observed as

India sat on the edge of the bed, straightening the jacket of the notorious pink suit. Had it only been yesterday that she and MacFarlane had been snarling like dogs at each other over it?

Now she understood that the tension between them was growing sexual awareness. It had been there from day one when MacFarlane had driven up to the house on his bike. While she'd been in denial, MacFarlane had exploited it during that humiliating picnic auction and at the dance afterwards. But, in doing so, had discovered to his cost that attraction was a double-edged sword. It compelled him to sit in the dark, watching India on the porch listening to Turandot. It made him kiss her in her aunt's kitchen and was responsible for him almost losing control this morning.

However, now was not the time for introspection, her aunt was the priority.

'I feel good, Aunt Elspeth, really good,' India laughed, taking her thin, dry hand in hers and massaging it. 'How about you?'

'Never mind me, I'm fine. I've told that fool doctor I'm not paying hundreds of dollars to sit in a hospital bed just so he can put his kids through college. I had a fall, nothing's broken, get over it. I want out of here, if not tomorrow then the day after.'

Looking at her redoubtable great-aunt, India saw the fighting spirit which had prolonged the feud between her and Judge MacFarlane.

'And what did the Doctor say?'

'He said to give up smoking, or I'll never see ninety.' She laughed at her own joke and started coughing, the loose chesty cough of an inveterate smoker. India poured her a glass of water from the jug on the bedside locker. The doctor was onto a loser, hadn't she'd been trying to persuade Elspeth to give up smoking for years?

While her great-aunt sipped the water, India read the cards on the flower arrangements.

'Impressive,' she observed, finding one from her parents. A great basket of regale lilies whose scent had reached her from the threshold of the room. She read the card, repeating dryly, 'Will get to visit you when my schedule is less hectic.'

'Where have we heard that one before?' Elspeth snorted, putting the glass of water down. 'I suppose, when it gets round to time for me to die, I'll have to phone his secretary and arrange a time convenient for your father.'

Grimacing at her aunt's black humour, India walked over to a basket of fruit wrapped in cellophane. She let out a shocked: 'I don't believe it. Old Judge MacFarlane sent you fruit and you accepted it?'

'Yeah. Life can be strange, can't it? I figured the old buzzard could part with some of his ill-gotten money.' Avoiding India's eye, she continued gruffly, 'The fruit's probably poisoned. Maybe he figures he'll get the house quicker that way.' India guessed the throw away remark was Elspeth's way of concealing how touched she was by the gift.

'Gardenias, too?'

'Yeah,' Elspeth shrugged. 'Who'd have thought it?' She

128

cocked her head, sending India a direct look. 'How come he knows I'm in hospital?'

Not wanting her great-aunt to know that she was staying with MacFarlane, India thought on her feet. 'Doctor Voss must have mentioned it. You know there are no secrets in MacFarlane's Landing.'

'Oh, so that's it. I thought you and the old varmint were in the habit of taking afternoon tea together.' India breathed a sigh of relief, glad that her aunt hadn't pursued the matter. However, the mention of tea drew India back to the cup of Earl Grey MacFarlane had brought to her that morning. Taking an apple from the cellophane and using the pretence of rinsing it under the tap, she escaped her aunt's all-knowing eyes.

'It doesn't taste poisoned,' she grinned, washing another before tossing it to her aunt. Elspeth put it on the bedside table and patted for India to come and sit down.

'You're too trusting, India. Come here and give me another hug.' India complied, taking care not to touch her great-aunt's bruises. 'Mm . . . that makes my old bones feel better.' She held India at arm's length. 'So, what have you been up to since I last saw you? You look blooming, child. You got a beau?' India laughed at her great-aunt's quizzing look and old-fashioned expression. 'Not that feller, Tim is it?'

India pretended to be cross. 'You know very well he's called *Tom*. So, stop it. As a matter of fact, Tom's in New York. And, despite all the encouragement my parents have given him, I'm going home in a week or two to make it plain to all parties that I'm just not interested. Apart from which, I've - well, I've pretty much decided to leave the auction house and put down roots in MacFarlane's Landing for the foreseeable future. In your house to be precise.'

Elspeth grasped India's hand and squeezed it.

'India, I'm so glad, about the house, and all. You deserve better than a man who, from everything you've told me, thinks civilisation begins and ends in New York. I hate snobs. No disrespect to you, honey, but I'm sure part of your attraction is the fact that your grandmother is Lady Meredith Fielding, your father is a senior member of *corps diplomatique* and can open doors for him. If he pesters you, stress the working-class roots of your Buchanan ancestors. The fact that they escaped poverty and deprivation by stowing away on a ship to America or stealing the money for their passage. History's a bit vague on that point. That'll get rid of him.'

'Aunt Elspeth.' India tutted at her great-aunt's acid tones and wagged a finger. However, there was more than a grain of truth in what she said. What a contrast to MacFarlane's dismissive comments of her English ancestry. He'd made it clear that his sympathies lay with the pioneering Buchanans, no matter how much of a rough diamond Jim Buchanan had been. India sighed; she couldn't please everyone no matter how hard she tried. But she felt she owed Tom something, getting back in touch with him when she returned to MacFarlane's Landing would be her number one priority.

Her aunt was on a roll. 'Not only did his ancestors come over in the Mayflower, they travelled first class.'

'Elspeth, Tom's a good man. He's loyal and dependable.'

'So's a Saint Bernard. And you can always send it back to the pound if you don't get on. Harvey's a limpet, you'll have trouble scraping him off your hull.' That made India laugh, where did her aunt get her expressions from? She sobered as Elspeth squeezed her hand. 'Seriously, Hun, he wouldn't make you happy. You need someone who'll stand up to you. Someone you can spark off; who'll love you but not give into you, except when it really matters. Maybe you'll fight, but so what? The making up'll be all that sweeter.'

Her voice trailed off.

For a brief second Elspeth's eyes held a faraway look. Intuitively, India guessed that her great-aunt was referring to some incident in her own past. India had often wondered why, despite being courted by the bachelors of Door County, Elspeth had chosen to remain single. Then the moment passed and Elspeth was her usual, no-nonsense self.

'Give me a cigarette before that fool doctor passes by. And open the window so the smoke blows out.'

'If he said no cigarettes . . .'

'India. I'm seventy-six, a little too old for smoking in the toilet. Do you think giving up smoking now will make any difference to my longevity? Stop acting like the Surgeon General and give me the cigarettes, girl.' Unwillingly, India did as she was told and watched as her great-aunt drew on one. 'So, sit down; sit down. Tell me where you're staying.'

Time to own up, India thought, sitting on the edge of the bed.

'You're not going to like it, Elspeth.' India wasn't worried that her great-aunt would sermonise over her staying in a man's apartment. She was too broad minded for that. What *would* matter, however, was that the man was a MacFarlane.

'So; surprise me.' Making herself more comfortable, Elspeth drew in a lungful of nicotine.

'I'm staying with Logan MacFarlane.'

For several long seconds Elspeth Buchanan didn't speak. Then, with characteristic bluntness: 'Have you taken leave of your senses India Jane Buchanan? After everything I've told you about the MacFarlanes and their double-dealing you go and do a fool thing like spending a night with one of them?' Stubbing out her cigarette she threw her hands up in horror and disbelief 'India, you've left me speechless, girl.'

'I said you weren't going to like it.'

'And you were right!' She gave India a shrewd once over, those clever blue eyes suddenly too knowing. 'And I suppose it's young Logan who's put the roses in your cheeks? India, I won't pretend I'm not sorry about you and Tom Harvey. But if it's Logan MacFarlane who's responsible for the change of heart . . .'

'He isn't 'responsible' for anything, for goodness sake Aunt Elspeth.' Her great-aunt raised an eyebrow and India continued a little less heatedly. 'He's merely been kind enough to let me have use of his guest room for a few nights. That's all,' she explained as her great-aunt gave her a sceptical look.

'Well India I may be old, but I'm not stupid. I can't believe a good-looking guy like MacFarlane and a beautiful girl like you could share an apartment without it resulting in fireworks.' Thinking of how close they'd come to pyrotechnics that very morning India turned away so her great-aunt couldn't read her expression.

'*Really*, Aunt Elspeth,' she protested and fiddled with the corner of the bed cover.

'Yes, really.' Elspeth took India's hands in hers and looked at her shrewdly. 'Honey, the only guy I'd trust enough to spend the night alone with you would be either a priest or a rabbi. Even then I wouldn't be so sure. And from what I hear of young MacFarlane he doesn't sound like he's ready to take Holy Orders.'

'Why? What have you heard?' India spoke too quickly and received a speculative glance from her great-aunt.

'It's common knowledge that after graduating from law school he took a sabbatical in MacFarlane's Landing. Folk say he spent hours at the County Record Office researching *their* claim to *my* house.' She gave a snort of righteous indignation before continuing. 'Didn't stop him from breaking the heart of every woman in MacFarlane's Landing, and beyond, who was fool enough to think he would date them. He's too clever for that.' She shook her head at the folly of her own sex. 'Mind you, you can't blame them for trying. MacFarlane's a good catch for a girl - and don't look at me like that, India. Not every woman wants to be, or can be, Miss Independent. Even these days.'

India didn't comment. She was thinking how close she'd come that morning to adding herself to that long list of MacFarlane's conquests. Forewarned is forearmed she thought, as Elspeth Buchanan continued.

'You only have to look at his parents to see why the boy's

never married or come close to it. His mother's as amoral as an alley cat, she's lived with a succession of men, young enough to be no good for her, in some expensive beach house on the Pacific Coast. His father's no better. Dumping the child with John while he pursued his high-flying career, as a Divorce Lawyer to people with more money than sense.'

Just like my parents, India thought, drawing a parallel between herself and MacFarlane.

Elspeth was in full flood. There was nothing more certain to raise her blood pressure than the subject of the MacFarlanes and, as she saw it, their double-dealing.

'The boy's got chutzpah, I'll give him that. One day he turned up at my house, bold and sassy as you please, and informed me that it was only a matter of time before he and his grandfather got the house back. How I'd better start looking for alternative accommodation! I chased him off my porch with a broom. Guess he couldn't have been more than ten years old, but he was every inch a MacFarlane.'

'I didn't know about that.'

'Yeah? Well, maybe you should have found out a bit more about him before spending the night in his fancy duplex,' her great-aunt sniffed. 'Listen to me, India; I've given you good advice all your life. He's a handsome boy, I'll give you that. Charming, too, when he sets his mind to it; but don't trust him. He's a rattlesnake, exactly like his grandfather.'

After her vehement speech Elspeth went quiet, and India was frightened that she'd exhausted herself. Then her great-aunt gave herself a shake as though, temporarily, she'd been whisked back to another time, another place and continued in a more subdued voice.

'India there's something you ought to know. Something I should have told you years ago. John MacFarlane and I were sweethearts.' Her face drooped as she remembered. 'Like Logan, he was a good looker and considered quite a catch. I guess he wanted me because I didn't run after him like the other girls. In fact, I made my opinion of him pretty clear.'

The parallel between MacFarlane and herself made for uncomfortable listening. Hadn't she made her opinion of him clear from the outset? Hadn't she gone out of her way to avoid him when practically every other woman he came across keeled over in front of him? Was history repeating itself?

'Go on,' she prompted.

'Then the whispering started; everyone saying how, if we wed, the MacFarlanes would get their house back, and the feud would be settled, once and for all. I began to wonder if it was me that John wanted or the house. I managed to convince myself that he was only courting me in order to get his hands on the property.' Sighing, she came to the end of her tale. 'So I told him what I thought. We had one hell of a row, John walked out in a blazing temper because I was unwilling to trust him. I felt bad, real bad, because he was on furlough from 'Nam, who knew what would happen to him on his next tour of duty? We parted on bad terms and within six months he'd married someone else.'

'*Six months?*' India couldn't believe what she was hearing.

'Yep. Showed his true colours I guess.' Even after all these years, his betrayal clearly still hurt and her voice trailed away. Plucking at the corner of her sheet she used it to wipe away an angry tear. 'There was other stuff, too. But I can't think about that today, India.'

'Oh, Elspeth.' India folded her great-aunt in her arms, laid her papery cheek against her own and stroked her back soothingly. 'You wounded his pride, I suppose. No man likes that.'

'The MacFarlanes all have pride in abundance,' Elspeth nodded.

Especially Logan MacFarlane, India's sixth sense warned. Almost against her will she recalled his words. *My grandfather said Buchanan women were ornery, that's when they weren't being downright stubborn.* And then later on: *Your great-aunt would burn the house down before she saw a MacFarlane set foot in it.*

Now India understood the reason for her great-aunt's vehemence concerning the MacFarlanes. It wasn't only family pride that kept the feud alive. She'd been hurt by old MacFarlane, and he by her lack of trust. The only thing she had left to wound him with was the house and the land he craved. The feud had festered on all these years fuelled by bitterness and mistrust. Now the toxic baton had been passed on to herself and Logan, the last of the Buchanans and MacFarlanes.

Would - *could* - things ever be resolved between them?

'India, I've been doing some thinking.' Elspeth broke into India's thoughts. 'I can't look after myself, not like I used to. Another Door County winter in my old house would kill me off, for sure. This bout of pneumonia has made that plain. So, I'm going to take up permanent residence in the residential nursing home in Green Bay. It's got everything laid on, for a price, and has great views of the lake. I checked it out before I was ill but didn't mention it to anyone. I've had a couple of sleep overs there to see if I'd like it.' She pulled a face at *sleep overs*. 'Hell, it was like going back to college, only this time the drugs are available on prescription and doled out by the nursing staff.'

'Elspeth . . .'

'Hear me out, Indy. The other inmates are sprightly Seniors like me. I'll have twenty-four-hour nursing, companionship and a degree of independence. In fact,' she gave a flirtatious look, 'a couple of the old boys made it plain that they'd be very happy if I moved in straightaway. Kinda makes me feel sixty again!'

'Elspeth, why haven't you discussed this with me, or my father?'

'Nothing to discuss. Unlike my mother, I won't be a burden on you.'

Was that another reason things hadn't worked out between her and John MacFarlane, India wondered? Elspeth had nursed her mother from the moment her dementia was first diagnosed until the day she died. It was expected of the daughter of the house in those days and Elspeth had turned her back on a promising teaching career in the local high school. Or maybe it was simply the case that Judge

MacFarlane couldn't face the thought of having an elderly cuckoo in their love nest?

'You wouldn't be a burden. No way.'

'You say that now. But I know how hard it can be and, for the record, your father was worse than useless. He threw money at the problem but hardly ever came to visit his grandmother. Left all the nursing to me. Anyway, my mind's made up. I want to sign the house over to you, and with it part of the legacy that will be yours when I've gone. Then you can start up your what'cha-ma-call-it?'

'Boutique Bed and Breakfast,' India supplied. 'Elspeth, are you sure?' She was touched by her generosity.

'Hell, don't thank me, girl. It'll be an albatross round your neck and will eat into your savings. I can't help you as much as I'd like because those residential homes don't come cheap. Especially when nursing care is needed, too.'

India was quick to reassure her great-aunt that she'd be fine.

'Granny Meredith says she'll help and she'll be in no hurry to have the money paid back. That'll give me time to get on my feet. She's a great believer in women doing things for themselves. And I do have some savings of my own. In fact, I thought I'd ask father if he would give me the money he and mother have put to one side for my wedding. He's already made it clear that he won't help with my project, although he could do so easily. I've no intention of marrying, now or ever. Using my *dowry*, for want of a better word, to restore the old house would be a much better use of it.'

'You're right honey. If - *when* - you find the right man, you can run away to - where's that place in Scotland?'

'Gretna Green,' India supplied. 'Or not get married at all.'

'Like me, you mean?' A shadow crossed Elspeth's face, suggesting that living a life devoid of love wasn't a course of action she'd recommend to anyone, let alone a much-loved great-niece.

The sorrow in her voice was palpable and India gave her a reassuring hug. Elspeth brushed away her thanks with customary gruffness. Then, banishing sombre thoughts she gave a mischievous smile. 'Say, why don't we ask one of the barracudas at MacFarlane, MacFarlane and Levison to handle the transaction for us? I'd get a great deal of satisfaction out of *that*. I like to rile the old rattlesnake when I can, keeps me on my toes.' She laughed at her own joke. 'Now, stop looking at your watch and go meet the MacFarlane boy.'

'I'm not . . .'

'Sure you are, you never could tell a convincing lie. Now, you tell young Logan from me that if he hurts you, plays you false, I'll come after him with my walking stick.' India didn't doubt it for a minute.

'You have nothing to worry about. Seriously, Elspeth.' She gave the old lady a loving, exasperated look. There was so much more she wanted to ask, so much she wanted to say. But that would keep for another time.

'I'm tired honey. Give me a kiss and come visit me in Green Bay, whenever they let me out of Alcatraz.'

139

'I will,' India assured, her face full of her love. 'Now be good and do what the doctors tell you.'

'Huh!'

Turning in the doorway she blew her great-aunt a kiss.

'Love you, Great-Aunt Elspeth.'

'Love you, too, India Jane Buchanan.'

It was a familiar leave-taking, one they'd observed since India was a child. Today, in view of her great-aunt's revelations, it seemed especially relevant. With these thoughts weighing heavily on her, India hailed a cab and returned to MacFarlane's condominium on Lake Shore Drive.

Chapter Nine

Late afternoon sunlight slanted across the white carpet and touched India's bare legs as she let herself into MacFarlane's apartment. The duplex felt strangely quiet and empty as if, like her, it was waiting for MacFarlane's return.

Now she was alone, India had a chance to study the apartment and learn more about the man who lived there.

The interior was classically masculine: black leather Le Corbusier chaise, a life-sized reproduction of Lichtenstein's 'WHAM!', Mayan masks and primitive Mexican statues scattered on low tables and the largest television India had ever seen. The decor emphasised the difference between them. MacFarlane was a man of this century while India drew comfort from the past and familiar things. Walking into the kitchen she cast an appreciate eye over the black marble worktops and glossy units which contrasted, somewhat clinically, with the stainless-steel appliances.

She'd lay good money that he rarely ate, let alone cooked, in there.

It was poles apart from Elspeth's homely kitchen, but India knew which one she preferred.

A huge bowl of Florida oranges provided a splash of colour in the monochrome setting and next to it an Alessi citrus press stood poised like a stainless-steel spider over the countertop. Attached to the citrus press, was a Post-it on which was scribbled: 'Hope you're great-aunt is okay. Don't believe everything she tells you about the MacFarlanes. See you around six.' It was signed with a bold: 'LOGAN.'

She said the name aloud: 'Logan.'

It was the first time she's used his Christian name and she shivered, knowing she would never willingly use his first name. It represented the final barrier between them and had to remain in place if she was to retain independence and sanity. Thank goodness he'd had the good sense to stop earlier in the bedroom. If they had become lovers the whole situation would have become intolerable.

Like Elspeth, she'd never know if it was her that MacFarlane desired, or the house.

She couldn't allow history to repeat itself.

Taking the Post-it off the citrus press she ripped it into shreds, then fed the paper into the waste disposal unit. If only she could dismiss her other problems so easily. Catching sight of her distorted reflection in the citrus press she pulled a wry face, then sighed.

Without a doubt MacFarlane was her biggest problem; she'd been thinking crazy thoughts about him all day. The more she thought about him, the more confused she became. How *could* she have acted so rashly this morning?

Easy, the answer came back.

MacFarlane made her feel wild, reckless, abandoned and with such devastating effect that she hardly recognised herself. Cool, assured India Jane Buchanan - always in command and in control - had been replaced by a flighty twenty-something, anxious about how the night was going to pan out. She covered her face with her hands, then dropped them. They smelled of the antiseptic hand gel she'd applied at the hospital and provided a timely reminder of Aunt Elspeth's warnings about the MacFarlanes. Another groan, although more of a whimper this time, as she glanced at her watch. MacFarlane would soon be home. How could she face him after everything that had happened in the bedroom? Should she act cool and haughty, countering his easy assurance with an attitude of her own?

Or, should she pretend nothing untoward had happened this morning?

They were attracted to each other. It was no big deal, they were grown-ups and free to act as they chose. Get over it.

However, it *was* a big deal - for her, at any rate. Casual sexual encounters had never been her style and she'd be sure to let MacFarlane know that. Glancing down, she saw that her hands were shaking. She wasn't sure if this was because of what she imagined MacFarlane might be expecting from her after this morning, or because she wasn't sure how long she could hold out against him.

She'd never invited the men she dated back to her apartment for coffee or spent romantic weekends with them in Country Inns. Not that she hadn't been tempted. She was, after all, a healthy young woman with all the usual feelings of attraction towards the opposite sex. In the past she'd formed

143

a couple of relationships which had lasted several months. But, while the love making had been pleasant and mutually satisfying it could hardly be described as earth shattering. In fact, the needle hadn't moved on the Richter Scale.

It might seem to others as though she had consciously avoided commitment. Truth was, until she'd gone to live in New York she'd been shifted around from pillar to post and never had the opportunity to put down roots. Because of her lifestyle it had seemed pointless to get involved, *seriously* involved with any man because she'd be moving on before any relationship had a chance to develop. As a result, she'd become so resourceful and self-reliant that it was difficult to let go. If some of the men she'd frozen out had put it about that she was a cold-assed British bitch because she wouldn't sleep with them, that was their problem.

Then she'd met Tom Harvey, director and heir apparent at the art auction house where she worked. Their relationship had progressed from mutual respect to an easy friendship. Tom had taken their friendship a step further by inviting India to spend Christmas with his family in Boston. They'd kissed under the mistletoe, and although the stars hadn't caught fire, they'd started to spend more time in each other's company.

And, superficially at least, it seemed a perfect match: the Harveys were an old Bostonian family of impeccable lineage, and India's mother's pedigree made her a suitable match for the son of the house. India, who considered such things unimportant, discovered that to some people they mattered a great deal. Every time she stayed with Tom's family it seemed as if she was living in a latter-day version of a Henry James novel.

Now everyone was waiting for them to send out SAVE THE DATE cards. How had things got that far? Time she went back to New York and made it plain to Tom and her parents that her life was taking a different direction. Maybe it was just as well she was thinking of making MacFarlane's Landing her home. Once she'd made her feelings clear to Tom, she suspected that her internship at his family's auction house would be terminated, citing the current economic uncertainty affecting all sections of society.

The time had come for her to empty her desk and sell the remaining lease on her apartment.

To jump before she was pushed.

Her mind drifted back to this morning and MacFarlane's hand on her breast. She'd never wanted to take her and Tom's relationship to the next level. If Tom had, then he'd never made it obvious in word or deed. That would make it easier to walk away from the relationship.

With MacFarlane it was different.

Within days - hours - of meeting him she was considering abandoning the code she lived by. Since they'd danced together at the picnic auction, all she could think of was having sex with him and knowing, instinctively, that it would be the best sex - ever!

Feeling feverish, in spite of the air conditioning, she snapped out of her reverie, walked over to the fridge and poured herself a glass of white wine. After the first sip she looked at the label appreciatively - of course, only the best for MacFarlane. Taking the glass into the sitting room, she stretched out on the Le Corbusier chaise.

What she saw on the wall opposite, made her sit bolt upright and spill wine down the front of her camisole. A watercolour of the house, lighthouse and jetty at MacFarlane's Landing displayed on an old-fashioned artist's easel. Why on earth was a painting of her family house on prominent display in enemy territory? She recognised the artist's signature, having seen it only minutes earlier on the post-it note stuck to the citrus press.

Logan MacFarlane.

Getting to her feet she took the painting from the easel to examine it with a professional eye. It was good. Very good. He'd caught the early afternoon light perfectly, the way the lighthouse cast a long shadow over the garden towards the artist. Artist? She'd love to know when - and how - he'd managed to paint the house from the jetty without her great-aunt setting the dogs on him. Raising the painting to eye level she read the date. The watercolour had been painted ten years earlier. The summer she'd taken the Baccalauréat and then flown to Italy to spend the vacation with her parents.

She took a step backwards and the floor creaked. Feeling guilty for snooping, she replaced the painting on the easel, glancing over her shoulder and half-expecting to see MacFarlane there. The painting raised more questions than answers. Shaking her head, she went into her bedroom to change her soaked camisole wondering what *exactly* made Logan MacFarlane tick.

*****

Ten minutes later, India opened heavy patio doors leading from the kitchen to the terrace and stepped out on to MacFarlane's rooftop garden. Leaning on the parapet at the very edge of the patio she looked down on Lake Michigan and its magnificent shoreline. Yachts, the colours of bright butterflies, moved across its surface. From thirty floors below the soft roar of the evening rush hour traffic rose to greet her. On the roofs of other apartment blocks she could see bright blue rectangles of swimming pools, the dark green of all-weather tennis courts, and people knocking off early to enjoy the weekend.

In so many ways, exactly like New York.

She thought of friends she'd left behind in Manhattan with mild regret. Right now they'd be meeting in some fashionable watering hole to drink cocktails and discuss the day's events. Within a month she'd be forgotten, or at least remembered as the girl who threw it all away: promising career, the boss's son, an opportunity to study for a further degree in London or Paris. And for what? The chance to run a Bed and Breakfast establishment, much as her Buchanan ancestors had done back in the 1890's, on a spit of land jutting into Green Bay.

Pur-leaze; gimme a break, she imagined mocking laughter and exaggerated eye rolls as they sipped their cocktails.

Perversely, even as she was planning her future in Wisconsin, thinking of that life in New York heightened her sense of dislocation. A wave of homesickness swamped her, made worse by waiting for the return of a man she barely knew. Despite the heat, she shivered, remembering MacFarlane's taunt that she would disappear as soon as the first snowflake landed on her eyelashes. She would hate to prove him right and that her enthusiasm for living in her great-aunt's house would disappear with the first fall of snow after Thanksgiving.

Shrugging off the mood, she wandered round the patio admiring terracotta pots full of geraniums and climbing plants wilting in the heat. Watering the plants while she waited for MacFarlane's return would give her something to do and go part way to repaying him for his hospitality.

Locating the hose, she connected it to a tap in the wall and turned it on, kicking off her expensive leather shoes, then watering each of the tubs and planters in turn. The terracotta pots turned dark red as the water soaked them and splashed on the tiled floor. The evocative smell of damp earth reminded her of an English wood in early spring, the scent of the bluebells in her grandparents' garden, wild garlic crushed underfoot.

England in the spring . . . New York in the summer heat . . . MacFarlane's Landing in the winter.

Where did she *really* belong?

'You don't have to do that.'

She reacted so violently to MacFarlane's greeting that

water splashed over her bare feet. Spinning round, she found him standing in the doorway, jacket slung over one shoulder, tie unknotted and slightly askew, and shirt sleeves rolled up to the elbow.

'MacFarlane! You gave me a start. You shouldn't go creeping up on people like that.'

Her voice shook, and she hoped he'd put it down to shock. His hair was ruffled and he looked tired, but so heart-crushingly handsome that for long seconds India could only look at him speechlessly while her heart performed flick-flacks.

'Your feet . . .' MacFarlane pointed down, then turned off the tap. India glanced down at the puddle of water she was standing in, holding onto the hosepipe as if it was a lifeline. He must think her an idiot, she thought despairingly, as he removed it from her slack fingers.

'I'm on a water meter, you know.' His quip a clear attempt to earth the electrical charge crackling between them. 'Guess I'll have to work extra hours at the office to pay for the hike in my utility bill.' It wasn't a particularly witty thing to say, but it filled the silence as they stood in the rapidly spreading puddle, oblivious to everything but each other. When India made no effort to move or join in the stilted conversation, he ran a finger down the side of his nose, revealing *his* indecision and uncertainty. 'I think, maybe, that . . .'

'Yes?' India saw her fears and reservations mirrored in his green eyes. If she'd spent the day beset by conflicting thoughts so, apparently, had MacFarlane. That made her feel better.

'I . . .' seemingly lost for words a second time, MacFarlane dropped his jacket onto a nearby lounger and let the hose pipe fall at their feet. Tension heightened as he took a step towards India. She swallowed, unsure of what was about to happen. 'I want to apologise for my behaviour this morning.' Reaching into his back pocket he pulled out an envelope and offered it to her.

'What's this?' Her heart sank. Was he paying her off?

Don't tell anyone what happened between us. Keep it secret.

'A junior suite at The Drake, reserved under your name. I'll call a cab to take you over there once you're packed.'

'Anyone would think you're trying to get rid of me, MacFarlane.' As always, a tart response was her first line of defence. There. That was easy. Keep it up, back to being *Mizz Buchanan*.

'But, this morning,' he nodded back over his shoulder towards the bedroom and flushed beneath his tan.

Seemingly of one mind, they both remembered his hand on her breast.

'What about it?'

'I overstepped a boundary -'

'It takes two to tango, doesn't it?'

'So I'm led to believe.' He stood, turning over the envelope containing the reservation in his hands, unsure of himself. 'So, you won't be needing this?'

India pretended to give the question some thought. 'Hm. Probably not.'

'Not?' His frown showed that he wasn't exactly sure what she meant.

'I felt sorry for your plants.' She moved the conversation onto less dangerous ground.

'I pay a gardener to take care of them.'

'Whatever you're paying him -'

'*Her*,' he corrected. Of course, *her*, India sent him an arch look.

'- is too much. Half the plants are dead.'

'That's your Scottish blood talking there, lassie.'

'They looked so dusty and neglected in the heat, I -' India's lips were dry so she moistened them with her tongue. The intimate gesture displaying an eroticism India hadn't intended and MacFarlane's eyes narrowed. Aware that she was sending out mixed messages, she tried to rein it in, and keep things on an even keel. Glancing down at the pool of water at her feet, she was amazed to find that it hadn't evaporated.

MacFarlane spoke first, his voice husky, Adam's apple moving up and down as he swallowed. 'You were saying?' Plainly, he wanted her to make the first move.

'What was I saying?' India asked, looking at him directly.

'That you don't want to spend the night in the Drake?'

'Correct.'

'Which kind of implies that you want to spend it here. With me.'

'Correct, on both counts, counsellor.' She sounded like the lawyer, not MacFarlane.

Her answer was the signal he'd been waiting for. Closing the gap between them, he drew India into his arms and kissed her with a thoroughness which demonstrated their minds had been running on the same dangerous track. Instinctively, India linked hands behind Logan's neck, curling her fingers in his hair to deepen and prolong the kiss. Tongues touched and desire lanced through India, making her gasp. Clearly, MacFarlane felt it too because he let out a groan and responded to India's kisses with such enthusiasm that the blood sang in her ears and lights flashed behind her closed eyelids.

When they pulled apart they had the dazed look of sleepwalkers.

'Are you going to tell me I shouldn't have done that?' MacFarlane's smouldering look dared her to contradict him.

'Should I?'

He looked at her consideringly. Then he bent his head towards her, before pausing inches above her lips and whispering: 'For both our sakes, I think you should.'

Before India could obey him, or the dictates of common sense, his next kiss destroyed the last shreds of resistance. They kissed for what seemed endless seconds, during which they rapidly approached the point of no return. India decided to call a halt to this all-too pleasurable madness. Using every ounce of willpower, she broke free of the embrace and walked unsteadily towards the table where she'd left her glass of wine.

'W - want some wine?' she asked in a voice that was surprisingly level, considering her heart was racing like a wild thing.

'Sure.' MacFarlane drew a steadying breath and a dangerous moment passed. India caught his reflection in the patio doors as she made her way towards the kitchen. His glance was admiring as he noted the way her bottom moved against the fabric of her tight, short skirt. Shaking his head, as though in disbelief, he grinned, unaware that he was being observed.

India smiled, too, as she walked into the kitchen and closed the doors. She needed a breathing space, time out to come to terms with her unbridled response to MacFarlane's kisses. Looking out through the small window that gave onto the patio she saw MacFarlane lean back against the balcony and rub his eyes with his knuckles.

That gesture made her heart contract with a tenderness that surprised her.

A warning bell sounded in the back of her mind.

This man affected her more than she was willing to acknowledge or allow. Until a few days ago she hadn't been aware of his existence and since then had come to view him as a formidable and determined adversary. Now here she was, stealing glances as gauche as a girl on her first date. Before she knew it, she'd be scribbling their names together on random pieces of paper: India MacFarlane, Mrs Logan MacFarlane, Ms India Buchanan-MacFarlane, just to see how it looked.

India's stomach lurched at the thought of spending two further nights alone with him.

She recalled his jibe last night: 'I won't knock on your door in the middle of the night if you promise not to knock on mine.' Then she'd been furious and the promise had been easy to keep. Tonight would be a different matter.

Catching sight of herself in the polished steel oven door, India felt she was looking at a stranger. Clothes were dishevelled, her lipstick was smudged and eyes were large in her pale face. Running fingers through her hair, she smoothed down her curls and then schooled her features before pouring two glasses of bone-dry Chablis and joining MacFarlane on the terrace.

He was sitting on a padded chair by one of the tables, loosening his tie while contemplating the city skyline. Taking the wine from her, he raised his glass 'Cheers,' he said, with an English accent which owed more to Dick Van Dyke in Mary Poppins than Hugh Grant. India grimaced and they both laughed, all awkwardness between them vanishing.

'Here's looking at you, kid,' she countered, chinking glasses together. She'd thought that MacFarlane was going to act as if the kiss hadn't happened, but he'd proved her wrong. Covering her free hand with his, he laced their fingers together. India's breath caught in her throat at the touch of his warm skin against her own and she covered her confusion by taking a sip of Chablis. When she glanced down, her hands were shaking. She knew that he was aware of it, too.

'India . . .' his soft voice caused a tingle of excitement to fizz along her spine. 'It took every ounce of my will power to leave you this morning. I almost rear ended two cars on the intersection because I couldn't get you out of my head.'

'Oh.' This time, she took a gulp of wine and tried to think of some witty response to this passionate declaration. But her mind had been wiped blank except for the image of

154

MacFarlane gently cupping her breast. In a heated rush, she blurted out: 'I went to see my great-aunt today and then I went shopping at the Water Tower Mall.'

She groaned inwardly. What was this? Show and Tell?

MacFarlane's teasing smile and the mischievous light dancing in his green eyes showed he recognised a diversionary tactic when he saw one. But for now, was prepared to play along.

'So, how was your great-aunt? And how was the Water Tower Mall?'

India laughed and managed a more relaxed, 'Both fine. And you?'

'I kinda got bogged down in a big corporate law issue we're handling at the moment. A fraud case; very interesting and very involved. But not, at this moment, what I feel like talking about.'

The ardent look he shot India left her under no illusion as to what he preferred to talk about. Her heart rate spiked alarmingly. Taking another large sip of wine, she warned herself to slow down. At this rate she'd be drunk as a skunk before she finished the glass. MacFarlane unlaced their fingers, reached into his wallet and drew out two tickets.

'I remembered that you liked Puccini.' He put the tickets on the table, seeming unsure of himself. As if mentioning Puccini would remind them of the night when she had listened to Turandot on her porch and he'd sat in the dark, watching her.

'I love Puccini,' she responded, seeing the tickets were

for *La Boheme*. 'Tonight? Oh.' Mentally, she ran through the scant wardrobe she'd packed. 'I've only brought casual clothes, hardly fit for the opera.'

'This isn't the Met or Covent Garden. And you looked pretty good to me this morning wearing a sheet.' MacFarlane laughed at her confusion. 'Why don't you go and have a shower and be ready in about an hour?'

'Okay,' India was only too glad to escape.

'We'll eat after the opera,' MacFarlane called after her.

As India ran the shower, her mind went into hyper-drive. This was all happening so fast. One minute she was trading insults with MacFarlane and threatening to see him in court. The next she was returning his kisses and going to the opera with him. With the cautionary tale of her great-aunt and the Judge giving food for thought, she stepped into the shower.

*****

Forty minutes later and feeling much more in charge, she joined MacFarlane in the airy sitting room. He was seated on the white leather sofa, dark head resting back against a bright red and cream Amish quilt draped over the back.

India coughed to announce her presence.

'Will I do?' she asked and gave a little twirl on the high heels of her soft kid sandals.

She wore a flowing dress with a shawl collar in different shades of indigo and jade green voile printed over with an ethnic design. It was currently her favourite, bought in London last summer. She blessed the impulse that had made her include it in her luggage; it was silk and almost uncrushable. Her make up complimented the colours of the Indian print; violet-blue eye shadow and eyeliner revealed the depth of colour of her irises. Light blusher and lip gloss completed the look and she'd applied mousse to her newly washed hair to give it extra volume. It framed her delicately made up face to perfection and MacFarlane's eyes widened in appreciation when she completed her pirouette.

Putting down the paperback he was pretending to read, he got to his feet.

'Lady,' he assured her, as he took her by the elbow, 'You'll do.' His all-encompassing look almost had her running back into the bathroom to stand under the cold shower. There was no mistaking the message burning in his eyes. 'Ready?' He picked up keys and wallet from a side table.

'Ready.' India replied and left the apartment, enjoying the light touch of his hand on her waist as they headed for the lift.

Chapter Ten

After the opera, a cab dropped India and MacFarlane outside a restaurant in a fashionable district of Chicago. The entrance was cordoned off by a crimson rope guarded by a muscular doorman. Groups of expensively dressed people stood on the sidewalk in the warmth of the summer's night waiting for a table, their tetchy expressions suggesting they'd been waiting quite some time. MacFarlane was greeted by the Maître d' who ushered them to a secluded banquette, amidst much protest from the others waiting in line. Within minutes, a glass of iced champagne appeared in front of them and then, with a slight bow, the Maître d' left them to contemplate the menu.

'Were we lucky to get a table?' India asked.

'Well, yes and no. Let's just say the owner owes me a rather large favour.' MacFarlane directed his attention towards the menu and India's appetite took a sudden dive, the glass in her hand feeling like a poisoned chalice. Forcing herself to snap out of the dreamlike state induced by La Boheme, MacFarlane's kisses and the way he'd held her hand all through the opera, she moved her brain up a gear. The deference shown to him by the Maître d' hinted at his standing in the community. She could only guess at the power the sway of law held in a city with a thousand restaurants, and she had no doubts over MacFarlane's skill as a lawyer. He was articulate, powerful - and she guessed - also ruthless and ambitious. Good qualities in an aspiring District Attorney, qualities he'd use without compunction to wrest her house away from her.

She'd do well to remember that.

On a first date, a girl needs to be level headed and wary, that was a lesson learned in New York. Tonight was no different. Putting her glass of champagne down on the table she pretended to read the menu.

'You okay, India?' MacFarlane asked, as the silence between them lengthened. India glanced up and caught his measuring look.

'Just translating the menu.' She smiled, and his expression lightened.

'No doubt you're fluent in French?' Plainly, he couldn't resist the opportunity to tease.

'And German and Italian. You don't have parents in the diplomatic service without picking up a smattering of most European languages.'

MacFarlane gave her a shrewd. 'Somehow I think your knowledge of languages goes beyond a smattering.' India sensed that he, too, was reminding himself of *her* capabilities; to be wary and not rush things tonight. 'A hundred dollars says you went to finishing school, Mizz Buchanan.' He held out his hand to seal the bet.

India's hand fitted into his like a glove, and despite the earlier resolution, her pulse quickened. 'You ask too many questions, MacFarlane, know that? Anyone would think you were a lawyer, or something.' She smiled to take the sting out of her words. 'Besides, I think there's been enough gambling between our two families to last a lifetime. Don't you?' He laughed, holding onto her hand and lazily tracing a whorl on her palm before raising it and kissing the underside of her wrist. He met her eyes and her breath caught at the message she read there.

'Guess you're right, it must be the lawyer in me,' he answered unrepentantly, covering her hand with both of his. India's heart changed rhythm, as though MacFarlane had trapped that, too, between his long fingers. She suspected he could feel her pulse beating quick and strong and knew how much his touch affected her. MacFarlane's mind must have been running on the same track because his eyes darkened, and he pressed home the advantage.

'India -'

'MacFarlane -'

Reluctantly he released her, his fingers trailing along the length of her palm before picking up the menu. He spent several minutes reading flowery descriptions of what was on offer and making fun of the more extravagant details, patently aware that they had to cool things down before the menus ignited in their hands. India took a deep breath and steered the conversation into safer channels.

'Where were you educated MacFarlane?'

'Out East. In a school right out of Dead Poet's Society. My mother came from New England, and didn't want me growing up a redneck.' He pulled a wry face at the expression. 'So, I was sent to boarding school to iron out any genes donated by my MacFarlane forbears. I swear she thought I'd break out in a broad Scots accent if I so much as saw a strip of plaid or caught a whiff of *uisge beatha*.' India's head came up sharply at his use of the Gaelic for *whisky*. Another reminder that he was smart, cultured, even if he chose to hide it.

'Sometimes, I think it would be a blessing to be hatched out of a pod, no ancestors, family history, nothing. Be free to go out into the world, making up the rules as you went along. Then we wouldn't be enemies . . .' Feeling she'd said too much, she looked away.

'Is that what we are? Enemies?'

'Adversaries, then,' India amended, not wanting to destroy the mood. 'Let's forget all about the house for tonight, just be ourselves?' She gestured towards MacFarlane with her champagne flute. He returned the favour by touching the rim of his glass lightly against hers. 'You were saying - Dead Poets' Society, posh boarding school? Then what?' His mouth quirked at her use of *posh* but bowed his head, acknowledging the temporary truce.

'I graduated, went to Law School. I'm a MacFarlane, it's expected.'

'And what if it hadn't been? Expected I mean?'

'I would have packed my backpack, sketch pad, pencils, box of paints and headed off into the wide blue yonder. Working my way round the world, earning my keep as I went, sketching everything I saw and - who knows, turning it into a book about my travels on my return. I'd grow my hair long, sport a grizzly beard and no one would recognise me when I got home. Like a sailor returning from a long sea voyage.' There was a note in his voice India had never heard before - wistfulness, regret.

'Really?'

He grinned and the moment was gone. 'I know that look, Mizz Buchanan. You think I couldn't survive without the luxuries that *I* - strike that - that my *interior designer* has assembled around me in my apartment? Well, you'd be wrong.'

'So, why don't you do it? Take off into the wild blue yonder?'

'Because . . .' he gave her a straight look, as if trying to figure out if bearing his soul was a good idea. 'How does the poem go? Something about *having promises to keep*? Dead Poets' Society, remember?' He raised his glass to her and India sensed the shutters were about to be pulled down, and so pressed home while she still had the advantage.

'Promises to whom?'

'To my family. It's the lot of the MacFarlanes to attend law school. So,' he let out a long breath, as if he'd made up his mind to tell her everything, 'here I am. A - what was it you called me - hot shot lawyer. End of story.' He took a large drink of champagne, then looked away, as though the truth made painful telling.

'Can I ask a supplementary question?'

'Go ahead.'

'Who painted the picture of MacFarlane's Landing and Aunt Elspeth's house displayed on the easel by the window?' She already knew the answer but wanted to hear it from his lips.

'I did.'

'It's good, very good in fact. Second question?'

'Last one. Then it's my turn.'

'How did you do it? I don't mean your technique, I'm wondering how you got close enough to the house to set up your stuff, get out your paints, and produce a painting. I remember Aunt Elspeth telling me that she chased you off her porch more than once. I can't see her letting you set up camp at the end of the drive for days on end.'

'You're right - she didn't. I printed off a photograph from the *Door County Advocate's* website and used that. So much for artistic ambitions, huh?'

'Not bothered by copyright, then?' she teased.

'Nah. I used the photograph as an aide memoire and more or less gave myself a free hand with the painting. I've been there enough times, often when old Mizz Buchanan wasn't around. She was pretty dangerous with that broom.' He didn't quite say that the image of the house was burned into the synapses of his brain and was there every time he closed his eyes. He didn't need to. He looked at her, waiting for a response. 'You liked it?'

'Very much. You have a gift MacFarlane, it's a shame not to use it.'

'Thanks.' He seemed genuinely pleased. Then, adopting an *aw, shucks ma'am, country boy* demeanour, he toyed with his napkin. 'I sure do appreciate that, ma'am - you being an art expert, an' all.'

'Don't push it MacFarlane.' A severe look. 'It's bloody good; okay?'

'I'll settle for *bloody good*.'

'Mind you, I hope the MacFarlanes don't regard the painting as a totem.'

'Meaning?'

'Meaning, that a totem can be the emblem of a family or clan and is often used as reminder of ancestry. Do you look at the painting to remind yourself what the MacFarlanes have lost and wonder if - how - they're going to get it back?'

'Shoot from the hip, don't ya?'

'Sure do,' she mimicked his drawl.

'Sleep easy, I think we both know the only ones really fired up over the house are my grandfather and your great-aunt. I'm going to Washington soon, you're heading back to New York.' He waited for her to contradict, then went on in a rush as though he had to say his piece, regardless of its effect on their burgeoning relationship. 'I was objectionable that day I caught you painting the fence. I hadn't seen my grandfather in a while and I didn't realise how ill he was. That day,' he rubbed his eyebrow with a finger, 'I took it out on you. There it is and I'm sorry. Grandfather's more frail each time I visit, and if there's a chance - however remote - that you or your aunt would be willing to sell then . . . then I'd like it to happen before he passes over.' His voice caught on the last sentence and he turned his head slightly to the left to hide the raw emotion in his eyes. 'You can't blame me for trying.'

'I don't. But you must accept that it will never happen. Aunt Elspeth is adamant on the point.'

'Stalemate?'

'Exactly.' India moved the conversation along, hoping he wouldn't ask her to comment on his statement that the only ones fired up over the house were John and Elspeth. Or to confirm that she'd be heading back to New York sometime soon. 'What about your parents?' she asked, although she already knew the facts, thanks to Lotte and Elspeth.

'What about them? Mother lives in Malibu, her hobby is adding to her collection of dim, beautiful young men. Father is a divorce lawyer, makes a killing in the divorce courts. The work's beneath him, and he could've been so much more - made Supreme Court judge, even. But my mother has screwed with his head over the years and destroyed him. So, he's settled for the easy life, and who can blame him.'

'Oh, MacFarlane.' She wished she hadn't started them off down this road, but now she sensed that he wanted to tell her everything.

'No, it's cool. It's the perfect marriage, actually, living three thousand miles apart and getting together at Thanksgiving for the annual row. Luckily, I'm of an age when I can choose not to be there, which they find disappointing; they always give a better performance in front of an audience.' There was emptiness in his eyes, a bitterness he made no effort to conceal.

'I'm sorry . . .'

He shrugged away her concern. 'Now you.'

'If you insist.'

'I do.'

'My parents are career diplomats. I was an unplanned and unwanted addition to their lives. Farmed out from an early age to a succession of nannies. Then boarding school . . . holidays with my English cousins . . . excruciating half terms because I didn't want to spend the holidays blasting pheasants out of the sky, or stand in the freezing cold cheering on chinless wonders trying to impress me with their sporting prowess. Like Lady Mary in Downton Abbey.'

'Chinless wonders? I guess you're one hard lady to impress, Mizz Buchanan?'

She dismissed the suggestion, making light of her lonely childhood though the pain still felt raw. 'Then, when I was old and determined enough, I chose where I wanted to spend my holidays.'

'Which was?'

'With great-aunt Elspeth. She had the swimming pool built especially for me. A couple of times she invited some of the local kids to come over for a play date. But it wasn't a success. They thought I was weird . . . strange name, odd clothes, even funnier accent. But, to be fair, Elspeth and I form a rather exclusive club of two, it's hard for others to break in.' She smiled at the admission. 'I stayed with her during most of my summer holidays until I was entered for public exams at sixteen and eighteen."

'You wanna know what's really weird? That you and I never ran into each other. As kids, I mean.'

'I suppose it is. But I guess Elspeth would have made it her business to ensure that didn't happen. And you'd be away at boarding school, or vacationing with your parents, wouldn't you?'

MacFarlane grimaced as though her words dredged up a gruesome memory.

'Some vacation! First of all, Mother'd drag me around all the fashionable west coast hot spots, all gussied up in the overpriced designer children's clothes she sold in her boutique, like I was a walking advert. I spent long nights alone in hotel rooms watching cable, eating room service while she was out somewhere with some guy she'd picked up in a bar.' He broke off, as though the conversation was becoming too personal, the memory too painful.

'While I was at university I travelled round Europe with great-aunt Elspeth. That is, before she became too infirm. When I graduated, I went to work in New York, got an internship at the art auction house, and have been there ever since.' She didn't mention the name: *Harvey's*, because the auction house was well known. Nor did she mention the man she'd left behind without a backward glance. MacFarlane didn't need to know everything about her. 'New York is a comfortable distance from my parents who are posted to Washington at the moment. They're moving to Paris in the autumn, their last post before retirement. It's something they've always yearned for. They'll soon forget about me and my p-plans for - for the future.'

She stumbled over the words and MacFarlane was quick to pick up on it.

'Plans?' He sent her a straight look. 'You've missed out the part about the house. But it's there, and it won't go away.' India's heart sank; and the champagne lost all taste. 'Level with me?'

Now was the time to lay cards on the table, but an instinct for preservation made her keep something in reserve, an ace up her sleeve. The rapport developing between them was new and untested, it wouldn't take much to destroy it.

'The House. I want to renovate it and live there, make it my home. I've no intention of selling it to you, now, or ever.' Her hands shook as she told him a half-truth and she hid them under the table, staring fixedly at the place mat instead of looking him in the eye. 'I want the house, *need* the house, because it's the only place where I feel I belong. Can you understand that?' Raising her head, she looked at him straight on, the light of battle in her eyes. 'And nothing, or no one will be allowed to take it away from me.'

It was such a relief to get it out into the open that she let out a great sigh at the end of the sentence. Instead of being furious, MacFarlane regarded her with a mixture of wry admiration and resignation.

'And I've got to accept it. That it?' He signalled the waiter to top up their glasses and India made a great play of watching bubbles effervesce and pop on the surface. Picking up her champagne she eyed MacFarlane covertly as he glanced back at the menu. Could she trust him? Really believe he was giving up his pursuit of the house and moving on? After their initial contentious meeting, it seemed unlikely. Maybe, like her, he was holding back? Oblivious to her inner turmoil, he continued. 'Getting the house back from the Buchanans is a point of honour for my grandfather. Like I said, he's past eighty, health isn't good and, lately, he doesn't seem to be able to think about anything else. How your family did the dirty on us by refusing to let our ancestor honour the IOU once the deadline had passed. How your aunt seriously annoyed him over the years by refusing to meet and discuss the matter.'

India remembered the conversation with her aunt in the hospital. Then she'd implied that John was the guilty party and he'd wronged *her*, that he wasn't to be trusted. She was just about to say: *snap*, when MacFarlane went on. 'As I've said, my career's taking me to other places. I've been offered a position in Washington; very junior of course, but a step towards Capitol Hill. I'd be a fool to let Grandfather's obsession over the old house, and his enmity with your great-aunt, get in the way.'

India experienced a sharp sense of loss. He was going

away before they had time to stop being enemies and become . . . what exactly?

'Will you accept it?'

'There's nothing to hold me here. Is there?' His expression was difficult to read. Almost as if he was waiting for her to say something; something that would make him change his mind. When she didn't speak he returned to the subject. 'If the house were mine I would have it renovated. And it would be there for me . . . waiting. Until I found a woman I wanted to settle down with, to have my children.'

India's womb contracted at the thought of MacFarlane living in *her* house with some woman with *long legs and brains*, and their cute children. MacFarlane showing the tenderness and consideration she'd only glimpsed at. The haunting image of them sleeping in the cool bedroom overlooking the lake, sharing love and confidences, the children playing in her yard and swimming in her pool made India's eyes blur with tears. A dart of jealousy, so strong it was almost a physical pain, lanced her heart.

She had to pull herself together. MacFarlane had got under her skin, making her think crazy thoughts, dream crazy dreams. They had no future together, best accept that and keep a cool head for the rest of the evening. The waiter placed their hors d'oeuvres in front of them and India's stomach lurched at the very thought of food.

Unaware of her inner turmoil, MacFarlane continued.

'I thought you were just another city slicker come down from New York for the summer to play house in MacFarlane's Landing.'

India experienced a sense of déjà vu. Wasn't that exactly what Tom Harvey and her parents had accused her of? Playing at Little House on the Prairie?

'And now?'

He paused before continuing, choosing words with care. 'I can see now that you mean to put down roots there. You're one very determined lady, India, and guess I've got to accept the inevitable with good grace.' He concentrated for a moment on his oysters and then, raising his head, sent her an uncompromising look. 'It will be your home, won't it, India? Somewhere you'll stay forever?'

'W - What do you mean?' India asked, a sudden chill striking her bones. She kept her expression neutral. MacFarlane had a way of looking straight into her eyes and reading her mind.

'You've had an expensive education, got a great job in New York, and have travelled the world. Somehow, I can't see you settling in MacFarlane's Landing with nothing to keep you busy. I'm sure you have plans for the house, to renovate and bring it into the twenty-first century. I hope that's where your plans begin and end. I'd hate to see the house turned into some god-awful Country Inn . . . all whirlpool baths, canopied beds and hand blocked wallpaper.' He said it with a laugh, but steeliness in his eyes made it plain he wasn't joking. 'Because if you do, I'll fight you every step of the way.' India's breath caught in her throat, the kid gloves were off and revealed an iron fist. 'That's a family home; *my* family home. If you don't want it, don't respect MacFarlane's

Landing and all it stands for, I'll make it my business to take it away from you.'

India's heart faltered, but she managed to swallow her oyster without gagging. 'Relax, MacFarlane you've got one hell of a suspicious mind.' Now she knew that if he so much as guessed at her plans for the house he'd make it his business to stop her. And all *this* - the opera, the candlelit dinner, the exchange of confidences wouldn't amount to a hill of beans.

It was that simple.

Smiling, she dabbed her lips with her napkin and hoped he wouldn't notice her hands trembling. What did it matter to him, she thought, bolstering up her courage. He was all set to go to Washington. He'd perhaps spend a week each year, two at most, at his grandfather's house once the old man passed away. All very well for him to be misty eyed and nostalgic about a house which had been in her family's possession longer than any MacFarlane had lived there.

He'd got his career mapped out, this was *her* chance to do what she wanted for the first time in her life.

And, if he tried to stop her, he'd find out that she could play hardball, too.

Despite these brave assertions India was alarmed by the thought of MacFarlane finding out about her plans. And, because she was by nature truthful and honest, lying - even by omission - weighed heavily on her. Sitting up in her chair, she straightened shoulders and injected some iron into her backbone. She'd have to toughen up if she wanted to realise her dream. Putting the thought from her mind she tried to enjoy the delicious food and allay his suspicions, but everything turned to ashes in her mouth.

'Having got the house out of the way, India, I've one more question. Is there anyone special in your life?' MacFarlane pushed his plate away and rested his elbows on the table, again giving her that fixed stare.

'Wh-why do you ask?' No doubt he was remembering that she'd called out Tom's name when he'd woken her this morning. MacFarlane leaned across the table and caught her hands.

'I'm not going to play games, India. Since I rode up to the house and saw you painting the fence - and acted like a complete jerk - I've wanted you more than I have ever wanted any woman.' He gave her one of his disarming smiles and India's heart rate doubled. Removing her hands in case they became sweaty and he guessed she was holding something back, she made a great show of placing her knife and fork at twenty-five-past-five on her plate. Exactly as her mother insisted a lady should, in order to let staff know she'd finished eating and the dishes could be cleared away. 'So, I'm asking you - is there anyone special in your life right now?'

'Anyone special?' she parried, playing for time.

'A significant other.' Grinning, he put his hand over his heart like a love-sick swain. 'Someone to whom you have plighted your troth? Isn't that how you say it in England?'

'Not for the last three hundred years, it isn't.'

'Well, is there?'

Tom Harvey's aggrieved features sprang to mind. Their

relationship was over, dead in the water. However, thanks to both sets of parents encouraging the match, he was proving difficult to shake off. As soon as she returned to Door County she'd ring him and make plain that they had no future and convince him that she meant it. This conversation with MacFarlane, the way her breast ached from his touch, his passionate words: *I want you more than I have ever wanted any woman*, put the final, irrevocable seal on her and Tom's disaster of a relationship.

'No one,' she said. Well, that was true, wasn't it?

MacFarlane let out a pent-up breath. 'Now for the hard part.'

'You mean, *that* wasn't the hard part?' she stammered, hardly daring to guess what he would say next. Clearly the lawyer in him wanted everything set out, so there could be no confusion, no equivocation. Signed, sealed and witnessed, in triplicate.

'The hard part is I can't be in the same room as you without wondering how it would feel to make love to you. I've spent all day thinking of nothing else. Kicking myself for leaving you alone this morning, parking my car and riding the 'L' to work, like it was just another day at the law firm. Acting as if nothing had happened between us but imagining what *would* have happened if my watch hadn't bleeped and broken the spell I'd fallen under. Your spell.' He looked about him distractedly and ran his hands through his hair. 'With any other woman . . . I'd wine and dine her, read the signs, know where I stood. But with you, it's different.'

'Different?' She marvelled that he didn't know she was on fire at the thought of them becoming lovers. Hadn't she spent all day torturing herself with the same thoughts?

'I don't know how to act with you, what to say. The usual rules don't apply. This business with the house has screwed things up between us.' His voice trailed away, but it seemed to India that the whole restaurant had stopped eating and was listening to their conversation. 'You want me, too, don't you, India?'

She hadn't anticipated such a leading question and blushed at his directness.

'MacFarlane, I - Oh God, MacFarlane.'

In response to MacFarlane's passionate, eloquent summing up India could only managed a garbled half sentence. But when she found the courage to look at him the world shrank to the few feet that separated them. MacFarlane screwed up his napkin and tossed it onto the table. Standing, he pushed back his chair and held his hand out to India.

'I shouldn't have said that. I've ruined the evening. Let's get out of here.'

'But the food . . .' Dazedly, she took his hand.

'Damn the food. I couldn't eat it. Could you?'

'No, but . . .'

'Fine. Then, let's go.' Signalling for the bill he paid it and escorted her out of the restaurant. He called for a cab and soon they were travelling through Chicago at speed, neither of them capable of speech or taking in the beauty of the balmy summer evening.

Then they were in the lift riding up to his apartment. The journey must have taken only seconds, but it seemed to go on forever. India was intensely conscious of MacFarlane in the enclosed space, his aftershave, the rise and fall of his chest beneath the fine cotton shirt, his breath on her collar bone as he turned towards her, smiling. Their eyes met, but his expression didn't alter. Instead, he sent India a look of such bone melting intensity that she had to turn away, or weep at the force of it.

Side by side, not touching, not speaking, they watched the numbers of the floors light up in ascending order. Pressing her sweating palms against the cool sides of the lift, India imagined she was vaporising in the heat coursing between them and when the doors opened there would be nothing left of her. She would pass through them as unsubstantial as a wraith.

'You okay?' MacFarlane turned towards her with a slow smile.

'Fine,' she lied. Every nerve in her body was aflame, sensitive to his presence. When the doors opened and he guided her onto the landing in front of his apartment, the light touch of his fingers on her elbow electrified her. After disarming the alarm, he tossed his keys on the table and reached for the light switch.

'Don't. The moonlight . . . It's perfect.'

It was like a scene from La Boheme. India's heightened senses imagined hearing Mimi and Rodolfo singing the famous duet, *your tiny hand is frozen*. Except, when she placed her burning palm on his arm, her body heat scorched MacFarlane's skin. She turned towards him, her face touched by the moonlight and he raised a hand to her cheek. When he spoke, his voice was husky with emotion.

'Is this what you want India? Sure?' She nodded and kissed him with such passion that he shuddered, moaning against her lips as they tumbled onto the wide leather sofa. His weight upon her was a joy, representing something so simple and fundamental that India gave herself up to it. As his questing fingers slid along her thigh, India's last coherent thought was: *only this matters; only this.*

Tomorrow there would be questions, doubts, regrets.

But tonight, there was just the two of them and the moonlight.

Chapter Eleven

India woke up and remembered. Last night she and MacFarlane became lovers.

Opening her eyes, she discovered she was in his large bed, alone, and gasped when she glanced at the clock on his bedside table.

Ten o'clock!

How had she managed to sleep so late?

And where was MacFarlane?

Surely he hadn't gone into work after - well, after everything? Bolt upright, she shook the last bit of sleep from her brain and took in the wreckage scattered around the room. The pizza MacFarlane had sent out for at three in the morning. The empty champagne bottle rolled on its side, tray of coffee cups and half-eaten chocolate chip cookies, an abandoned tub of Ben and Jerry's Phish Food, half-full of melted ice cream. Smiling, she scrunched down under the covers, remembering how they'd used the ice cream in ways the Boys from Vermont had probably never imagined.

Last night they'd spent hours in the semi darkness talking

to each other, until it felt as if she'd known MacFarlane all her life.

Widening her sweep of his bedroom, India saw clothes lying abandoned. She'd been responsible for that, losing patience with buttons that couldn't be found, fingers turning into clumsy thumbs as she wanted to remove all barriers between them. She stretched luxuriantly in the wide bed, feeling at peace, yet buoyed up with a feeling of anticipation, as if this was Christmas morning and further treats lay in store.

Today, life stretched out before her, like a great adventure to be embarked upon and enjoyed.

The phone on the bedside table warbled. Gingerly, India picked it up. 'Hello?'

'Hi there sleepy head. Did I wake you?' A squadron of butterflies performed victory rolls in the pit of her stomach at the sound of her lover's voice. *Her lover!* Sinking lower in the bed, she hugged a pillow which smelled of his aftershave, cradling the phone as she conjured up his presence.

'No, you didn't wake me. I was just lying here looking at the mess we made last night. Please tell me this isn't your cleaning lady's day. I'd die if she turned up at the bedroom door with mop and bucket and found me in your bed.'

'Cleaning lady?' he laughed. '*Cleaning lady.* I love that.'

'What would you call her, then?'

After last night's intimacy it felt strange to be talking about housework - and on the phone, too. How was she going to face him in the cold light of day after last night's passionate lovemaking? Right now, was he thinking that becoming lovers had been a big mistake? Did he regret moving their relationship up to the next level? Screwing up her eyes and pulling a face, India reined in her inner turmoil. Thinking like this would drive her crazy. Another breath and then she continued in a more practical tone.

'Your bedroom looks like the dog's dinner. Time I got up and started tidying, if your cleaning lady isn't calling.' She said the words as if they were in inverted commas.

'Dog's dinner? You sound very *British* this morning.' He paused as if choosing words carefully. 'I guess I always find that a surprise. And you are certainly one for surprises aren't you, India?' His voice deepened, becoming more intimate and India knew then that he hadn't rung her to inquire after her health. Perhaps he wanted reassurance, too; wanted to know where this relationship was going. 'It's weird talking to you on the phone, after last night.' There was a pause when neither of them spoke as they thought back to their lovemaking. Then he continued in matter of fact tone. 'I had a breakfast appointment I couldn't get out of, and my secretary had arranged interviews with two important clients. So, I left you sleeping.'

India imagined MacFarlane stealing out of the room, turning at the door to look at her - just once, before leaving. She heard the teasing, passionate note in his voice and was overwhelmed by a sudden need to touch him, hold him.

'When will you be home?' She was unable to keep the longing out of her voice.

MacFarlane, clearly affected by her tone answered with a groan of despair. 'I've got enough work in front of me to last a week. And all I can think of, is you in my bed.' Then his voice took on a rougher, edge. 'God, wish I was lying there beside you, India.' A buzz of sheer pleasure coursed through her as MacFarlane coughed and recovered himself, and then continued in a steadier tone. 'But that's not why I rang.'

'It isn't?'

'No. I want to buy you lunch. As I recall, we ate an amazing amount of junk last night. Exercise makes you hungry, I guess.' There was a long pause while they both remembered, and India imagined him smiling down the phone.

'Where are you calling from?' She had a vision of him sitting in a busy office with his colleagues listening to every word.

'Relax. One of the perks of being the boss is that you give yourself a coffee break when you feel like it. I'm in my office, the door's shut, and I'm alone. So, I can say just about anything I want.'

'I hope your phone isn't tapped.' India gave a husky little laugh.

'If it is then this has got to be the most interesting conversation the Russians, or Chinese, will have heard in a long time. I'll be through here about two o'clock. I could meet somewhere for a late lunch? Better make it somewhere pretty public, I can't guarantee my behaviour.'

India wanted to say that she didn't mind how badly he

behaved but chickened out at the last minute. 'You choose,' she said, happiness spreading through her at the promise in his voice.

'Okay, I'll pick you up from my apartment.' India heard a buzz in the background, and MacFarlane's reply to his secretary. 'Thanks Janet, send him through in two minutes. India, Gotta go. Is a quarter after two good for you?'

Little did he know that if he'd said: two minutes to midnight, her reply would have been the same.

'Yes.'

There was a disconnecting click. For almost a minute she didn't move, cradling the telephone to her breast, unwilling to sever the link between them. Then she lay back in his comfortable bed, head filled with pleasurable dreams and body aching for his touch.

*****

India put the finishing touches to the lunch she'd set out on the black marble counter: tomatoes and mozzarella drizzled in extra virgin olive oil, fettuccine and a sauce, green salad, and zabaglione. She frowned in concentration as she checked the food. She didn't want to go to an expensive restaurant; she wanted them to spend their last few hours alone before flying back to Green Bay. She knew that once back in Door County, this beautiful interlude would be over.

Would MacFarlane think it presumptuous of her to use his apartment as though she belonged there? How many other women, she wondered, had prepared food in this kitchen - full of high hopes and expectations, only to have them dashed when the relationship ended?

Was her great-aunt guilty of exaggeration, or had he really broken the hearts of most of the women in MacFarlane's Landing? Lotte Erikson had warned her about MacFarlane when she'd first arrived in Door County. How he was considered the best catch in the county - and knew it. That he had arrogance in abundance, but also charm and a sassy smile that always got him what he wanted. The tape in her head ran on, and earlier feelings of euphoria and optimism evaporated.

Well, she'd certainly experienced the charm and the arrogance, she thought, walking through to his bedroom to strip and remake the bed. And the sassy smile, too, for good measure. But, nothing her great-aunt or Lotte had said could have prepared her for MacFarlane's skill as a lover. Last night he had been tender and considerate, overcoming her initial shyness and hesitation with a reassuring word and gentle touch. Afterwards he'd made her laugh by telling her outrageously exaggerated accounts of some of the cases he'd taken to court. He'd fed her ice cream and fetched coffee and biscuits when she'd asked for them. Later he encouraged her to take the initiative in their lovemaking, to relax, and to respond instinctively to the passion he aroused in her.

Giving a little sigh, she sat down on the edge of the rumpled bed and kicked away the empty champagne bottle.

Who was the real MacFarlane?

Last night's tender, considerate lover? The man whose

women friends were legion? The determined adversary who would wrest the house away from her if he learned the truth?

She took in the bedroom with its dark navy and white colour scheme, college photos and racing pennants on the wall. The mahogany book case, television and MacBook on the desk by the window. There were no feminine touches here, nor in any of the other rooms. No pastel colour schemes, soft cushions, curtains with tie-back, frills or ribbons. Magazines neatly arranged on low tables were all solidly male: yachting, classic cars, up market periodicals and legal quarterlies.

If any woman *had* shared his life then she'd left nothing behind to mark her passage. And when *she* left, would it be the same? The thought depressed her.

Sighing, she took down a framed photograph from the book case. MacFarlane in skiing gear, face tanned by winter sun and wind. Ski goggles hid those amazing green eyes, but his white smile, and relaxed attitude as he leaned on his ski sticks showed that he was at ease with the photographer. Just looking at his image made India's heart beat faster. He was the most devastating man she'd ever met. He made her feel utterly feminine, putting her in touch with a sensual side of herself that she didn't recognise.

He only had to look at her and she was lost.

It occurred to her that the photograph could have been taken by one of his women friends. Perhaps, someone like her, who'd shared MacFarlane's bed. The very thought, made India sick - sick and jealous. Looking at his photograph, she could no longer hide from the truth. She was falling for MacFarlane, falling hard.

The realisation had crept up on her but made complete sense. Why else would she be living in a state of heightened emotions and all-consuming sexual desire? Longing for his return, yet almost dreading it? Gamely, she made an effort to pull herself together and call time on these tumultuous feelings. *She* was the one in control; the one who always called the shots in relationships.

Wasn't she?

Until she'd met MacFarlane she'd always been assured, capable of ordering her own life. Her future was all mapped out and there was no room for romance, emotional entanglement or serious commitment. Not for years to come. One night with MacFarlane, though, had changed all that. Walking into the kitchen she poured herself a glass of wine. *At this time in the morning, India?* She could hear her mother's censorious tone. However, right now, a glass of wine was just what she craved. Perhaps alcohol would settle her churning stomach and calm her turmoil.

She had to give it a try.

*****

India was tasting the pasta sauce before adding a spoonful of pesto when MacFarlane's key turned in the door. 'Honey, I'm home,' he called from the kitchen doorway, grinning. Then, 'Are we having a party?'

'Kind've,' India said, swallowing her joy at seeing him.

'Do I get a balloon and a piece of cake to take home? Or do you have something better in mind?' MacFarlane hung his jacket over one of the kitchen stools, making no attempt to hide how pleased he was to see her. Sniffing appreciatively at the pasta sauce he loosened his tie and then beckoned to India: 'What happened to my taking you out to lunch?'

'I - I thought this was more fun.'

'Come here kid, you've got spaghetti sauce on your face.'

The affectionate, teasing note in his voice was more affecting than any passionate greeting. As India walked towards him, he gave her such a look of shining promise and remembrance that her knees buckled. Dutifully, while inwardly trembling at his nearness, she held up her face to have him wipe away the sauce. Ignoring the kitchen towel, he pulled her to him and licked the sauce off the corner of her mouth.

'You taste real good, India.'

Then his mouth was on hers. She gave a gasp of pleasure as his tongue found the erogenous zones of her mouth and his hands fanned over her buttocks. When he pulled her close she felt the strength of his arousal. Putting all doubts from her mind, India responded in kind, arching and moulding her body into his. At that, their kiss became a heated fusion of tongue, lips, teeth - earth shattering in its intensity, as though neither could draw enough sweetness from the other to satisfy the need within.

'India,' he murmured, his hand seeking out the warm body beneath her silk camisole.

The timer sounded on the oven, shrilly demanding attention. They kissed on; then with a supreme effort India broke free. Straightening her camisole which had rucked up during the passionate exchange of kisses, she switched off the timer.

'Lunch?' A steadying breath and she drew her eyes away from MacFarlane's mouth. It was drawn back in one of his quirky smiles, as if he knew what was going through her mind and enjoyed knowing he was responsible for it. 'I hope you like Italian food.'

'Love it.' As usual, MacFarlane was first to regain his equilibrium. Dazedly, still buzzing from his kisses, India put the mozzarella on the table.

'Allow me, Signora,' he said and chivalrously pulled out her chair. Shaking out her napkin, he draped it over her knees and then, standing behind her, bent his head and kissed her collar bone exposed above the silk camisole. 'Cute little outfit, Mizz Buchanan,' he breathed in her ear as though he'd never seen it before.

'You don't think it too provocative?' Poker faced, she entered into the spirit of the game as he took his place opposite her.

He appeared to give the question serious thought and then he took her hand in his and turned it over, tracing a line from her wrist to the tip of her longest finger. A delicious tremor ran through India and it took all of her effort not to throw her head back and close her eyes, relishing the touch. Then, as if it was the most natural thing in the world, he raised her hand and kissed the palm. The gesture was a heady mixture of old world courtesy, and eroticism. Spontaneously, India's fingers curled into her palm holding the kiss there.

'Provocative? You are the most provocative woman I've ever known. Just when I think I've got you all figured out you do something like this, and I'm left wondering who you really are; what makes you tick.' He filled their glasses with Chianti Classico, then savoured the garlic, oil and basil dressing on the tomatoes and cheese. 'So, where did you learn to cook like this, Mizz Buchanan?'

'Italy. I spent two long summer holidays there when my parents were posted to Rome. Usually I spent my summers with Elspeth but, on this occasion, my parents thought a dose of 'culture' would be good for me.' A fond smile crossed India's face. 'I must have explored every inch of the eternal city. But I remembered being very disappointed because the Trevi Fountain was switched off for cleaning and covered in scaffolding.'

MacFarlane took a sip of wine and shot her a surprised look. 'You went round on your own?' How old were you?'

'Sixteen; quite grown up.' She spoke brightly, not wanting him to think that she was another rich kid whose parents didn't have time for her. 'But I didn't mind being on my own. Mother would only have complained about the heat and Father would have been glancing at his watch every five minutes.'

'Sixteen seems pretty young to be wandering round Rome on your own.' MacFarlane observed, touching India with his show of concern. 'No wonder you've turned out to be such a tough cookie.'

Tough cookie. Is that what she was? How he saw her?

'I was fine.' She made light of the danger, conveniently forgetting the sinister, dirty streets hung with washing where she'd wandered for hours, lost. 'The Italian chef at the embassy taught me a few neat phrases of street Italian, guaranteed to cool the ardour of the most persistent Romeo. *And* he taught me to cook Italian. Although this is just stuff I bought in the local deli. When we get back to MacFarlane's Landing I'll cook you a real Italian meal.'

Bending her head over her food she bit her lip, the words had slipped out almost before she had time to call them back. Now he'd think she was making plans for their future, had booked the church and chosen the names of their first three children.

Fool! she scolded herself.

'I'll hold you to that,' MacFarlane smiled and attacked his lunch.

'Have you ever been to Europe?' India asked, to cover her gaffe.

He hesitated. 'When I graduated from High School my mother took me to Britain. My father was furious because he'd been promising to take me to Scotland to trace our roots ever since I can remember. But she deliberately beat him to it, thus scoring a couple of points in their game of marital bliss.'

'That's crazy!'

'You think so?' MacFarlane broke in on her. 'Well, get this. I'd been back home two days when the old man comes in and tells me to pack. We're going to Scotland, he says. I spent two miserable weeks, double jetlagged in drenching rain trailing round Scotland after my father who was in serious danger of overdosing on tartan and nostalgia. He insisted that I phone my mother each night when we got back to the hotel, just to let her know how much I was enjoying myself.'

He told the story in a self-deprecating manner, clearly designed to make India laugh. But her heart went out to the young MacFarlane, pulled apart by selfish parents and their bizarre tug-of-love.

'Poor you.' She squeezed his hand comfortingly and MacFarlane twined fingers in hers, prolonging the contact.

'That was the last holiday I spent with them. I wasn't going to be used as a pawn in their game. But they could play the game without me. On my twenty first birthday I got two power boats. When I graduated law school, each gave me a sports car. I sold the boats and the cars and bought the lease on this apartment. A much better use for the money.'

'How awful.' India was shocked by their behaviour and their extravagance and left wondering how they could afford to throw money around like that. Apparently reading her mind, MacFarlane filled in the gaps.

'Mother inherited money from her parents. Father, as I mentioned before, handles divorces of the rich and famous. Money is no object, for either of them. Tell me,' he moved the conversation forward and ate the last of the mozzarella and tomatoes, 'why are we eating in the kitchen when I have a perfectly good dining room?'

'I like kitchens. They're friendly.' Raising her head, India smiled. She'd found his dining room, with its huge table which could comfortably seat twelve, too overwhelming for the simple meal she'd prepared. This kitchen was much more intimate. 'The kitchen should be the heart of the house; warm and filled with the smell of cooking. People relax in kitchens. I like my friends to bring their drinks through and talk to me while I'm cooking dinner for them.' She thought of some of the successful suppers she'd cooked for colleagues from the auction house. Then, before she could stop herself, asked: 'When you were a child didn't you help your mother in the kitchen when she was making biscuits?'

'Mom bake cookies?' MacFarlane gave an incredulous laugh. 'I swear the only time she ever went into the kitchen was on the help's day off to find ice to put in her drink.' He poured himself another glass of Chianti. 'When she *did* cook it tasted so goddam awful that none of us could eat it. My father would complain; she'd laugh in his face and then he'd slam out of the house.'

'Couldn't she cook? '

'Sure she could. She did it just to drive my father crazy.'

'Where were you living then?'

'Western Springs, just outside Chicago.' He swirled the Chianti round in the glass staring into the wine, a faraway look in his eye. 'I was six years old when they split up. In the beginning I thought it was something I'd done; something

191

I'd said that made them argue. But looking back I realise they were completely incompatible. Mother relished the social cachet of being wife to one of the best divorce lawyers in the business, the circles he moved in. What she didn't bargain for was being left alone at night with a five-year-old while my father worked late.'

India ate her food quietly. She hadn't meant to open old wounds, but MacFarlane seemed unable to stop the bitter biography of his parents' marriage.

'She'd leave me with a baby sitter and stay out late. That's how I got this,' he touched the crescent shape scar on his upper lip. 'The babysitter was making out with her boyfriend in front of the TV. I snuck out and went to play with next door's Doberman and it bit me. My father went ape. Called her an unsuitable mother.'

'Oh, no!'

'Then the rows got worse. Father knew she'd been cheating on him. Finally, he's just had enough. One day, he arrived home early and found her in bed with some guy. They couldn't find me, cue panic stations. I was hiding from the shouting and recriminations in my bedroom, in the toy fort grandfather had custom-built for me. I guess I was waiting for the seventh cavalry to come over the hill and rescue me. My going 'missing' was a shock neither of them got over, and after that everything changed. Father walked out on her, on us, and I was sent to live with Gramps and Grammy MacFarlane until I was old enough to attend boarding school.'

India recalled what her great-aunt had said about

MacFarlane running wild before being packed up and sent to prep school back east.

'They've never divorced?'

'No. You see, if they divorced there would be no one to fight with, and the whole point *is* the fighting. It's like foreplay to them. They can inflict more pain and hurt on each other as husband and wife than they could as ex-partners.'

Hating the bleakness in his eyes, India gave his hand a reassuring squeeze. Then she cleared away their first course, leaned back against the sink and told him something of her own upbringing. 'Incredible as it may sound, I've never heard my parents argue. They've perfected the art of the stony silence. I've sat through meals where you could cut the atmosphere with a knife. I wanted to scream sometimes, but that would be unladylike. And in my mother's book, one must act the lady at all times.' She switched on the coffee filter and took her place at the table. 'Father retreats to his study to tie fishing flies and mother makes lists. Lists of people to cultivate, people to avoid. Then she counts the linen and checks the store cupboard against her inventory to see if the staff are ripping her off.'

'So that's how civilised people do it, huh?' MacFarlane undid his tie and looped it over the back of his chair 'I've often wondered.'

'Yes.' India brought the conversation to a close.

Pushing his plate away, MacFarlane shook off the sombre mood which had settled on them. 'That was a delicious meal and I didn't mean to spoil it by exorcising old ghosts. Guess

I just find you easy to talk to, India. Come on,' he took her hand, leading her into the sitting room. 'I've got something for you. To say thank you.'

'Thank you for what?' India asked, knowing he was referring to last night. She blushed as she ripped open the ribbon-tied package. It was a CD of La Boheme, recorded at La Scala.

'I know you could download it from iTunes, but I'm Old School.' He watched as she wound the scarlet ribbon round her knuckles before slipping it into her pocket. 'My apartment's never going to look the same in the moonlight.' His tone was light, but his expression was serious.

'But I haven't got anything for you.'

'Oh, I wouldn't say that.' His look made India's stomach flip over and, as one, they glanced at the sofa where they'd made love last night. India had restored it to order this morning, plumping the cushions and neatly folding the red and white Amish quilt before laying it over the back. Last night, in the moonlight, it had covered their nakedness.

Her skin prickled at the memory.

Pulling her into his arms, MacFarlane buried his face in her hair. For the moment it seemed that it was enough just to hold each other. India laid her head on his chest and during the stretched-out seconds felt so close to him that her heart swelled.

Now is the time to tell him how I feel . . . level with him about the house. Then her great-aunt's warning came unbidden into her mind: *Don't trust him. He's a rattle snake. Exactly like his grandfather.* India hesitated and instead of following

194

her instincts, allowed doubts and questions to fill her head. Could she trust him? Was he capable of forming a lasting relationship with *any* woman after years of watching his parents tearing each other apart?

It was difficult to reconcile her growing feelings for him against the prejudice fostered by years of her great-aunt's bitter animosity towards the MacFarlanes. Not to mention her own fear of revisiting the rejection she'd known as a child.

Catch-22.

If she told MacFarlane about the business, despite all that had passed between them, he would make sure that she did not succeed. In order to trade from the house, she needed to satisfy the historic district planning committee and zoning regulations. He had the necessary financial and legal clout to block her. They could spend years in expensive litigation burning through money she didn't have. If she *didn't* tell him, she was only postponing the moment when he discovered the truth for himself.

Then she would lose him forever.

Soon she would have to make a choice. She could have the business. She could have MacFarlane. She couldn't have both.

'You look miles away, India. What's up, honey?' Holding her chin in his hand, he looked into her troubled eyes. If she told him the truth now, and their relationship foundered, she would be left with nothing. Intuition, and an instinct for self-preservation held her back.

Hating herself, but sure that she was doing the right

thing, she told a different truth. 'I'm frightened that when we get back to MacFarlane's Landing, *this,*' she struggled to find the right words, 'will come to an end.'

MacFarlane's expression was hard to read. When at last he spoke, it was with slow deliberation. 'We don't have to go back today, India. I could ring and change our reservations for the first flight tomorrow.' The way he looked at her made tiny hairs on the nape of her neck curl in on themselves. 'We could have one more night.' His smile was unexpectedly rakish as he continued: 'If that's what you want.'

Her words came out huskily. 'That's what I want.'

He walked over to the phone, tapped out the number and made the necessary arrangements. She'd gained herself time; a breathing space, she didn't have to choose right now. Tomorrow she would make the right decision. As MacFarlane had said, they could have one more night - together.

For now, that was enough.

A click as he replaced the telephone and folded the tickets back inside his wallet.

'No problemo.' Standing next to India, he twisted the thin strap of her camisole round his finger. Then, drawing it off her shoulder, he kissed where it had been. 'Why don't you come and help me pack?' Sliding the other strap down, MacFarlane led her into his bedroom. The room was full of harsh afternoon sunlight and he drew down the blinds to make the light softer. Then, turning back to where India was waiting for him: 'India, honey, take off your clothes.'

'Like this?' In one fluid movement she shrugged the silk

off her shoulders and let it fall in rippling folds around her waist. She didn't want to appear passive and anxious in his arms, she wanted to make love as much as he did. For one long, breathless moment MacFarlane was transfixed by her nakedness. When at last he spoke, desire roughened his voice.

'Christ, you are beautiful India.' He swiftly closed the gap between them.

The touch of his hands on her skin was a delight and their lips met in another drawn out kiss. With teasing deliberation, she untucked his shirt from the waistband of his trousers and flattened her hands against the strong muscles of his lower back which flexed at her touch. MacFarlane whispered something against her lips, then guided her towards the bed.

Lowering her onto it, he removed his shirt before joining her. The contrast of the soft quilted comforter under her nakedness and the rough caress of MacFarlane's body against her breasts drew a wordless moan from India. Taking that as encouragement, MacFarlane encircled her breast with his hand. Her senses were so heightened that she felt the sailing calluses which scarred his palms as they drew across the sensitive skin of her nipples. When his mouth followed the same path, warm and moist, India curled fingers in his thick, dark hair and cradled his head there.

After a few delirious moments, he raised his head and looked down into her face. Slowly, without taking his eyes away for a second, he unzipped her skirt, drew it over her hips and dropped it onto the floor. His fingers feathered lightly across her flat stomach, and India's womb contracted in a spasm of pleasure. Shivering with delight, she closed her eyes and arched her back like a contented cat.

'God, India, but you are perfect,' MacFarlane whispered in her ear, openly pleased by her responsiveness. 'I want to keep you here, in this bed, forever.'

Opening her eyes, India traced the line of his mouth with her finger. Suddenly it didn't matter if he'd said the same words to a thousand different women, in that instant he was saying them to her, and his smile was for her alone. Nothing else counted. Consigning doubts and uncertainties to the back of her mind she held out her arms, inviting MacFarlane to bury his face in her breasts while she focused on the one thing she knew for certain.

She wanted MacFarlane as much as he desired her.

For now, that would have to be enough.

*****

That evening, Logan insisted on taking India out to dinner. She had run out of clean clothes and was forced to wash lingerie in the bathroom sink and leave it to dry over the shower rail, much to MacFarlane's amusement. Her silk dress passed muster after being shaken out and sprayed with perfume. Picking up her clutch bag, she walked into the sitting room where he was stretched out on the Le Corbusier chaise. Seeing her, he dropped his paperback onto the floor and sat upright.

'You look beautiful, India.' He sent her an admiring glance and getting to his feet appeared to reach a decision. 'Come on, there's something I want to show you.' Taking her hand, he guided her towards a door on the far side of the room. 'Now, close your eyes and don't open them until I tell you.' Puzzled, she did as asked, standing still until she heard the door open. 'You can look now.' Pushing it open he stood to one side and indicated that she should enter. India held her breath, sensing that she was about to be shown something significant, something private and personal to MacFarlane.

She wasn't sure what she'd expected, but it certainly wasn't a fully equipped artist's studio. Dropping MacFarlane's hand, she stepped into the room, her high heeled shoes snagging on plastic sheeting laid down to protect the woodblock floor from paint splashes.

'Go ahead, look around.' He made it seem as if being ushered into his inner sanctum was no big deal. However, India guessed it was a privilege granted to few - if any, other women. What did this show of trust signify? What was he trying to tell her?

Standing in the middle of the studio illuminated by cool north light, India almost destroyed the mood by remarking that Old Dutch Masters, such as Vermeer, painted by the same light because it was devoid of changing shadows. Instead, she walked over to a large trestle table supported on splayed, steel legs and touched his paints and brushes with a reverential hand. Underneath the table were wicker baskets crammed with all kinds of things: sketch books, a jointed wooden artist's model, empty jars, unused canvasses and, incongruously, a baseball catcher's mitt. A row of low lights with brass shades, the kind seen in French cafes, hung over the table, giving it an air of antiquity.

'I love it,' she said, honestly.

This, she realised was the real MacFarlane, the one who'd painted the water colour of her great-aunt's house. The one who would have followed his dreams and become an artist if it hadn't been written in letters of stone that MacFarlanes became lawyers.

She remembered what he'd said in the restaurant - *I would have packed my backpack, sketch pad, pencils, box of paints and headed off into the wide blue yonder. Working my way round the world . . . sketching everything I saw and - who knows, turning it into a book on my return. I'd grow my hair long, sport a grizzly beard and no one would recognise me when I got home. Like a sailor returning from a long sea voyage.*

Smiling at him over her shoulder, she walked to the end of the trestle table where a Mac computer was in sleep mode. She would have loved to have awoken it and seen what was on the screen, but that would have been a step too far. Nearby a huge, antique easel held a half-finished canvas of a seascape. She recalled him saying that his mother hailed from the eastern seaboard, Nantucket most likely, judging by the seascape. It was good; better than good. *She'd* been able to shake off her parents' expectations and follow her dream. MacFarlane hadn't, and that made her sad.

She turned, trying to communicate her feelings with an empathetic look.

Making slow progress round the studio admiring and touching things as she went, India stopped by an artist's work station on casters.

'I simply adore *this*. A tabouret.' She pronounced it a la française - tahb-ou-ray. 'I can't believe you have one.'

'Round here, ma'am, we call it a tab-ou-ret.'

Laughing, she replied: 'You say tom-ay-to and I -'

'Say tom-ah-to?' MacFarlane finished her sentence and then added *jazz hands*. 'Go on, open it. I can tell you're itching to.'

'Oh-kay.'

India opened the doors of the tabouret revealing several sets of drawers, each filled with artists' materials: tubes of paint, pencils, a palette. On either side was space for rolled up sheets of paper and small canvasses. It was exquisite, and she envied MacFarlane's ownership of it.

'Et voila.' He reached into a space above the top drawer and pulled out a draughtsman's board. Pinned to it was a half-finished charcoal sketch of the Chicago skyline. 'Permettez moi, Mademoiselle,' he said in a faux French accent. 'Regardez, le piece de resistance.' Moving her gently to one side he slid the top of the tabouret open, separating the two halves, then extracted and assembled a miniature folding easel concealed within.

India clapped hands in delight. 'It's perfect. The art auction house I work for has an antique tabouret in a glass cabinet at the front of house. But not half as good as this one. Where did you get it?'

'I wish I could say that I found it in a junk shop, languishing in a dark corner, unloved and unwanted. That I restored it and brought it back to life. In reality, I paid a fortune for it in an on-line auction.'

201

'But you *have* brought it back to life, haven't you?'

'I guess so.'

'Oh -' she walked over to a table by the window. 'What are these?' She indicated a collection of mixed media drawings of mythical beasts and sea creatures executed on pages ripped out of an antique dictionary.

'Now *this* I did find in a thrift shop, a dictionary about one hundred and fifty years old. I thought it'd be a good idea to sketch a pen and ink drawing on the page giving the dictionary definition of the object. Don't worry, the dictionary was falling to bits and half its pages were missing when I bought it. I'm not a complete Philistine.'

'Sorry.' India realised that her face had revealed too much of what she was thinking.

'See this one?' On the page giving the dictionary definition for *SEAHORSE*, he'd drawn two seahorses frolicking at low tide in a rock pool. It was reproduced on the sepia-coloured six by eight page and beautifully executed. 'It's one of my favourites. The pages are quite small so I'm experimenting with working on antique parchment which has been digitally printed with the original dictionary page, only much, much larger.'

'I see.'

'Each one takes me hours, so sometimes I leave it for a few weeks and paint something else, a seascape for example, just to save my eyes.'

'You love painting, don't you?'

'It takes my mind off the day job. As does skiing and

sailing my boat. He walked over to the seascape on the easel and India followed.

'New England?' she asked.

'How did you guess. Yes, it's the beach near my mother's family home.' His mood changed, becoming sombre as he seemingly remembered unhappy childhood vacations spent with his warring parents. Then he exhaled and returned to the drawings on the dictionary pages. 'I want you to have this one.' He handed India a pen and ink drawing of an Earl Grey teabag, steeping in his granny's china cup. 'To remind you of that morning, when . . .'

'Do you think I could forget? *Ever*?' She blushed.

For a moment, he was lost in his own thoughts. As if there were things he wanted to say but knew this wasn't the time or place. Breaking the mood, he walked over to a counter top running the length of one wall. It had a sink and a draining board and drying racks of different sizes ranged along it. Stacked in one corner were shop-bought clip frames. Picking up a cloth, he dusted one of the smaller frames, sandwiched the print between the sheets of glass, replaced the clips and then handed the framed print to India.

'Pour vous, Mademoiselle.' He bowed with a flourish.

India took the framed print. 'Oh, but you haven't signed it.'

'I'll sign it when we return to MacFarlane's Landing.'

She nodded, understanding his meaning.

These last few days had been unreal – *surreal*. She'd discovered MacFarlane the adversary, MacFarlane the passionate and tender lover and now, MacFarlane the artist.

Which was the *real Logan MacFarlane*? She suspected that MacFarlane was wondering the same things, about her. Wondering if their new-found relationship would survive being uprooted and transplanted in Door County. They'd had passion-filled days, romantic nights at the opera and meals in high-end restaurants. But did they have the commitment necessary to ensure that what had passed between them was more than just a summer fling?

He was destined for Washington. *She* wanted to stay in Door County. The demands of his high-powered job would keep him away from her. She had the house to renovate, her aunt to settle in the nursing home in Green Bay, and the detritus of her life in New York to deal with. Only then could she get her Boutique Bed and Breakfast project off the ground.

She pushed his family's claim on her great-aunt's house and land to the back of her mind. It was too big a problem to think about right now. Perhaps, like MacFarlane's signature on the print, it should be left until they returned home?

Home. The very word made her heart swell, filling her with such optimism that every obstacle seemed surmountable. She looked at MacFarlane, eyes shining, and hoped that he would read the message in them: she loved him and wanted them to stay together.

'*Now* what's made you smile?' he asked, grinning back at her.

'I was thinking . . . never mind *what* I was thinking. Thank you for the print, for showing me this room and – oh, I don't know, *everything.*'

He was about to say something but put his finger on her lips. As if he understood the tumultuous thoughts and feelings running through her mind, had experienced them himself. No need to put them into words. Glancing at his watch he led India back into the sitting room.

'I've booked a table for eight o'clock. If we don't turn up I'll never be able to go to that restaurant again.'

'Seriously?'

'Seriously. The Maître d' is still upset about us walking out the other evening. He had a member of staff ring me at the office the next morning to check if he – they had done something to offend me. I couldn't say that his oysters and champagne came a very poor second to my hot date.'

'Indeed,' was his *hot date's* response.

Leaving the framed print on the side table she picked up her clutch bag and followed MacFarlane out of the apartment and into the lift. This was her last night in Chicago and she was determined to enjoy it and try very hard not to think about what the future might hold.

Chapter Twelve

Fine red dust powdered the paintwork of MacFarlane's car as it approached Aunt Elspeth's home from the main road. As the car neared the old house, India experienced a strong sense of homecoming. She'd only been away for a few days, but seeing it now, basking in the sun, she felt fiercely protective of it.

This was hers.

Somewhere where she belonged.

A place to make a *real* life for herself.

MacFarlane caught her look and must have guessed something of what she was feeling because he caught her hand and gave it a reassuring squeeze.

'Home, India.'

'Home,' she echoed.

Now, the time was right. She would tell him the truth about the house and her love for him, her plans for the future, everything. Here, on her own territory it would be easier. If the relationship foundered, she'd have the house for solace and comfort. But, somehow, she believed it *would* work out, she *could* have it all . . . MacFarlane, the house, a future together.

Killing the sports car's powerful engine, MacFarlane walked round to the back of the vehicle and opened the boot. 'Go along in, I'll bring our bags.'

Our bags – India beamed, she liked that.

'Cool. I'll fetch a couple of cold beers and we can sit on the verandah and watch the sun go down.'

'Mad dogs and Englishmen sit on the 'verandah', dear lady,' MacFarlane mimicked Noel Coward's clipped tones. Then, switching to an exaggerated Mid-Western drawl. 'Out here, ma'am, we sit on the porch.'

India got out of the car and came round to his side, entering into the spirit of things.

'Think you're pretty smart, don't ya mister?' She struck a Barbara Stanwyck pose, hands on hips.

'I must be pretty smart to catch the best girl in town,' MacFarlane said in similar vein. Happiness bubbled up and India moved closer to him.

'Oh yeah?' she asked, mock-belligerence behind the laughter in her eyes.

'Oh, ye-ah.' MacFarlane said, in a similar tone.

Hot dry wind made the dust swirl around them and teased a long strand of India's hair across her eyes. Tenderly, MacFarlane tucked it behind her ear, his eyes ranging over her face, drinking in every detail. Then the laughter died and they were suddenly serious, aware of the pull of sexual attraction which was never far away. Now, though, something else underscored that undeniable tug of sexual awareness. Something gentler, more subtle. A heart wrenching feeling which made India's eyes fill with tears and her heart swell at the thought of what was changing between them. Lust was turning to love, she could feel it. Clearly, MacFarlane felt it, too. Leaning against his dusty car, not caring that he'd ruin his suit he pulled India into his arms in one swift movement. Taking her by surprise, he kissed her with such passion that everything else was forgotten.

'Let's go in, out of the sun,' she suggested at last, breathless from his kisses. Taking MacFarlane's hand she led him up the steps and into her house. Pulling her closer, he put his arm around her waist and they crossed the threshold together, entering the cool darkness of the hall where the old staircase led to India's bedroom.

A feeling of presentiment washed over her. As if, once before, she'd stood in this hall, ready to climb the stairs to the bedroom overlooking the lake. A bride on the brink of a new life with the man that she loved. She shook off the feeling, putting it down to whimsy and wish fulfillment on her part. Breaking free of MacFarlane's grasp she turned to face him, suddenly serious.

'What is it?' MacFarlane regarded her with a mixture of puzzlement and anxiety.

'I . . . I have something to tell you.' The speech she'd been rehearsing in her head all the way from Chicago needed to be said, right now. Before she ran out of courage and the moment was lost.

'What is it?'

'It's about us. The house. You see, I need to tell you . . . to explain.'

'Explain what?'

Her reply was interrupted by an impatient rat-a-tat-tat at the door. The sound reverberated round the old hall with its wooden floors and panelled walls. Reluctantly, India left MacFarlane's arms and ran to look out of the hall window. She saw a taxi making its way down the drive.

'You expecting visitors?' MacFarlane frowned at the unwelcome intrusion.

India shook her head. Only Lotte knew that she was coming home today and had called by earlier to put a few basic provisions in the fridge. The knocking continued, now accompanied by the staccato ringing of the doorbell. Sighing, India moved towards the front door but MacFarlane pulled her back into his arms, giving her a rough kiss.

'Get rid of them,' he ordered, sending her an ardent look. 'Set the dogs on them, if necessary.'

She was just about to protest that she didn't have any dogs when MacFarlane propelled her forward with a light tap on her derriere. 'I'll try,' she promised, wanting nothing more than to be alone with him.

When she opened the door her world came crashing down around her ears.

Standing on the threshold fresh from New York and clearly expectant of a lover's welcome was Tom Harvey.

*****

'T- Tom,' India managed after a few stunned seconds.

Harvey didn't look like he'd travelled the best part of a thousand miles by plane and automobile during the driest summer on record. He appeared untouched by the heat and dust of MacFarlane's Landing. His fine blonde hair was immaculate, and as he bent towards India she caught the subtle scent of his personally blended aftershave. Blinking in the harsh sunlight, she stared at him with a mix of disbelief and incredulity. And, as the silence stretched between them, her bubble of happiness burst.

Why was he here? What did he want?

It was as if some powerful magic had spirited him from New York and deposited him here, on her doorstep - a ghost from the past, sent to jeopardize her future. He brought with him the smell and taste of New York and the life she'd left behind. The wheeling and dealing, the desire to be best, the ambition that drove her contemporaries to designer drugs and burn out, before they reached thirty.

Pulse racing, taking a steadying breath, India stretched her frozen face muscles into a welcoming smile.

'Tom. How lovely - lovely to see you.'

Stepping over the threshold, Harvey dropped his expensive luggage at India's feet, closed the door behind him with a deft foot movement, took her into his arms and kissed her. The kiss was lingering, proprietary and unwelcome, his mouth tasting horribly of the breath freshener it was his habit to use before he kissed her. India opened her mouth to protest and, taking this as an invitation, his kiss became more intimate. His hot hands seeking for her buttocks, pushing her into his groin.

What? India's head jerked back in revulsion. He'd never done that before, what gave him the right to -

'India. Honey.' Oblivious to her offended expression and the fact that she was stiff and unyielding in his arms, he moved in for another kiss. 'I've missed you so much.' He kissed the top of her head, held her at arm's length to get a good look at her. 'We *all* have. I've come to take you away from Hicksville and back to New York, where you belong.'

Taking a step away, India pressed her cold hands against flushed cheeks. Anger replaced the shock of finding him on her doorstep, an unforeseen and unwanted complication.

'Have you indeed?' she said with a touch of asperity.

'I'm going to take good care of you, India darling. I should never have let you slip through my careless fingers.' He attempted to fold her in another unwelcome embrace but this time India managed to dodge it.

'India?' MacFarlane growled from the depths of the shadowy hall, his voice low, but with an edge to it. It was apparent from his tone that he was trying to figure out who this untimely visitor was - and why he had the right to kiss India so intimately. Emerging from the shadows he walked towards them and India blanched at the cold calculation evident on his face. Knowing MacFarlane, he'd be adding two and two - and making five.

India had to act quickly. Eyes widening in appeal, she begged for a chance - for the right to explain who Harvey was and why he assumed he had the right to kiss her in such a familiar fashion. No fool, Harvey was quick to pick up on how she and MacFarlane communicated, wordlessly - like lovers.

His self-satisfied smile vanished and, evidently summing up the situation, he took a step towards India, intent on staking his claim.

'Have I caught you at a bad moment?' He was noticing how India kept glancing at MacFarlane for guidance and reassurance. His stress on *caught*, made it seem as if he'd walked in on them having sex. He glanced across the hall to where India's powder blue leather overnight case lay close to the MacFarlane's brown leather grip on the wooden floorboards. Both pieces of luggage had the same airline labels fixed to their handles and it was plain that India and MacFarlane had spent the weekend together. 'Have I, India?'

'No - Don't be silly; of course you haven't!' India's brain went into hyper-drive wondering how she was going to explain the existence of Harvey to MacFarlane, and vice-versa.

What could she say? Oh, by the way MacFarlane, when you asked me if there was anyone special in my life, I neglected to tell you about the man I left behind in New York. The man everyone expected me to marry. Everyone, that is, except me.

Or, Tom this is Logan MacFarlane the man I've spent the weekend with. My lover. The man who has it in his power to make me happier than I have ever been, or to crush my dreams with a word, or gesture. Taking a step back, she positioned herself between the two men, fervently wishing herself back in MacFarlane's arms, with Harvey on the next plane to New York.

'Tom Harvey; Logan MacFarlane.'

Neither man made any attempt to shake the other's hand but stood face to face, like duellists waiting for the signal to draw their pistols, take aim and fire.

MacFarlane had the advantage of being several inches taller than Harvey and had a firm, athletic built. Harvey was slighter but in good shape from jogging and working out at his private members' gym. There was a fastidiousness about him that India had previously never noticed. Now, as he stood opposite MacFarlane, he was shown for the city creature he was, out of place here in the Mid-West. MacFarlane's sexual magnetism was made all the more apparent by the contrast between them, his jacket creased, his dark hair untidy where she had wound her fingers in it, boots covered in dust. Harvey, smooth and urbane in his two-thousand-dollar suit, taking it all in his stride. His woman had erred, so what? He was willing to forgive, she was worth that, surely?

'MacFarlane.'

'Harvey.'

Both snarled the required response, gave a curt nod in the other's direction and then turned their attention towards India. She swallowed nervously, now the time for explanations had arrived, she had none to give. One thing however was certain, the hall was not the place to make a stand, to fight for the new beginning that had seemed tantalisingly within her reach, just minutes earlier. Nor the moment to declare her love for MacFarlane.

'I . . . think we'd better go into the kitchen,' she stammered.

MacFarlane allowed Harvey to precede him to show that he was master of the situation and Harvey an unwelcome guest. India indicated they should take a seat at the old scrub top table, but neither was willing to sit down and give up pole position. Consequently, all three stood round the table as the tension racked up.

Walking to the fridge, India took out three cans of beer and placed them on the table. With a calm deliberation which hid her inner terror, she pushed back the ring pull on her beer can. As she'd hoped, the tiny explosion of escaping gas broke the impasse.

Harvey spoke first. 'I take it,' he said in a superior tone, 'that you're the MacFarlane who's been hassling India over the house?' Clearly feeling master of the situation, he pulled back a chair, sat down and stretched legs out in front of him. Picking up the can of beer, he glanced at MacFarlane's dusty Western boots and then back at his own polished Gucci loafers, staring just long enough to make it plain that MacFarlane was just a hick from the sticks.

Outwardly, MacFarlane appeared to ignore the insult, but there was a dangerous glint in his eyes as he looked at India, waiting for some form of explanation. The silence stretched out between them, heavy and ominous until he broke it.

'You seem to know a hell of a lot about India's business.' His warning growl inferred that Harvey should take great care over what he said next.

Harvey tried to stare him down, but MacFarlane had stood in too many courts and experienced first-hand the biting sarcasm of crusty old judges and wily prosecutors. He wasn't about to be browbeaten by the likes of Tom Harvey. Their eyes locked and as MacFarlane's straight, dark eyebrows drew together, Harvey was the first to look away.

'I have the right to know about India's affairs,' he began, flushing an angry red and putting his can down on the table.

'What right?' MacFarlane demanded, his expression making plain that he already knew the answer.

'The right as her future husband.'

India gave out a soft cry, pulled out a chair and sank down on it, unable to meet MacFarlane's eyes.

Harvey gave an incredulous laugh. 'You didn't know?'

'No,' was MacFarlane's grim response. 'I didn't.'

'MacFarlane . . .' India started to explain. The precious moments they had shared in Chicago, the touch of his skilled hands on her yearning body, the drugging power of his kisses, were slipping away. Even though he was furious with her, she'd never found him more attractive. Nor, she realised with a weakening pulse of desire, had ever wanted him more.

But she put that thought aside knowing she was in trouble, big trouble. Even if she hadn't told him outright lies, she had at the very least been guilty of the sin of omission.

MacFarlane's searing regard stripped away the layers of pretence she'd built around herself. Defensive layers she'd hoped would protect her against her growing feelings for him. Frantically, she searched MacFarlane's implacable expression for some sign, some hope that he would listen to her explanation. But, it was too late; he'd already taken a step away. Barely fifteen minutes earlier they'd been laughing and kissing on the dusty drive. Now they faced each other like enemies.

India felt sick to her core at Logan's bleak expression. As if his dysfunctional childhood, his parents' infidelities, the rows, the scenes, his father finding his mother in bed with another man had returned to haunt him. History was repeating itself and without meaning to, she was responsible for it. Yet, during those drawn out seconds, it was apparent that he was also remembering how it had been between them. The undeniable physical attraction, the lovemaking they'd shared. Then the moment passed, his expression hardened and he put those memories from him, forever.

When he next looked at India controlled anger darkened his expression.

'I can explain . . .'

'Explain?'

'Yes! Everything . . .'

'I don't think that's possible. And,' he paused for effect before continuing, 'you don't have to. I get it. Save your explanations for your - your *fiancé*.' He nodded in Harvey's direction.

'That's just it. He isn't my fiancé!' India declared passionately. This was her last chance to explain before MacFarlane walked out of her life. 'He never was, despite what our families may have wanted.' She knew she was gabbling, digging a deeper hole for herself, but she had to make MacFarlane listen. She was losing him, perhaps had already lost him. What happened in the next few seconds would set the seal on their relationship.

'Not your fiancé? India, you know that isn't true.' Tom delivered the sucker punch and India rounded on him.

'You knew things were over between us when I left New York. Why have you come here?'

'I've come because I was worried about you, baby. I couldn't reach you by phone; you didn't answer my emails. What was I to think? I didn't know how you were, what you were doing.' He made India sound selfish and inconsiderate. The eloquent look he shot MacFarlane made it plain he had a pretty good idea of what she'd been up to, and with whom.

'My parents knew where I was. Why didn't you ring them?'

'I did. They are as concerned about you as I am. This . . . going off piste without an explanation, isn't like you, Baby.' Reaching out, he took hold of India's hand and moved closer, evidently feeling it was time to stake his claim and make everything quite clear to MacFarlane.

'I'm not your Baby! I'm nobody's *Baby*,' she spat out.

Undeterred, he grabbed both her hands and pulled her towards him. 'I'm forgiving, India. I get where you're coming from. You want your own business, and it makes sense to

217

remove all obstacles in your way.' He nodded towards MacFarlane, making it plain that he was one of the obstacles. 'I'm cool with that.'

India stiffened. No.No.No.

If he mentioned her plans for the house all would be lost. All she needed was a few minutes alone with MacFarlane. One last chance to explain things, to redeem the situation.

'All of this has nothing to do with you,' she said, desperate to stem the flow of words. 'I don't want to discuss it, Tom.' Pulling her hands free, she turned towards MacFarlane with a pleading look.

'Isn't she the most stubborn woman you've ever met?' Harvey asked MacFarlane in a jocular, patronising tone. As if they were a couple of regular guys in a bar discussing how to deal with the shortcomings and idiosyncrasies of the opposite sex. 'We've all tried to talk her out of this crazy idea of hers.' He cast his eyes over the peeling wallpaper in the kitchen and then back to MacFarlane.

Having been fed the line, MacFarlane had to respond.

'And what crazy idea would that be?'

'You mean you don't know? She hasn't told you?'

'Evidently not,' MacFarlane ground out. 'It must have slipped her mind.'

'Really? Usually we have to stop her talking about her great plan to move here and run a Bed and Breakfast from her great-aunt Elspeth's home.' Harvey's look implied that MacFarlane and India might have shared a bed, but she'd kept her innermost thoughts and ambitions to herself.

'Is this true, India?' MacFarlane asked quietly.

'Yes,' she whispered, her voice husky and barely audible, unable to look at him.

'Let me get this straight,' MacFarlane began, as though he was unravelling a particularly difficult puzzle. 'That night, when I asked you if there was anyone special in your life and you said there wasn't. That was a downright lie, right?'

'Yes; well no, not exactly. Because Tom and I were never engaged, despite what he says - and, we were *over*.' India flushed under MacFarlane's look of utter disbelief. Even to her ears the excuse sounded lame, making her appear like a teenager hiding the truth from her parents. She sent MacFarlane a plaintive look begging him to dismiss the thoughts rushing through his head, and to remember what they had. What they'd shared.

'And when I asked you if you were going to turn the house into a family home and not some goddam Country Inn you lied then, too. Huh, India?'

'I - I did.' India's mouth went dry, unable to summon up the words in her defence. 'But only because I didn't want to ruin what we had. I wanted to be sure - to know where I stood with you before I told you everything. You would have done your worst to stop me. Wouldn't you?' India flinched from MacFarlane's contemptuous look and hot, salty tears stung her eyes. But no; she wouldn't cry in front of him. She would not. From somewhere she found an extra reserve of courage to frame the words of her denial. 'I *was* going to tell you about my plans. I tried to

219

several times - but I couldn't. Then Tom knocked on the door and . . .'

She sent MacFarlane a melting look, begging him to believe, to understand her dilemma. Raw emotions crackled between them: desire, longing, need. An unspoken wish that this was a nightmare they'd wake from to find themselves in bed, wrapped in each other's arms.

'Wouldn't you?' India prompted, desperate for him to deny it.

'I would,' he admitted, unmistakably hardening his heart against her. 'God, India you've played me for a fool. And I fell for it. Fell as hard as any man who has ever fallen for a scheming woman with a beautiful face and heart of stone.' Then, as the full realisation of what he believed she'd done to him began to sink in, he walked over to the sink and stood gazing out across the land that had once belonged to the MacFarlanes. Land that should still be theirs, if there was any justice in the world. When he turned back there was a ruthlessness that India had never seen before and she knew something precious had been lost.

'I'll block you every which way. You know that don't you?' His voice was quiet and steady and frightened India far more than shouting and recriminations. 'I know the law. I'll use it to prevent you from treating my family's home like an amusing hobby, gussying it up and playing lady of the manor until you grow tired of it and return to New York and your life there.'

A life, his expression suggested, which included this pale excuse of a man who was so desperate to marry her that he'd followed her all the way to Wisconsin, unasked for, uninvited.

'I know you will,' India returned evenly, though her knees were knocking and hands shaking. Clasping them behind her she mirrored his determined expression and stepped back from the invisible line that marked the distance between them. 'But understand this. I intend to succeed. So you'd better get used to the idea.'

Raising her head, she regarded him with a hauteur that concealed her breaking heart. It had been in this kitchen that MacFarlane had mocked her mother's ancestry. Now India drew strength from her Fielding blood line, and from the centuries' old belief that Fieldlings had an inalienable right to do as they damn well pleased. She wouldn't let him see how deeply his words had cut her. That her fears had been justified and, in the end, she'd been right not to trust him.

'Not this time, lady.' MacFarlane drawled. 'You're a foreigner, an outsider; I'm an American. That'll go against you when you try to get past the historical district planning committee to open your house up for trade. Not to mention the zoning regulations. And don't go bringing your great-aunt into this. She might be American but she's old and infirm and that'll go against you, too. Dragging an old lady out of a nursing home to justify your right to open up a goddam Country Inn. How would that look?'

That made her sound like a calculating bitch and warned her that he would use every legal trick and loophole in the statute book against her.

India's confidence took a nosedive. 'I don't give up that easily, MacFarlane and you know it.'

He shrugged dismissively.' You don't have a chance in hell of succeeding, Mizz Buchanan. And you know it.'

'We'll see, MacFarlane.' India shot him a look of pure defiance, a sliver of ice piercing her heart at his return to *Mizz Buchanan*.

'What are you going to do? Sleep with every male under sixty on the committee to get your way? That's how you operate, isn't it?' His expression was bitter, yet there was something in his tone which almost begged her to contradict him. When she didn't, he repeated the question as a statement of fact. 'Isn't it?'

Harvey re-entered the conversation, pushing back his chair and rounding on India as he realised what MacFarlane was implying.

'India? Have you slept with him?'

'For God's sake Tom.' India brushed him aside as if he and his concerns were of no consequence. 'Not now.'

'I think now's a pretty good time to have that particular question answered.'

Pushed beyond endurance India rounded on him.

'Yes. I slept with MacFarlane. If that's a problem for you, then I'm sorry. I told you that we were over back in New York, why won't you accept it.' Harvey's expression demonstrated that he didn't care for this India - fiery, passionate and assertive. He just stood there, his mouth opening and closing like a landed fish.

'*Slept* with him?' he repeated, stunned.

'It doesn't matter. Not now.' India rubbed a weary hand over her eyes, unable to forget that there'd been little sleeping involved once she'd lain in MacFarlane's bed.

'I think it does. We were - *are* engaged after all.' He hastily corrected the tense and then baulked under India's furious, direct gaze. Then, continuing in a conciliatory tone which was even more irritating, 'Don't get the wrong idea, MacFarlane. The only reason India slept with you was to get you to drop the litigation. Well, I guess I can understand that,' he said magnanimously. 'She's nothing if not ambitious.'

But, in spite of his words, Harvey's expression showed that he didn't quite comprehend *why* India had slept with MacFarlane . . . when she had barely allowed him to kiss her goodnight. MacFarlane regarded them both with burning contempt but reserved his most coruscating look for India.

'Thanks for summing it all up so succinctly, Harvey.' MacFarlane's tone made it clear that Tom had put into words what he'd been thinking. 'I congratulate you on having such an understanding fiancé who shares your pragmatic approach to business, Mizz Buchanan.' Giving her a look of absolute loathing, he strode into the hall.

India raced after him. She couldn't let it end like this. She had to try one last time to convince him of how it had *really* been. How she had been afraid of revealing the truth; of losing him. She stood between MacFarlane and his leather grip, but he pushed her roughly aside.

'Don't do this; don't humiliate both of us. Go back to your fiancé. You deserve each other.'

'MacFarlane - for the last time - he's not . . .' she grasped his arm, desperate to make him believe her.

'Not another word. You've pushed the boundaries today,

lady. Now, get out of my way before I do something we'll both regret.' India flinched as he grasped her by the elbows and moved her to one side. Then, picking up his bag, he headed for the front door.

'Please . . .' she called after him. 'Logan.'

Although he struggled to hide it, India's use of his Christian name affected him profoundly. A shudder ran through him and his body slumped. For one heart-stopping moment India thought that all anger was spent and he was going to give her a second chance. But, when he turned to face her, his expression was as implacable as before. Then anger returned, fuelled by what he plainly regarded as a further example of India's deceitfulness. Swallowing hard, he picked up the leather grip.

'Sure know all the tricks, don't you India?' His voice rough with emotion. 'I've been waiting for you to use my name. But no, it was always MacFarlane. Even when you called out as we made love.'

In a flashback that was almost cinematic, India saw them lying on the floor of the sitting room covered by the red and white Amish quilt. Their bodies pale in the moonlight, their breathing rapid, her face buried in the hollow of MacFarlane's collar bone, her body replete, yet already craving for his touch.

MacFarlane broke into her thoughts.

'Is that how you reminded yourself of your purpose? How you kept it all business like and professional? By deliberately never using my first name, were you reminding yourself of the feud - even as we came together?'

'How can you believe that?' India asked brokenly, eyes bright with the tears she no longer bothered to hide, sliding down her cheeks.

'I believe it because it's true,' he told her ruthlessly. 'Isn't it?' Not waiting to hear her denial, he walked towards the door and onto the porch.

'Logan - please,' India ran after him.

He turned and placed a small gift-wrapped package on the table with a bitter laugh that mocked his own foolishness. 'That's for you. I'd thought to give it to you under slightly different circumstances. Shows how well you had me hooked, I guess.'

'I don't want your present.' India pushed it back towards him but he took no notice.

'Take it; you've earned it. What kind of business woman will you make if you give your services for free?' His tone deliberately insulting, he gave her one last look which undressed her, as though she was a commodity to be bought and sold.

'You b - bastard MacFarlane.' Her voice broke.

'I guess that kinda goes for the both of us, doesn't it?' India took a step towards him and slapped his face. The report of it echoed round the hall and up into the stair well. 'Feel better?' he asked, as though she were a spoiled child stamping her foot. He rubbed the red mark tenderly, like a love token.

'Get off my land MacFarlane. Get off and don't ever come back,' India's voice cracked with emotion as she watched him walk down her path and through the picket gate.

Through a sheen of tears, she saw the livid hand mark where she'd slapped him and was ashamed of her own behaviour. This was real life, not some appalling soap opera where most characters were out of control.

Reaching his car, he turned. 'I'll be back. Next time I walk through that door it'll be as owner of this house.'

Getting into his car he gunned the throttle and drove towards the lake, wheels spinning on the unmade road. India was left clutching the fretwork rail of the verandah, sick to her stomach at what had just passed between them. A discreet cough behind her alerted to Harvey's presence.

'He's gone then?' he asked, unnecessarily.

'Looks like it.' They stood shoulder to shoulder watching the dusty wake created by MacFarlane's car.

'Are you going to come back to New York with me, India honey?'

He obviously believed that with MacFarlane out of her life India would be able to chalk it all down to experience and they could restore their on/off relationship to its default setting.

'No.'

'He won't be back. Not without an army of lawyers.'

'Don't you think I know that?' Harvey registered the forlorn note in her voice and the truth finally dawned on him.

'India you didn't; couldn't - love him, surely?'

India turned her face towards him and lifted her shoulders in a hopeless, little shrug. 'That's just it, Tom. I do.'

'Jesus, India.' He sat down on the swing seat, lost for words. 'This has all been a real shock to me. You know?'

'Yes; I know.' Absentmindedly she patted his arm as though he was a child deprived of his favourite toy.

'But you've got to admit India. He was only too willing to believe the worst of you.' He pursued his point, every word a knife thrust into India's heart. 'Almost like he'd been expecting it?' His voice rose at the end of the sentence.

India nodded, Tom wasn't usually so perceptive, but he was right. MacFarlane had been expecting her to revert to type and for Buchanan blood to show, sooner or later. He'd thought everything between them was an act and that in time she'd drop the pretence and show her true colours. And, to be fair, hadn't she thought the same of him? It made it worse to know, in spite of everything they'd shared, they'd both been anticipating this moment.

Overwhelmed by the need to be alone, she walked up to the swing seat.

'Come on, Tom. I'll drive you into Green Bay. You can get a hotel there and book a flight home.'

'But India, you gotta come back with me, honey.'

India gave him a second look. Had she underestimated all this time? Did he really love her so much that he'd take her back under any circumstances? Even if it meant accepting she'd slept with another man and was in love with him?

'*Got* to, Tom?' She looked straight at him and his blue eyes shifted, guiltily.

'India . . . Look, I'm going to level with you. It was my father's idea for me to bring you back to New York.' There was an edge of desperation in his voice.

'*What*!'

'No, listen. The auction house's been losing commissions since you left. Everyone knows you've got an instinct for what's fake. We've sold a couple of duds at auction recently. Clever forgeries which would never have gotten past you. We've had them returned by angry clients. They're threatening to sue our asses off, if -'

'Know what? I don't care. And as for spotting a fake,' she thought of Logan Macfarlane. 'Looks like I've lost my touch.'

'Jesus, India . . . don't be so heartless.'

India saw his petulant, almost sulky expression and realised that he was totally unaware of the damage he'd caused by turning up unannounced. He was so consumed with pleasing his father and safeguarding his inheritance, he couldn't see that he'd destroyed her only chance of happiness.

She had no problem in denying his request.

'Right now, I feel pretty heartless. Heart*broken* if you must know. Don't you realise what you've done?' But he wasn't listening.

'But, India. Baby. I love you. I miss you. Please - I need you.' Then, a gulp. 'If I don't bring you back, my father's threatening all kinds of stuff. You wouldn't want to see him cutting me off without a penny? Would you?'

So, that was what had brought him all the way from New York and made him knock on her front door, just as she was going to level with MacFarlane.

Kismet.

'Actually, Tom, right at this moment, nothing would give me greater pleasure.'

Perhaps she should thank him. At least he'd stopped her

making a total fool of herself by telling MacFarlane that she loved him. And she'd been spared the humiliation of having her love rejected. In that moment, she felt used by both men.

Harvey only wanted her to gain favour with his father.

And as for MacFarlane - had she ever been more to him than a piece of real estate?

'Get your bags Tom. You're going to Green Bay,' she said firmly.

'India - Sweetie . . .'

'Your bags.'

Evidently realising at last that the lady wasn't for turning, Harvey did as commanded. India left MacFarlane's package on the rail of the verandah. She'd return it unopened, that'd be a shot across his bows, a declaration of war. Show him she meant business. However, there was no joy in that course of action. Only a terrible aching emptiness that had her gazing unseeingly towards the lake as she prepared to drive Harvey to Green Bay for an overnight stay before catching a direct flight to New York.

*****

Several hours later, she was sitting on the verandah lost in her own thoughts. Fleetwood Mac was playing in the background on the radio. She was emotionally drained, too tired to think of anything beyond the fact that she and MacFarlane were over. Finished before they'd even started. Anger at Harvey's unexpected arrival ebbed away, leaving her bereft and capable of little else than listening to the gentle lap of the waves against the wooden jetty projecting out into the lake.

She sipped her wine but it tasted bitter and oxidized. Putting the glass on the floor beside her she allowed her attention to wander over to MacFarlane's gift on the verandah rail where she'd left it. The foil gift-wrap changed colour as the sun sank below the rim of the lake. The feminist in her wanted to throw it back in MacFarlane's face; however, the woman she was wanted to know what it contained. Stretching out her hand she picked up the package, untied the bow and slipped off the wrapping paper. Inside was a soft dark blue leather box. Elevating the box to see it more clearly by the bulkhead light over by the kitchen door, she raised the lid. The light revealed a yellow gold band, set with a circlet of garnets. The breath caught in her throat as she identified it as an early nineteenth century betrothal ring, dating roughly from the time when Jim Buchanan and Sean MacFarlane established a trading post and livery stables at MacFarlane's Landing.

She slipped it on her finger. It felt heavy and cold, like her heart. India searched the box for a message, but there was none. The ring *was* the message, a declaration of MacFarlane's intent. Christine McVie's pure tones came through the radio, as she sang about the consequences of telling sweet little lies. Maybe, as the song suggested, they were better off apart?

She'd told lies all right; sweet, little lies, designed to save her from pain and betrayal. But lies nonetheless. Now she was being punished for being economical with the truth, for daring to believe she could have it all: MacFarlane, the house, her business. Logan had warned her that lying and infidelity were the enemies of love. His mother's lies and affairs had destroyed his father's love and ruined his childhood. Now it must seem that the pattern was repeating itself.

'Logan,' she spoke his name shakily on an exhaled breath, rocking the swing seat consolingly, as a child might. But it was a woman's tears which blurred her vision and, as the last of the light slipped below the rim of the darkening lake, she knew it was what she *hadn't* told MacFarlane and what she hadn't said which had cost her a future with the man she loved.

Chapter Thirteen

Logan drove his sports car at breakneck speed along the lake shore, keen to put India Buchanan and her web of deceit behind him. How could he have been so stupid? Allowing himself to be taken in by a pretty face and winsome manner? Hadn't his grandfather warned him that Buchanan women were poison?

He should've listened.

Reaching his grandfather's house, he pressed the remote, waited for the garage doors to open and then drove in with exaggerated care. If he dented the classic Corvette, mothballed under canvas, his grandfather would make good on his half-serious threat to cross Logan's name out of the family bible. Today, the old joke no longer seemed amusing. The names in that bible stretched back to when MacFarlane and Buchanan had first opened their trading post and made a life for themselves in Sturgeon Bay.

What would his forebears think of the mess he'd gotten himself into?

Bringing fists down on the steering wheel he vented

some of his hurt and anger on the vinyl. In that moment, driving full tilt at the wall and bending the BMW into shards of twisted metal - himself along with it, seemed a good idea. At least it would release some of the pent-up fury and hurt tightening his chest and making red spots dance before his eyes. Then, common sense kicking in, he dropped hands onto his knees and waited for his breathing to return to normal.

Was this how his father had felt every time his mother had cheated on him? Like the heart had been ripped out of his chest and thrown pumping and bleeding into the trash can? He focused on the rack of tools arranged along the back wall until his vision blurred and eyes ached. For the first time, he felt empathy for his father. MacFarlane men were lousy judges when it came to choosing the women they loved, weren't they? *Loved?* The word hit him with the force of a sledgehammer and he swiftly sought a substitution: lust, want, need, craving, sex.

But what he felt for India Jane Buchanan, was more than the sum of all those adjectives.

He had fallen in love during their brief sojourn in Chicago. Now it was messed up and ruined forever. Raising his hand to the red mark on his cheek he acknowledged that he'd deserved the slap.

What kind of businesswoman will you make if you give your services for free?

How *could* he have said that?

That wasn't who he was.

Releasing a shuddering breath, he got out of the car

and entered the house via a side door. It was time for his grandfather's nap and he was anxious not to disturb him. Not that he'd be lying down in bed, all neatly tucked in by his nurse. He was more likely to be found in his den, watching horse operas - just to vex her, and prove there was still fire in his belly. Even if he generally fell asleep before Randolph Scott or John Wayne chased off renegades and rescued the homesteaders.

MacFarlane men were obstinate and mule-headed, Logan acknowledged, tiptoeing to the icebox to fetch a beer. Just as Buchanan women were - how had the Judge put it? Ornery and downright stubborn.

An explosive combination.

Best not let his grandfather know what had transpired between himself and India. Hell, he couldn't think about her without his guts churning and a sour taste filling his mouth. How could he explain everything to his grandfather when *he* hardly understood what had gone wrong? The official line would be that he'd taken his leave at the airport after hailing a cab to take India to the hospital. After that, they'd returned to Green Bay on different flights. More lies, white ones this time, designed to save his grandfather's blood pressure and keep from the world that Logan MacFarlane had made a bloody fool of himself.

*****

Whatever problem dogged him, Logan usually found that sailing his boat down the inlet and into Green Bay provided him with a solution. However, today was the exception and despite the glorious sunset and wind singing in the sails, he cut his trip short and headed home. As he walked the short distance from the jetty to the house he could smell cigar smoke and caught his grandfather on the deck drawing on a forbidden cheroot and drinking a can of beer.

'I'm guessing it's your nurse's evening off?' Logan climbed onto the deck and gave the old man's shoulder an affectionate squeeze.

'Damn woman, she'll be the death of me. No tobacco, alcohol or salty food. You're right, it's her half-day but she continues to torture me, leaving a dinner in the icebox I wouldn't serve to a dog. Leaves, rice and some goddam tofu burger, or worse still that stuff with the unpronounceable name. Qui-'

'Quinoa?'

'That's it. I told her I'd had my fill of lentils, mung beans and macrobiotic junk back in the sixties, and at least then I could smoke dope to take the taste away. But she doesn't listen. It's like I've become invisible. Jeez, I must've been an evil bastard when I was in court because God's sure punishing me for it, now. But, let's put *Nurse Rached,*' he pulled a face at the nickname, 'out of mind and tell me what you've been doing? I have to live vicariously these days, seeing as I'm not allowed out of the house without an army of carers. I sure would like to sail in that boat of yours, one last time.'

One last time?

Fear gripped Logan's heart, putting everything else into

perspective. His grandfather had always been a part of his life – dependable, reassuring. Standing in for his parents more times than not when they were off pursuing their own dreams and didn't want a small boy in tow. Pulling up a stool, Logan sat at his grandfather's feet, and shook his head. He wasn't ready to admit that his grandfather might not be here for another Thanksgiving, let alone another birthday. Having suffered enough shocks for one day he put the thought from his mind.

'If that's what you want, I could arrange it, providing the Bay was calm and I used my outboard motor instead of the sails. I'm sure a couple of guys from Sturgeon Bay Yacht Club would come along, too. Just like the old days?' His forced jollity hiding that his fellow yachtsmen would include a doctor and a paramedic, and that there would be a defibrillator hidden in the bunk.

Just in case -

'No Nurse Rached?'

'Shiver me timbers, matey, the high seas ain't no place for a woman. If you 'ave a mind, me hearty, we could make her walk the plank.' Logan felt mean for wanting to consign the conscientious nurse to Davy Jones's Locker, she was only doing her job after all – and under very difficult circumstances. However, he'd made his grandfather smile and that was good enough.

'You make a pretty good pirate, Logan. You've got the scar and everything.' He gestured towards the crescent shaped mark on Logan's lip. 'Glad to see that wearing a suit hasn't diminished you. The MacFarlanes weren't meant to be pen pushers, pouring over legal papers, arguing the toss in court. We've got wild blood in our veins and we've had to deny it. We should be -'

'Riding the range? Taking off into the Badlands?' Knowing his grandfather's penchant for Westerns Logan attempted a weak joke.

'I'd agree with you, son, except the Badlands have relocated to Chicago and we handle the fallout. At a price. Right?'

'Right.'

There was a brief silence which the judge broke with, 'So, you gonna tell me what happened in Chicago?'

'Chicago?'

'Big city on the shores of Lake Michigan?'

'I know where Chicago is.' Logan smiled and shrugged away his interest. 'Nothing out of the ordinary. I told you, I travelled over with Ind - Mizz Buchanan, she took a cab straight from the airport to check up on her great-aunt. I never saw her after that.' He looked away to hide his expression; he'd never been good at lying to his grandfather. Maybe he should take lessons from India Buchanan, she was a past mistress in that dark art. Somehow that thought didn't bring him any cheer and he concentrated on what his grandfather was saying.

'So, the Logan MacFarlane seen wining and dining someone whose description exactly matches India Buchanan, wasn't you? Huh?'

'How -'

'How the hell do I know? If you want to keep your relationship with a woman secret, you don't take her to a restaurant patronised by Chicago's legal profession. Especially not a looker like Mizz Buchanan, with her red hair and all. Good thing you're a lawyer and not a spy, Logan.' He laughed, his breath rattling in his chest. Waving away Logan's concern, he took a medicinal slug of beer. 'You'd 'a been shot, your pockets filled with lead and then dropped silently into Lake Michigan, to swim with the fishes.' Seemingly, he was amused that his highly qualified grandson had no more sense than a fly.

'I was just -'

'Yeah, I can imagine what you were 'just' doing. I warned you about Buchanan women, yet you saw fit to ignore me. You've known the girl how long, couple of days? I've known her aunt my whole life, went to the same church, attended the same youth groups. Just when you think you've got the Buchanans all figured out, they have a way of pulling the rug out from under you. And, if you're not careful, they'll break your goddam heart, just for the hell of it.'

There was a story here, one John had never seen fit to share. Perhaps the old man had an inkling of what had happened in Chicago and had words of wisdom to offer? Right now, Logan would take advice from anyone, providing it poured balm on the pain scouring through him like cleansing fire. Or maybe it was simply the case that his grandfather was aware he was running out of time and wanted to share old stories. Logan shivered, he didn't need to see the grim reaper standing with a hand on his grandfather's shoulder to know that John wouldn't be with him forever.

'You can't trust them or get involved with them. Jim Buchanan reneged on a gentleman's agreement all those years ago and they've been double-dealers ever since, Now, for Pete's sake, tell me you didn't sleep with the girl?' He cocked an eyebrow and Logan squirmed under the too-knowing scrutiny. 'Don't answer, I can work it out for myself. And, judging from your expression, something went wrong?'

Logan ran a weary hand across his eyes. 'I can't talk about it right now, Gramps.'

'You haven't called me Gramps for years, so I'm guessing something pretty bad happened. We've all been crossed in love, Logan, and you're no different.' Something in his tone made Logan give him a searching look.

'You talking from experience?'

'Pour us both a Bourbon and I'll tell you a story. One full of missed opportunities, breakups and crossed wires. Better than any goddam soap on cable.' Logan didn't think twice about getting his grandfather the Bourbon. If he had words of wisdom to offer, Logan wanted to hear them. Aside from which, he had too much respect for the old man to act as his wet nurse. If his days on earth were numbered, Logan figured he was better off enjoying such time as was left to him. When he returned with the Bourbon, his grandfather had drawn a woollen comforter across his knees, although it was sixty degrees on the deck. That gave Logan another scare, ice replacing blood in his veins.

'You okay?'

'Don't fuss, Logan, I'm fine. Come, sit here - it's time I told you what really happened between me and Elspeth Buchanan. Your Grandma's been gone these last fifteen years, so I don't feel I'm being disrespectful to her memory by raking over the past.'

Logan clinked glasses with him. '*Slainte*,' they shared the Gaelic toast.

'Where to start . . . if this sounds like a history lesson, forgive me, but you need to know everything in order to understand.' He sipped his bourbon and looked out across the lake. 'Back in '64 I was an up and coming young advocate, practising law in D.C. I was headhunted; drafted in to prepare the groundwork for the Gulf of Tonkin Resolution.'

'Time out. Gulf of Tonkin Resolution?'

'Guess they didn't teach you about that in Constitutional History, huh? A chapter in U.S history many would prefer to forget. Sorry, I'm rambling . . . the Resolution.' With some effort, he focused on the subject. 'Earlier that year, three North Vietnamese PT boats allegedly fired torpedoes at the USS Maddox in the international waters of the Tonkin Gulf, thirty miles off the coast of North Vietnam.'

'*Allegedly*?' Logan's legal brain picked up on the word.

'You decide, councillor. The attack came after six months of covert U.S and South Vietnamese naval operations. A second, even more highly disputed attack, is supposed to have taken place on August 4th. Then when L.B.J. -'

'Lyndon Johnson?' Logan said, almost to himself, keen to get everything straight in his mind.

'The same. He used the attacks as justification to wage

war against North Vietnam, without securing a formal Declaration of War from Congress.'

'So, what was your role in this?'

'Like I said, I was recruited onto the legal team to observe the niceties and draw up the Resolution. Make sure it was watertight. In retrospect, I'm not sure it was. Some conspiracy theorists allege the attack never took place and – well, we'll let history be the judge of *that*. Like you, I was ambitious, I wanted to cut corners and climb the greasy pole as fast as I could. That outweighed everything else. I knew that if I turned down the chance to be part of the team, there were hundreds of young lawyers only too eager to take my place.'

Logan looked at his grandfather speculatively. John MacFarlane was single-minded and had a ruthless streak. If it suited his purpose, he could find a legal precedent for arguing black was white.

'What happened next?

'L.B.J. was elected President and, in February of the following year, sustained bombing of North Vietnam began. American troops were deployed to protect the airfield at Da Nang and before long, over two hundred thousand troops were defending Vietnam against the Vietcong.'

He paused, seemingly wondering if his legal team had done the right thing.

'I see. But what does all this have to do with the Buchanans?' The judge gave a harrumph of displeasure at Logan's impatience, plainly wanting to tell the story at his own pace.

'Long story short? Elspeth Buchanan and I were

sweethearts. Okay, you're old enough to know the truth, we were lovers.' Logan made no comment, wanting his grandfather to finish the story before he ran out of energy. 'We got engaged. Elspeth was in her senior year at the University of Michigan studying politics and economics, so we decided to wait until she'd graduated before we got married. Big mistake. While I was in Washington she'd gotten involved with the anti-war movement, attended a teach-in at Ann Arbor, and set about organising teach-ins in other universities.'

Reaching over, he picked up a well-thumbed John Grisham from the table next to his chair. Opening it, he fished out a faded photograph and handed it to Logan. It featured a group of students - all long hair, flared jeans and tie-dye t-shirts - lining the steps of some municipal building. One of the women, in a t-shirt emblazoned with Che Guevara's image, and sporting a black beret at a jaunty angle, was punching the air with a clenched fist.

Even the faded Kodak colours couldn't disguise the copper-red hair, defiant stance and fierce blue-eyed gaze.

'Old Mizz Buchanan?'

'Yep. Elspeth. She'd written an end of term paper disputing the Domino Theory . . .'

'. . . that if one country in a region came under the influence of communism, then surrounding countries would fall in a so-called domino effect? Yes, yes, I know all about it. But what does any of this have to do with the MacFarlanes?'

With me and India – the question hung in the air.

His grandfather sent him a reproving look, then carried on at his own pace

'Elspeth had her fifteen minutes of fame.' A snort of derision. 'She spent most of that summer lecturing radical groups, arguing that the domino theory was no more than a ploy used by successive United States administrations to justify American intervention around the world. When I came home from Washington we wasted time arguing over the legality of the Tonkin Resolution when we shoulda been making love. She told me I was naïve, a fool for buying into the whole Gulf of Tonkin fiasco, and allowing ambition to get in the way of common sense and morality. I told her she was nothing more than an armchair revolutionary; a Pinko. That the troops were there to stop the spread of communism and bring democracy to the people of Vietnam. She told me I was supporting imperialism without understanding the repercussions of the U.S. getting involved in a costly foreign war.'

Logan gave a long, low whistle, remembering the times Elspeth Buchanan had chased him off her pontoon with a broom. He could well imagine her standing up to his grandfather and giving him an ear-bashing.

'We had a humdinger of a row next day when I found her painting a political banner to use at a rally in Chicago. How did it go - *Hey, Hey, LBJ, how many kids did you kill today?* He held out his hand for the photograph, gave it one last, long look and then tucked it back inside the pages of the Grisham. Logan guessed that he'd hidden it there from Grammy

MacFarlane all these years. And he could understand why.

'Go on.'

'We broke up, I was drafted and sent over to Vietnam. Karma, you could say. Guess history's proved her right, huh?'

'The jury's still out. You returned from your tour of duty in one piece, but I'm guessing you never made up with her?'

'Worse than that.'

'Worse?' Logan shuffled closer, it was the first time his grandfather has ever opened up to him like this.

'I was wounded during my tour of duty. Nothing serious, some shrapnel in my back and legs. I was treated in a field hospital, met a hot combat nurse who made me feel like a war hero, not a gullible fool and -' he hesitated.

'And?'

'We had an affair, more of a fling if you really wanna know. She fell pregnant, was shipped back home. We got married on my next leave and six months later your father was born.'

'That was *Grammy MacFarlane?* Logan tried to marry the image of the *hot combat nurse* with the thin, embittered woman who'd hated the world and everything in it. Starting with his grandfather and finishing with himself. Now, for the first time, everything made sense.

Grimacing, John continued. 'We were ill suited but, in those days, a man was expected to do the right thing; the honourable thing. I'd gotten her pregnant and it was my job to make everything good.'

'So . . . Elspeth?'

'Once I came home with a pregnant bride it was over between us. Elspeth sent me a terse note which read: *you're a bigger fool than I took you for.* She was right, of course.' He sighed, stared into the middle distance across the lake where, in the descending dusk, the buoy at the end of MacFarlane's Landing winked back at them, an all-knowing eye.

'Go on . . .' another sigh.

'Elspeth graduated, summa cum laude, naturally; taught economics at senior high and that was that. We never spoke again. Over the years I've seen her from a distance and always wanted to explain how I *was* a gullible fool, just like she said. How I ruined everything because she'd rejected me, and your Grammy was only too keen to take her place.' Falling silent, he pulled the comforter higher up his legs, as if recounting the story had drained him of all energy. Logan's heart contracted with love and concern and he knew it was time to draw the conversation to a close and settle the old man for the night.

'You can tell me more tomorrow. But for now -' He got to his feet and stood by his grandfather's chair. Catching him by the sleeve, his grandfather pulled him close.

'It isn't too late, is it Logan?'

'Too late for what?'

'For you and young Miss Buchanan. Don't let history repeat itself.'

Logan sighed. 'I think it's gone past that. I . . . I said things I shouldn't've said.'

'Go back. Tell her how you feel.'

245

'I don't think that'll work. A so-called fiancé has come out of the woodwork.' Logan felt physically sick as he imagined them tumbling onto India's bed, making love, just as *they* had. No - nothing like they had. That physical connection, the fact that he enjoyed time in her company, didn't happen with everyone, did it? What they'd had was precious and he was man enough to acknowledge that. Also, to know that wounded male pride and hot-headedness had made him throw it away.

Just like his grandfather.

'It's never too late, Logan.'

'I think it is, for me. I should've . . . But don't worry, I'll sort out the house, get it back for you if it's the last thing I do. The fiancé let slip that she had plans to open the house up as some kind of *English-style Bed and Breakfast*. A Country Inn by any other name. I'll make it my business to ensure she hasn't got a snowball in hell's chance of achieving that ambition. We'll send her scuttling back to New York, along with her fiancé.'

John MacFarlane passed a weary hand over his eyes. 'You don't get it, do ya, son?'

Logan only half-registered his grandfather's whispered remark. 'Get what?'

'It's not about the house. It's *never* been about the house.'

'I don't understand. I was brought up on stories of the feud, how the Buchanans had done the dirty on us. Hasn't every MacFarlane since that poker game been trying to get the house back? By fair means or foul? My parents couldn't take any more of it, it's one reason they moved away from Sturgeon Bay and Door County.'

'Any excuse is a good excuse in your father's case. He always hankered after the high life and, for a time, it seemed that's what your mother wanted, too. I've been using a century old dispute as a contrivance, an excuse to get Elspeth Buchanan back into in my life. Your Grammy's gone and Elspeth and I are knocking on heaven's door.' He waved away Logan's protests. 'I want one last shot at explaining why I acted as I did. One last chance to make things right between us, to admit that she was right and I was wrong. I want *you* to make it happen, Logan. Will you do that for me, son?'

A shadow passed over them and Logan shuddered. His grandfather, evidently sharing the moment of prescience, clutched Logan's hand almost like a lifeline. His fingers were cold and dry and all colour had drained from his cheeks.

What choice did Logan have?

'Sure - I can set it up. Bring you and old Mizz Buchanan together. If that's what you want.'

'It's what I want.'

'Only -'

'Only? Come on, be honest with me, but remember, I have a weak heart.' His grandfather put his hand over his breast pocket in a half-joking gesture.

'I might not be here to see it through.'

'How's that?'

Logan wanted to level with his grandfather, tell him that what he really wanted to do was forget torts, codicils and *Buchanan versus MacFarlane*. For a while at least. Showing India round his studio had reawakened his dream of being an artist. He'd only become a lawyer to please his family because that's what MacFarlanes *did*, it was in their DNA. The first MacFarlane had passed his law exams at the turn of the century believing it would make it easier to win back the house. After that, the career path for subsequent generations had been set, in stone.

Now his grandfather was saying that repossessing the house no longer mattered? That what *really* mattered was putting the record straight; grabbing one last chance of happiness with Elspeth Buchanan? It would take some time to get his head round that.

Maybe the time was right for *him* to realise the dream he'd shared with India.

I would have packed my backpack, sketch pad, pencils, box of paints and headed off into the wide blue yonder. Working my way round the world . . . sketching everything I saw and - who knows, turning it into a book on my return. I'd grow my hair long, sport a grizzly beard and no one would recognise me when I got home. Like a sailor returning from a long sea voyage.

Could he do that? *Really* do it? Turn his back on everything he'd achieved since leaving Law School, the promised position in Washington, a chance to join a team of high flyers. Just as his grandfather had done nearly half a century earlier? He shook his head free of the idea - it was too much for his tired brain to process.

'I . . . I'm thinking of taking a sabbatical. Renting out the duplex, putting my furniture into storage. Selling my cars and the boat, if necessary.' Logan was thinking on his feet but it all made perfect sense. He had to get away, lick his wounds, sort himself out. 'But, if you need me, really need me I'll catch the first flight home and . . .'

'Logan, I squandered my chance of happiness. If you want to travel the world, live in a shack on a beach, watch the sun come up over a foreign sea, do it. I won't stand in your way. It'll jeopardise your chances in Washington of course; they might even withdraw their offer. But you know that, and I'm sensing you don't give a damn.'

'Not anymore.'

'So, what's brought this on? Let me guess. It's the Buchanan girl, isn't it?'

'I . . .'

Judge MacFarlane became thoughtful. 'Do you love the girl?'

'I think I do.'

'Then go tell her.'

'I can't. Not after everything's that's happened. I've got to take some time, think it through.'

'What's to think about?'

'Mother wrecked Father's life with lies and deceit. I don't want my life to be a case of different scene, same movie. I thought we had *something,* now I know I was wrong.'

'Logan, there are no certainties in this world. If you want this girl badly enough, go tell her. Or history really *will* be repeating itself.'

'Maybe . . .'

'Procrastination is the thief of time. Isn't that how the saying goes?'

Logan didn't answer straight away. Tenderly, he removed the blanket from his grandfather's knees, folded it and placed it over the back of the chair. Then, sliding his hands under his grandfather's armpits, helped him to his feet, taking care to give the old man time to steady himself.

'How about a movie?'

'You want to change the subject. I get that. But I'll be damned if I'll allow you to tuck me up in bed with a glass of hot milk like a geriatric baby.' His grandfather's severe look dared him to try.

'I wasn't planning on it.' Logan managed a weak grin. 'So, tell me what you want.'

'What I want is to watch a movie with you in the den, and then for you to set up a meeting with Elspeth Buchanan. ASAP. But it won't be easy, she's tougher than she looks. Deal?'

'Deal.' Gently, Logan fist bumped his grandfather, then led him from the deck, through the kitchen and down the steps, into the den. The room was a mini cinema with massive television screen and bookcases filled with DVDs arranged in alphabetical order. After settling his grandfather on the sofa, Logan walked over to the largest bookcase and scanned the shelves.

'How about, She Wore a Yellow Ribbon?' It was one of John's favourites and usually distracted him from pain and worry. Tonight, though, not even that seemed to work. His mind was firmly fixed on events of that summer in 1965.

'Elspeth ruined that movie for me. Said it was propaganda, designed to manipulate U.S. citizens into uniting against communism. That, when the cavalry drives off the Native Americans' horses and defeats them, it's a metaphor. According to Elspeth, Ford, the director, is suggesting that the only way to protect the U.S is by removing the communists' strength, in this case the atomic bomb.'

Logan let out a long, slow whistle. 'That's quite a theory.'

'She wrote a paper on the subject.' He pulled a face, showing that age hadn't mellowed him or made him change his opinion of her politics. Getting John and Elspeth into the same room would take some doing. Bringing about a rapprochement would be even trickier. 'I'm only telling you this because I want you to know who you're dealing with. She's not your average septuagenarian with a walking frame. She should've been a lawyer, or a university teacher. Instead she had to settle for teaching high school and marking SAT papers in the vacation to provide extra funds for her mom's medical care. She developed early-onset dementia around about the time I went to Washington and needed twenty-four-hour nursing.'

Logan loaded the DVD and started credits rolling before returning to the kitchen to freshen their drinks.

'Go on, I'm listening,' he said.

'I should've apologised then. Supported her through a difficult time; we were friends, after all, old friends. But with a new wife and a baby of my own, my plate was pretty full. And Elspeth made pretty clear that she wanted nothing

251

more to do with me. Still can't get over the fact that I let her down . . .' The judge's voice faded into the background and theme music from the film drifted out from the den instead.

Standing by the kitchen sink, Logan looked out across the lake to MacFarlane's Landing. His grandfather's story had been a distraction, allowing him to forget what an unholy mess he'd made of things himself. His world had turned upside down the moment he and India stepped over the threshold of her great-aunt's home. Instead of a new beginning, as he'd hoped, everything'd come crashing down around them.

Was it really as simple as the judge made out? Just drive over there and tell her he'd acted rashly and said things he didn't mean? That he should've given her a chance to explain? He frowned, what about the fiancé? He couldn't be explained away with a few words or made to vanish in a puff of smoke. How could a relationship work, based on lies and dissemblance? If she *had* any feelings for him, surely, she should have told him the truth, long before Hardy's appearance?

'You coming, Logan?' his grandfather called from the den.

Picking up two watered down bourbons, Logan turned his back on the winking light across the bay and the brief, disastrous affair between himself and India Buchanan. He'd do as his grandfather asked: take him out on his boat, arrange a meeting with Elspeth Buchan and then . . .

Then what?

He couldn't think beyond that. At least, not today.

All he knew for certain was that he wanted to put as many miles as he could between himself and MacFarlane's Landing. Once he'd done that, he could view his life with detachment and dispassion while figuring out how he'd ever be able to trust anyone again.

Chapter Fourteen

'That's great, India. One last shot, if you don't mind.'

'I don't mind in the least.'

India smiled at the photographer from upmarket periodical, *By Design,* a magazine specialising in high-end interior design projects. A former colleague had brought India's bed and breakfast establishment to the attention of the editorial team and they'd jumped at the chance to feature *Buchanan's* in their Thanksgiving Edition.

The feature had all the elements of a great article: her father's recent posting to Paris, the family connection to English gentry via Granny Meredith - and a century old feud. *Exactly* the sort of thing *By Design's* subscribers loved to read. As the editor put it, India's story was the *'perfect storm of creativity, history, and a modern woman's determination to succeed'.*

Added to which, the proprietor of *Buchanan's Bed and Breakfast Establishment* was well educated, easy on the eye, and had connections with the Old Country and the doughty pioneers who'd opened up the wilderness in the nineteenth century. All the story lacked was Prince Charming, an omission India was in no hurry to rectify.

Once bitten, twice shy - wasn't that how it went?

'Hold it, India, that's it.' The camera's flash dazzled as she posed next to the fireplace in the newly decorated sitting room. The mantelpiece held Granny Meredith's precious collection of Staffordshire cows and milkmaids and India was keen to show them off. She hoped that state of the art plumbing and central heating, comfortable beds and great cooked breakfasts, coupled with family antiques and the best of modern contemporary furniture would make her establishment stand out from other Country Inns in Door County.

Country Inn.

The very word brought MacFarlane to mind.

'I'm sure you have plans for the house, to renovate and bring it into the twenty-first century. I hope that's where your plans begin and end. I'd hate to see the house turned into some god-awful Country Inn . . . all whirlpool baths, canopied beds and hand blocked wallpaper . . . if you do, I'll fight you every step of the way.'

'S-sorry,' India stammered. 'Could you repeat the question?'

'Of course. Could you tell our subscribers how you gained the necessary permissions to trade as a bed and breakfast? It's the sort of detail they *adore*. Many of them dream of doing something similar.'

By Design's director and India exchanged a wry look, acknowledging the hard work necessary to establish an enterprise such as *Buchanan's*. India had put in eighteen-hour days in an attempt to get the bed and breakfast ready for

Thanksgiving. It wasn't a project for the faint hearted, but that wasn't what people wanted to hear.

Taking a breath, she wondered how to condense five months of hard slog into a couple of sentences.

During the unhappy weeks after her return from Chicago she'd kept busy, hoping to exorcize MacFarlane's ghost from the house. That was when she'd discovered documents, dating back to the turn of the century, stored in a tin chest in the cellar. Documents which proved *Buchanan's* had once held the necessary permission for running a business from the house. It was a small step from there to taking professional advice, then updating the documentation to ensure everything was legal and water-tight. Luckily, Door County's Planning and Zoning Department had been keen to see the old establishment back on the map, knowing *Buchanan's* would provide much needed accommodation during the busy tourist season from Memorial Day in May, through to Labour Day Weekend in September.

'There's been a livery stable here since the late eighteen-nineties,' India explained. 'When the steamers from Chicago brought summer visitors to Door County, they landed at Ephraim. My great-great grandfather took them to their holiday cottages along the shore. He started out with horse and buggy and later on bought an automobile. Between the turn of the century and the Great War, my family offered accommodation during the summer months.'

The editor pushed the tape recorder closer as India explained how no one had raised any objections and, as the newly-found deeds revealed, the house had once held 'industrial zoning'.

- no one had raised any objections -

India frowned as the editor fiddled with the tape recorder. She'd expected the MacFarlanes to block her every step of the way. Yet, nothing; *nada*; not a word. As if they'd lost interest in the house and, by association, *her*.

The editor sent India an apologetic smile. 'I hope you don't mind the feature mentioning the dispute over ownership of the house.' A good reporter, she evidently sensed a human-interest angle to the story. 'Our readers love that sort of detail.'

India waved away her interest. 'Ancient history. I'd much rather we concentrated on my plans for welcoming the first guests over Thanksgiving Weekend. To which end, I'd like to offer a complimentary weekend break to one of your subscribers and a plus one. Perhaps you'd like to join us, as our guest, for the annual cross-country ski run in December?'

The distraction worked and the editor didn't pursue the Buchanan/MacFarlane story. 'I'd love to, this bed and breakfast is *so* romantic. A cut above the others. So, tell me more about the cross-country ski run. That'd be a great follow up piece. Thanks, India, this is going to be a super cool edition.'

*****

Eventually, India waved goodbye to the design team, her face frozen in a fixed smile. She'd planned to drive over to

Green Bay to visit Elspeth in her Assisted Living Apartment in Belvoir Park, but the photo shoot had taken longer than expected. Now she was too exhausted to fetch the Buick out of the garage. She'd ring Elspeth and explain. Her aunt would be disappointed but she'd understand. Tomorrow was *Buchanan's Bed and Breakfast's* Open Day, complete with a piper playing reels to welcome the guests, and Elspeth would be joining India for that. She checked her watch. Time for a long, lingering bath followed by an early night with a book. She had to be up early to supervise the outside caterers and appear bright eyed and bushy-tailed by the time her guests arrived. Lotte Erikson and other ladies from the community had volunteered to help, too - and for that she was grateful.

Sleep eluded her. Every time she closed her eyes haunting images of Chicago rose to torment her . . . MacFarlane licking the spaghetti sauce off her face . . . her, exploring every inch of him with a teasing touch which had driven him wild . . . him, rolling her under his naked body and bringing them both to a state of delirious, unbridled passion.

Then, like a douche of cold water, his insulting: *What kind of business woman will you make if you give your services for free?*

MacFarlane had said things which had cut her to the bone. By falling in love with him she'd overruled common sense and sound judgement, and lain herself open to pain. She felt no sense of triumph in realising her plans for the house, just a numbing sense of loss. Lying in the darkness she looked into the inner-most corners of her heart and admitted that some small part of her had hoped that applying for commercial zoning might have brought Logan back into her life. Given her a second chance to explain why she hadn't been honest and up front over her plans for the business.

Punching her pillow into a more comfortable shape, she stopped beating herself up over what couldn't be changed and willed herself to sleep.

*****

'Did you send the MacFarlanes an invitation to your open day, India?' one of the women helping set out the buffet inquired. India was still getting used to the directness of local inhabitants. If they wanted to know something, they came right out and asked. That wasn't her way, the English way, and at times she found their directness disconcerting.

'Of course, I try to be a good neighbour. Whether the judge or his grandson,' she couldn't bear to say his name, 'choose to accept, is entirely up to them.' Smiling coolly, she took a step back from her inquisitor and glanced at her watch. 'Will you excuse me? The first guests will be arriving and I have some last minute things to check.' She walked away, aware of how like her mother she sounded - and groaned. Daphne Buchanan had taught her well and, it seemed, blood will out.

After checking that the hired help were carrying out her wishes to the letter, India walked over to great-aunt Elspeth and Lotte, seated at the kitchen table. Elspeth wouldn't have missed this Open Day for the world and had come over from Green Bay in Belvoir Park's minibus with nurse in attendance, complete with a wheelchair - which she flatly refused to use.

Elspeth beckoned India forward. 'I'm real proud of you, honey bun, and what you've achieved.' Bending, India kissed Elspeth on the cheek; she smelled deliciously of Chanel No 5. The kiss evoked a memory; at the end of every holiday, Elspeth had driven India to Green Bay airport, kissed her goodbye and put her onto the flight to Chicago, both women counting the days until India's return.

'*Are* you, Elspeth?' India sought Elspeth's reassurance.

'Sure am! You showed that MacFarlane boy what it means to take on a Buchanan,' she asserted, a combative light in her eye. Then, with a frown, 'What I can't figure out is why you don't look happy. Isn't this what you wanted, darling?'

'Of course, it is,' India responded with false brightness. 'I'm just tired, it's been an exhausting few months.' She tried to inject a positive note into her voice but Elspeth, obviously sensing who was at the root of her unhappiness, made her feelings plain.

'India, back at the hospital in Chicago, didn't I tell you not to trust the MacFarlanes? They're double-dealing rattlesnakes, every last one.' Reaching out, she held India's hands in her own, clearly trying to figure out what had happened between her great-niece and the MacFarlane boy. 'You're a Buchanan, India; full of pride and obstinacy! And I guess you wouldn't be a Buchanan if you didn't have a streak of cussedness, too.' Then, sobering, 'But, India honey, - sometimes getting what you want, can mean losing what you most desire.' Sharp blue eyes regarded India for long, drawn-out seconds. 'Did you really think you could have it all? The bed and breakfast business, *and* young MacFarlane?'

Just hearing his name caused familiar feelings of sick excitement and yearning to swamp India. She wanted to confide in Elspeth, but couldn't admit, even to her loving aunt, what a fool she'd been. Instead she deflected her great-aunt's interest with: 'Oh Elspeth, let's not talk about it now. Here's Lotte's husband Eddie with their kids.'

Their arrival provided a timely distraction and India made the most of the opportunity to move out of the kitchen and away from her perceptive great-aunt. Did she really wear her heart so clearly on her sleeve? Or, did Elspeth simply know her too well?

'How's the latest addition to the family?' she asked Eddie, returning his hug as he handed the baby over to Lotte.

'She's just had a feed and will sleep for a few hours if we're lucky,' Lotte answered for him. 'At the moment I feel as if I'm sleep walking. She woke every two hours last night. If she starts yelling, I'll take her home. Show Eddie around, Indy.'

Taking Eddie's arm, India guided him through the open plan, downstairs rooms.

'Wow!' Eddy responded, giving her arm an enthusiastic squeeze. 'India, honey, you gotta come and do up our place.'

'I'm so glad you like it. I've managed to redecorate all the downstairs rooms and three of the bedrooms, making them en suite. Once paying guests start arriving and I repay the money I owe my family, I hope to renovate the other rooms in turn. And one day, to convert the stables and buggy sheds into self-catering holiday accommodation.'

'It's adorable,' Lotte put in, joining them in the sitting room after handing the baby over to her eldest for a few minutes. 'What's not to like?'

The sitting room was decorated in the style of an English country rectory, inspired in no small part by Granny Meredith's Queen Anne house in Berkshire. It had a look of Jane Austen, which India hoped tourists would appreciate. She'd persuaded her parents to let her have some family antiques and a couple of well-executed nineteenth century landscapes on permanent loan to complete the image. The rest was achieved through subtle use of soft furnishings and India's own eye for detail and colour. She could almost imagine that a frosty Berkshire morning, perfect for a day's hunting, lay beyond the windows, not a cool Wisconsin afternoon in mid-October.

'Come and see the kitchen and the dining room, Eddie. I'll serve breakfast in the kitchen to my guests every morning but evening meals will be taken in the dining room.'

'Very ambitious, India honey. I just *know* you'll be a great success. Any advertising you want, just you let me know, I'll give a good rate at my agency.'

'Miss Buchanan,' one of the hired staff drew India away from the Eriksons. 'Your guests are arriving and the piper wants to know if he should start playing his reels?'

'Ask him to pipe them into the house, please, I'll be along directly.' India turned back to Eddie, gesturing towards the newly decorated kitchen. 'This is my 'Shaker' room. Let me know what you think.' Leaving them, she walked into the hall where the first visitors were handing over their coats and accepting a glass of wine. The brass-faced grandfather clock, an heirloom from her rough-diamond Buchanan ancestors, chimed the hour as she joined them.

*****

By the end of the afternoon, India felt tired but triumphant. Guests took their leave after signing the visitors' book and leaving favourable comments. Handbills and business cards advertising *Buchanan's* had all but disappeared from the hall table, a good omen. India crossed her fingers, hoping the Open Day coupled with the spread in *By Design*, would be enough to send her bed and breakfast on its way.

She sipped tepid wine and nibbled a left over canapé, realising that she was ravenous.

Then, as had been the pattern over the last few months, her mood of euphoria evaporated. Shoulders drooped and all those feelings of loss and desolation returned. She raised her hand to the scarlet ribbon at her neck, the one wrapped around the CD of La Boheme that MacFarlane had given her the day after they'd been to the opera. Dangling from the ribbon was the ring he'd left on the verandah rail before driving off in a cloud of dust.

She knew she should return the ring to the MacFarlanes, suspecting it to be a family heirloom. However, she'd kept it, in the vain hope that MacFarlane returned to claim it and give her a chance to make things right between them. Maybe even start over. But the odds were stacked against that ever happening. He believed she'd deceived him in order to outmanoeuvre him over the house and there was no going back.

If she was proud and bloody-minded, so was MacFarlane.

On several occasions over the last, lonely months, she'd parcelled up the ring to send back with a curt message. But it was a letter that refused to be written. She'd got no further than writing Logan, before remembering his departing shot: I've been waiting for the last three days to hear you use my name. But no, it was always MacFarlane. Even when you called out as we made love.

Her bottom lip quivered and she blinked away ever-threatening tears. Closing fingers round the ring, she drew strength from it, as if it was a talisman. Then she dashed away the tears with the knuckles of her right hand and stiffened her resolve. She had to stop all this introspection; it was border-line masochistic, a daily fix of pain she could well do without. Time for her to write off those three days in Chicago with MacFarlane as a hurtful and bitter experience.

One that she'd get over, though, given time.

'India. Look!' Grabbing her arm, Lotte pointed out through the sitting room window and down the long drive where a black limousine bouncing hard on its suspension, was making stately procession to her front door.

'Who is it?'

'MacFarlane,' Lotte said.

'Logan?' India managed in a choked voice, her heart almost stuttering to a halt.

Lotte looked at her with gentle compassion and squeezed her hand. Perhaps, like Elspeth, she'd half-guessed the reason behind India's recent, unexplained melancholy.

'No, Hun, old Judge MacFarlane.'

'What!?' Detecting the note of panic in her great-aunt's voice, India spun round to face her. Between them, Lotte and India helped her to walk over to the window. 'He's not setting foot inside this house,' Elspeth vowed as his chauffeur opened the car door and helped him climb the steps to the porch. When John MacFarlane entered the hall, the Buchanan women were waiting to receive him.

Judge MacFarlane was taller and more upright than India had imagined. Even in his mid-eighties he was a handsome man with thick white hair and a commanding presence. India felt her great-aunt tremble beside her. However, when Elspeth spoke it was anger that made her voice quiver, not trepidation.

'You've got some nerve coming here, John MacFarlane,' she said. 'If you've come to make trouble for India - you can get back in your fancy limo and git off my land.' She gave the limousine parked on India's drive a scathing once over, as though it was *just* the kind of car he would own.

'I believe it's your niece's land now Ellie,' the judge observed with fine regard for legal niceties. 'Maybe it's for *her* to order me off?' He gave India a searching look, his eyes as green and disconcertingly all-seeing as his grandson's, even if age had dimmed their brightness.

'This is Buchanan land.' India refused to let herself be brow beaten by that inimical stare 'I think that's been established beyond any doubt.' She sounded cool and collected, her voice clipped and very English next to her great-aunt's Mid-Western drawl. 'If you've come to upset my great-aunt and make trouble, you'd better leave now. I'm sure I don't have to tell you that MacFarlanes aren't welcome in this house.'

That took him by surprise, as if he hadn't expected such a show of spirit. Giving India a more thorough glance he nodded, as though her reaction was well-deserved - considering the history between their families.

He turned to Elspeth. 'You've taught the child well.'

'As you have your grandson.'

'Humph,' he grunted, leaning on his walking stick.

'What do you want, John?' she asked.

'I've come to see what's been done to my great-grandfather's house. It sounds as though it's been turned into a three-ring circus by the Buchanans.'

'If we'd decided to raze it to the ground it'd be none of your damned business. The MacFarlanes have always been sore losers, and you're no exception. Never could admit when you'd had a licking.'

That brought angry colour to the judge's cheeks, as he and Elspeth seemingly remembered an incident long buried in the past. He gave her a straight look and made a less than flattering observation. 'I thought old age and illness might have mellowed you, Elspeth. But you're just as ornery as you've always been.'

That venomous little dart struck home. No woman,

even in her mid-seventies, likes to be reminded of age and infirmity. It surprised India to discover that her great-aunt minded what he said, and minded very much, too.

'I'm sorry if my attitude doesn't suit.' Her withering tone conveyed the exact opposite. 'But after all that's passed between us do you really think I'm prepared to let bygones be bygones? I'm sure as hell not going to invite you to come swing on *my* porch!'

The old-fashioned expression left no one in any doubt as to her opinion. But he wasn't prepared to let her have the last word.

'How come you haven't responded to the letters from Logan, suggesting we meet?'

Logan had been writing to her aunt! And Elspeth hadn't mentioned it?

Elspeth was quick to answer. 'I don't dance to your tune, MacFarlane. Never have; never will.'

'That much is obvious.' This time the corners of his mouth lifted in a wry, half smile. 'So, I figured – if the mountain won't come to Mohammed, then . . .'

'I'm a mountain now. Is that it?'

'Yes! Immovable, unbending stubborn . . . You don't deny it?'

'Can't say I do.' There was a twinkle in Elspeth's eye and some of her anger dissipated. 'Come on, you old fool, sit down before you fall down.' Dismissing the nurse and chauffeur she led the way to India's private sitting room at the back of the house. There they took up warring positions either side of the fire, glaring at each other in the gathering dusk, neither willing to concede ground.

This was the showdown they'd waited long years for, years during which enmity and animosity had festered. They were going to have their head-to-head and nothing was going to get in their way. Is this how it would be, India wondered, if she and MacFarlane met again? Unresolved issues destroying them, eating into their happiness like battery acid?

A sigh, and she left them, closing the door quietly behind her to return to her guests, and check that the catering staff were following her instructions to the letter.

Chapter Fifteen

Finally, the last guests drifted home. Relieved, India took a calming breath, allowing herself to savour the silence settling on the old house. Then the sound of hired help in the kitchen washing up and Judge MacFarlane and Elspeth arguing in her sitting room reminded her that the day wasn't over.

Returning to the sitting room she found Elspeth and the judge regaling Eddie and Lotte with tales of the old days.

'My ancestor, Sean MacFarlane - after whom MacFarlane's Landing is named, of course - can claim to be the first Scot to have set foot in these parts,' the judge explained.

'And *my* ancestor, Jim Buchanan was right by his side. Probably fighting off a grizzly while MacFarlane cowered behind a tree. We Buchanans don't need places named after us to remember *our* place in history.'

'True, you wear . . . what-do-you-call-those things - *pashminas* - in Buchanan plaid, overload the house with tartan cushions, and have a piper at the door to remind everyone there's Scottish blood running through your veins.'

'India gave me this shawl,' Elspeth bit back. 'And I hardly call three scatter cushions on a window seat *overloading the house.*'

'I rest my case,' came the judge's dry response.

Time to break up the party before insults got out of hand.

'It's getting late, Elspeth . . .'

'India Jane Buchanan, don't you go ordering me to bed, Missy. I'm not senile yet!'

'I'll attest to that.' He sent India a look of fellow-feeling.

India turned to Lotte, soliciting sympathy. 'See what I get for following doctor's orders.'

'Doctors. Schmoctors!' the judge dismissed them contemptuously. 'What do they know? Tried to stop me drinking good Bourbon and made me give up driving.'

'Tried to get me to quit smoking. Much good it did 'em.' Elspeth sent India a defiant look, then she and John exchanged a conspiratorial smile. 'Doctors? Hah! My Daddy always referred to them as quacks.' She laughed the husky, throaty laugh of a lifetime smoker. 'Remember?'

'Charlatans,' he joined in with her laughter.

India looked on in astonishment. Whatever they had been talking about while she'd been busy with her guests seemed to have brought the cold war to an end - cushions, pipers and pashminas, notwithstanding.

'So, your honour, what do you think of my business venture?' India asked, testing the water.

'I think you did well to get planning permission, Miss Buchanan. But the law says you have a right to it; and who are we MacFarlanes to argue with the law?' His thick white eyebrows drew together in a frown. Then a straight look, reminding India so much of MacFarlane and her heart lurched. 'But I didn't come here to discuss the bed and breakfast with you, it's a done deal. I want to ask about Logan.'

He glanced over at Elspeth who nodded her approval, willing India to listen.

'Yes?' India's breathing became rapid and her heart skipped another beat.

'What did you do to get him all fired up?'

'Fired up?' India pretended she didn't understand.

'That's what I said.' He gave her a chance to respond and when she didn't, carried on. 'He's madder than hell, and not just over the house - although that's reason enough.' Evidently, he couldn't resist one last dig. 'There's something eating him. Wanna tell us what it is?'

'I --- I' India faltered under his interrogation. Eddie and Lotte, correctly assuming that this was a family moment, slipped out of the room. India sent them an apologetic look over her shoulder as they left and then returned to the conversation.

'Leave the girl alone John.'

'No, this needs to be discussed, Ellie. I care for my grandson as much as you care for your niece. All I know is that when Logan returned from Chicago, he'd changed. Turned his back on everything he'd striven for since leaving law school. Including a post in Washington he'd spent a

271

year and countless lobbying to acquire.' Then he clammed up, perhaps thinking he was giving too much information away in exchange for little in return. 'Something's eating him, wanna tell us what it is, India.'

He sent her a searching look and then his eyes lit on the ring at the end of the scarlet ribbon. There was a flash of recognition and understanding, and then his expression softened, as if the ring provided him with all the answer he needed.

'Now hold it there. If your grandson has a quarrel with India it's not for us to go interfering. No matter how much we'd like to,' Elspeth added, letting India know that she shared the judge's concern.

Seemingly, Elspeth had been keeping her counsel, hoping that India would open up and confide in *her*. When India glanced at the judge the same concerned look was on his face. So much for believing she'd kept her pain and misery secret.

'Where . . . is Logan?' she managed to choke out.

'In the Far East, living in some artistic community. Sketching, painting, taking time out to decide what he wants to do with his life.'

'How -'

'Do I know all this? He Skypes and emails me photographs a couple of times a week. Bet you'd got me down as some old timer who doesn't know how to operate an iPad. Huh?'

'I -'

'Back off. Maybe you should ask your grandson the same question, John MacFarlane? If they want us to know what happened between them, they'd tell us. Right?' Elspeth's look willed India to spill the beans. India lowered her eyes and didn't respond. She and MacFarlane had drawn a line in the sand, put '*Chicago*' behind them and were getting on with their, very different, lives.

That was all anyone needed to know.

Her bed and breakfast business had the potential to become a success. She should focus on that and forget all about MacFarlane and Chicago. Be happy. Instead, a great lump of misery wedged behind her breastbone, making it hard to swallow - or to focus on what Elspeth was saying. Pain and anguish for her situation overwhelmed her. She had to escape from their concerned, searching glances before she broke down in front of them.

'I . . . I have things to check. Please . . . excuse me.' Her voice snagging, she turned on her heel and fled, not for the kitchen, but the sanctuary of her bedroom.

Closing the door behind her, she sank down on the padded window seat and, drawing her knees up, pulled a cushion towards her, hugging it for comfort. Resting her head back against the heavy shutters she looked out into a vermilion and gold sunset where islands and peninsulas jutted out into the bay. However, the beauty of the scene was lost. All she could think of was how different the sunset must look from MacFarlane's beach hut, thousands of miles away.

The low rumble of the Judge's voice and her great-aunt's

response reached her from the sitting room below. Elspeth had always been her role model - fiery, principled, scared of nothing. If only she'd had the strength to stand up for herself when Tom Harvey had knocked on the door and set in motion a chain of events which had destroyed her hopes and dreams, things might have turned out differently.

Truth was, she'd fought harder for her business than for the man she loved. As her great-aunt had so aptly put it - surely, she didn't think she could have it all?

Arrogantly, she'd assumed she could - and this was her comeuppance.

Cool air blew off the lake and through the open window, stirring the muslin draping her cast iron four poster bed. Getting up to wipe her eyes on the corner of her pashmina, she caught sight of herself in the cheval mirror. Backlit by the sunset, with filmy drapes billowing around her, she seemed as unsubstantial as a ghost. A mere shadow of her former self. Dark circles under her eyes, skin without its youthful luminescence, violet eyes huge in her pale face.

She'd conned herself into believing that if she kept her anguish hidden, and let no one guess at her unhappiness, it would pass. Believing that, if she won the right to trade from the house and bury herself in work, it would be enough. Instead, the only person she'd fooled had been herself.

He's all fired up . . . madder than hell with you . . . It's not just the house. It's something else.

The nightmare was just beginning. A dark future stretched ahead of her, a future without MacFarlane. Then, unbidden, she heard her mother's voice in her head: *India Jane, you're neglecting your guests. Tidy yourself up, apply fresh lipstick, go downstairs and do your duty as a hostess.* Turning her back on the room with a heavy heart, she prepared to do just that.

*****

The following morning India poured coffee for Elspeth and the Judge in the kitchen. With painful tact they avoided any mention of India's 'time out' last night. Still, it hung in the air between them. Once the coffee was poured and the battered biscuit barrel passed round, India sat down.

It was then that her great-aunt dropped her bombshell.

'India honey, John and I have decided to go away together.' She sent India an anxious look, clearly worried about her reaction. 'On an extended vacation,' she explained, her voice trailing off.

'Vacation!' India couldn't keep the astonishment out of her own voice. 'Where?'

Her great-aunt faltered and John supplied the details. 'There's this place in Palm Springs - kind of an elephant's graveyard,' he observed with gallows humour. 'It takes in old folks and provides them with twenty-four-hour nursing, until the end.'

The end? Were they repaying her reticence by keeping bad news from *her?*

'John don't tease,' Elspeth chastised, reaching over for India's hand. 'It's a five star assisted nursing hotel, with its own golf course and swimming pool and fully qualified staff.

275

We've reached the conclusion that we're too old for another Wisconsin winter.'

'It's time we enjoyed the years we've got left. Together,' the Judge added. 'We've been foolish and stubborn. Wasted precious years fighting when we should have been . . . friends.' The Judge struggled to find the right word; but his look showed Elspeth that his regard went beyond friendship. 'It's taken me over fifty years to apologise to your great-aunt for something I said in the heat of the moment. Fifty years to admit that I married the wrong woman.'

'Hush, it doesn't matter now,' Elspeth interrupted gently. She sent India another anxious look. 'You don't think we're crazy, do you?'

'Sometimes, crazy's the only way to go. Anything that makes you happy gets the thumbs up from me, my darling, you know that.' India hugged and kissed her great-aunt, then after a moment's hesitation kissed Judge John MacFarlane on the cheek, too.

'Thank you for that, India,' he responded gruffly. Then he pulled a dog-eared diary out of the breast pocket of his sports jacket and continued in a business-like manner. 'We're planning a family get together at my house before we fly to Palm Springs. They let you have a few weeks there - a trial period before you commit to buying one of the villas in the 'village'.'

'Twenty-four seven care doesn't come cheap, so we have to be sure.'

John reached across the table for her hand. 'We *are* sure, Elspeth.'

'Yes. I guess we are.'

India marvelled at how often the pronoun 'we' peppered their conversation. They were acting like a couple of kids, newly in love. It made her eyes brim with tears so, turning away, she walked over to the Welsh Dresser and fetched her desk diary.

'When do you plan on flying down there? I'll have to organise nurses, tickets and . . .'

'You don't have to worry about any of that, India. I'll take care of everything.' He shot her a look from beneath thick, white brows which told her that from now on, Elspeth was *his* responsibility. Then he made a joke, guessing she'd find that hard to accept and wanting to soften the blow. 'I'll probably give my bank manager a heart attack with the amount of money I'm spending. But, hell, we've waited long enough for this moment. We're going to enjoy every minute of it.'

India could see that his - *their* - minds were made up. She flipped open the pages of her diary and retrieved a pencil from behind her ear. 'When were you thinking of holding the dinner party?'

'Tuesday of Thanksgiving Week - twenty-second of November.'

'The twenty-second? But, that's just *weeks* away, the run-up to my opening weekend, I can't spare the -'

'Sure, you can. That's why *I'm* organising the vacation; you don't need to get involved. As for the dinner, my housekeeper Martha will see to that. From what I've seen and from what Ellie's told me, your bed and breakfast business is good to go. I'm sure Lotte Erikson is capable of holding the fort for a few hours while you have dinner at my place?'

India nodded. Lotte would be only too happy to help.'

'It'll be a very low-key affair, just you two ladies, myself, and Logan of course.' He spoke as if it was the most natural thing in the world for over a hundred years of feuding to be resolved over dinner at his house. He glanced over at India, seemingly to gauge her reaction to Logan being the third guest.

Then he slipped on his reading glasses and scribbled in his diary, diplomatically giving her a moment to assimilate everything he'd said.

'Yes. Yes, of course. Logan. Logan, too. Naturally.' India bent her head and made a great show of writing until she'd regained her composure. All she could think of was the livid mark on Logan MacFarlane's cheek where she'd slapped him, calling him a bastard. The thought of sitting across the table from him and making polite conversation over Thanksgiving dinner filled her with dread. *Thanks*giving? No *thanks*.

'India?' Her great-aunt brought her back into the conversation. 'Are you listening, child? I asked you if you'd take me back to Green Bay.'

'I'm sorry Aunt Elspeth, of course I will.' India managed a bright smile, although she suddenly felt in need of fresh air. 'I - I'll go and fetch the car round.' When she tried to move, her legs almost buckled under her.

'No need, India. My chauffeur will see us both home.'

With that, Judge MacFarlane took charge. Elspeth collected their coats, called their nurses through from the sitting room and left India in the empty kitchen, lost for words.

278

Chapter Sixteen

India drove the Buick through the red-gold and ochre of the autumn evening. Fallen leaves trailed in the wake of the vintage vehicle, swirling and dancing in the tail lights.

'India. You're mighty quiet, honey. You okay?'

'Just concentrating. I hate driving in the dusk, you know that.' Turning, she smiled at Elspeth. 'Probably time I had my eyes checked at the optometrist's in Sturgeon Bay.' She wiped suddenly moist palms down the sides of her wool coat.

Used to being completely open and honest with her great-aunt, India was finding it hard to hide the thought that meeting MacFarlane filled her with sick apprehension. Switching on the radio to fill the silence and take her mind off the ordeal ahead, she swung onto the long drive up from the shore road to the MacFarlane house. She'd no sooner parked than the judge came out to greet them, making plain he'd been waiting for their arrival with some impatience.

'Elspeth. India. Welcome. Come on in.' He ushered them into an oak-panelled hall dominated by a stone fireplace in which a welcoming fire burned. The house was pure Norman

Rockwell, and India's professional interest overcame her anxiety as she took in the panelling, stained glass and hand-painted floor tiles.

'It's an historic house, India,' Judge MacFarlane put in proudly.

'A house I vowed I'd never set foot in, after you returned from your tour of duty with your new bride.'

'It's very beautiful,' India gushed, anxious to cover her aunt's bitter aside.

'Now, Ellie . . . I thought we agreed to let bygones be bygones.'

'You're right. It's Thanksgiving, so let's be thankful that we've been given a second chance to be together.'

'Give your coats to Martha, come through and we'll drink to that.'

He gestured for them to precede him into a large sitting room overlooking the lake. As the housekeeper came forward to help Elspeth out of her thick coat, India hung back, allowing her great-aunt to enter the sitting room ahead of her. This was Elspeth's moment, and this evening she was happy to take a back seat.

Another beautiful room. This time with one wall comprising entirely of glass, through which shore lights twinkled like brightly coloured lanterns. Beyond that, the light at MacFarlane's Landing beat towards them, strong and steady - as it had done for the last one hundred and fifty years. Crossing her fingers, India hoped that her heart would beat as steadily tonight. How the judge had stood it all these years knowing that the woman he loved was so near, yet out of reach, India couldn't imagine. *She* couldn't live in close proximity to MacFarlane, watch him marry and set up home in this grand old house. She tortured herself imagining a scenario where she bumped into Logan and his new wife coming out of the Inn at Cedar Crossing in Sturgeon Bay, pushing a baby buggy.

If that happened she'd close down her business, sell the house and give up on her dream.

Whoa . . . she was getting ahead of herself. MacFarlane would never settle in Door County, it couldn't contain him, or his ambitions. The sick feeling abated, her pulse rate slowed and she turned towards the elderly couple with a false, bright smile. 'Something smells good.'

'Martha's famous Thanksgiving turkey. I hope nobody minds, we're going to have to wait dinner because Logan's been delayed. He's catching a late flight from Chicago, and he'll join us as soon as he can.'

He'll join us as soon as he can . . .

India's stomach lurched as disappointment and relief washed over her in conflicting waves. How on earth could she eat Thanksgiving dinner with MacFarlane, let alone keep it down?

'Our first Thanksgiving Dinner together Elspeth. Whatd'ya think of that?' He raised a toast to her, as if she was still eighteen and, in his eyes, the most beautiful woman in the world.

'I think it's fine. Mighty fine.' Elspeth sent India a

concerned look, as if sensing her inner turmoil. 'And has young Logan enjoyed his time abroad?'

'He's having a great time.' A stab of pain lanced through India's heart. 'Skypes me from all the places he's been. He's taken a pilgrimage to some of the old haunts on my behalf, looking up places where I spent my last tour of duty in 'Nam. Laying ghosts, Elspeth,' he was quick to reassure her, 'nothing more. He sent me a bunch of photos on-line, but I hardly recognised any of the buildings. Those I do remember have either been swallowed up by the jungle or razed to the ground and replaced by modern dwellings.'

He stopped talking, plainly thinking back to those days, remembering.

'That's only to be expected, John. It is a long time ago, after all.' Reaching out, Elspeth touched his hand, comfortingly. 'Water under the bridge, laddie,' she joked, referencing their Scottish ancestry.

'You're right, Ellie.' Shaking off his introspective mood, he squeezed her hand in silent communication before moving the conversation along. 'Last time we spoke, Logan was in Penang, Malaysia, where he's renting an old colonial villa. He's gotten involved with a group of ex-pats there - writers and artists, all living the dream. Here's a photo he emailed a couple of weeks back. I had it printed off and framed.' Releasing Elspeth's hand, he got to his feet and walked stiffly over to a baby grand piano where a collection of silver framed photos was displayed. Picking one up, he handed it to India. 'This was taken outside Logan's villa.'

She examined the photograph with hungry eyes, taking in every detail. Logan looked fit and tanned, surrounded by half a dozen young women dressed in typical Boho fashion: baggy trousers, fringed batik patterned skirts, or chopped off shorts and skimpy tops which revealed tattoos, multiple piercings, and sun-kissed skin.

'Very nice' she choked out, keeping her expression neutral.

'Logan has been helping some young Australians on their gap year. They've gotten into difficulties because visas - and money – have run out. It's typical of Logan that he's offered food and shelter to young strangers, keeping them safe until documentation is sorted out, or Mom and Dad send enough money to fly them home. I warned him to tread carefully, not upset the local judiciary by overstepping the mark. Being a westerner in that part of the world, let alone an American, brings attendant problems these days.'

'Let me see, India,' Elspeth held out her hand for the framed photograph which was in danger of slipping from India's slack fingers.

'He's having a ball . . . sketching, painting, exploring - and in no hurry to come home.' The judge drove another nail into India's heart. 'However, once I told him of our plans to move to Palm Springs, he was anxious to spend one last Thanksgiving in the old house.' His gaze ranged round the room, capturing it in his memory.

'And then?' Intuitively, Elspeth raised the question that India couldn't bring herself to ask. Questions were too revealing, too exposing; she was just managing to hold it all together, but it wouldn't take much for her control to slip.

'I don't know. Chicago? Once the wanderlust is out of his system? Or, maybe try for that position in Washington he put on hold. He's well respected and has a network of contacts in D.C. I can't imagine they'd hold this sabbatical against him. Once, moving to Washington was all he wanted. But now?' He fixed a penetrating stare on India, as if suspecting she knew the reason for Logan's change of heart.

Elspeth, however, was having none of the blame landing on her great-niece's shoulders. 'Logan's almost thirty-five, John, so I guess he knows what he's doing. It's a long time since you changed his diaper, if you ever did. We gotta let young folk make their own mistakes.'

'You're right, Ellie. And, much as I miss Logan, I don't want him hurrying back before he's good and ready. He's spent the last fifteen years dragging MacFarlane, MacFarlane and Levison into the twenty-first century. He's due some time-out. Time to figure out what he *really* wants to do with his life. Unlike India who's got hers all sorted out, with the bed and breakfast and all?' He exchanged a look with Elspeth. They were happy and clearly wanted to see Logan and India settled before they left for Florida.

'India's working like a Trojan. I swear to God she'll burn herself out before she's thirty.'

'Really Aunt Elspeth. Hard work never hurt anyone.'

Having raised the subject, the judge was in no hurry to drop it. 'Wish I knew what demons are keeping Logan away from MacFarlane's Landing. I figure, once I leave the house and Martha stays on as housekeeper/custodian, there'll be nothing to draw him back here. What do you say, India?' Another questioning look, willing India to put their minds at rest.

Using the excuse of returning the photograph to the baby grand, India escaped their loving interrogation, walking over to the window and looking out over the lake. Suddenly fearful of the future, she reflectively twined the ribbon holding MacFarlane's ring around her fingers, drawing solace from touching it. She'd spent many sleepless hours deliberating if she should wear it tonight, afraid that he might interpret it as somehow provocative. As if she was flaunting herself and her business in his face, or wearing the ring to taunt him.

She suspected, after seeing the judge's reaction, that Logan had removed the ring from the family vault at the end of their idyllic stay in Chicago. A time when they'd been happy and he'd evidently thought their relationship had a future. Now, having had time to think things over, he probably regarded their time together, India's passionate response to his lovemaking, and her agreeing to prolong their stay in Chicago, as nothing more than a ruse. A ploy to gain time for her to carry out background checks into zoning regulations and the viability of her business scheme.

His bitter parting shot: *'God, India you sure took me for a ride, didn't you? I fell for it as hard as any man has ever fallen for a scheming woman'*, showed he regarded himself as a sucker, taken in by her sweet little lies.

India wished she could shut her mind to everything

that'd happened between them, all the hurtful things he had said. However, almost masochistically, she kept prodding the memory, keeping it alive. Because, no matter how painful her soul searching was, it was preferable to the emptiness of her days when she couldn't get him out of her head. Or those long, sleepless nights when she longed for him; wanted him so badly that her whole body ached and burned . . . until she buried her face in the pillow waiting for sleep to finally claim her.

Pressing her head against the cold window she closed her eyes. Surely, MacFarlane must feel something of this terrible desolation - the blackness that sucked the joy out of things: music, books, plans for the future. He must know that it had been more than just good sex between them. Although God knows, she thought as an unbidden frisson of desire travelled her length, that part had been good; so good.

By wearing the ring tonight, she hoped to show MacFarlane that she wanted a chance to talk things through. To say what she should've said before they left Chicago.

That she loved him.

If he ignored the gesture, rejected her for a second time, she'd admit defeat and return the ring. She had no right to it. Even though it represented a time when the world had seemed full of endless opportunity and she'd been at her happiest. Her heart contracted with love for MacFarlane, a love that wouldn't go away. For a few, ecstatic seconds her soul soared, filling her with euphoria and dizzying optimism.

She'd imagined countless times how this evening would

unfold but had never got past the part where she told him that she loved him and asked if they could put the past behind them. Just as John and Elspeth had. Even during the darkest moments of despair, she couldn't admit the possibility that he'd reject her a second time. Now the waiting and wondering was about to end.

The front door opened and closed and Martha call out joyously, 'Logan's home.'

'Logan!' The judge prised himself out of his chair and walked stiffly into the hall, leaning heavily on his cane. 'Come on through, son, we're in here!'

Now the moment had arrived, India's confidence plummeted and fear and doubt crowded in. The evening was going to end badly, she *knew* it. However, she was no quitter and determined to give it her best shot. She paused briefly to compose herself before turning back towards the room.

Her first glimpse of MacFarlane was his image reflected back at her from the window. Even through the glass darkly, framed in the archway linking the sitting room to the hall, he looked better than she remembered - in jeans, scuffed leather jacket over a micro-fleece, with a cashmere scarf wound round his lower face. India was hit by a rush of feeling, a hormone-induced high as real as any addiction. Breathing snagged, her skin became suffused with heat and blood sang in her ears.

Earlier feelings of optimism returned.

She'd *make* him listen. *Make* him believe.

Unwinding his scarf, Logan dropped his leather grip

onto the floor and shrugged off his jacket. In her heightened state, India imagined she could smell the cold breath of autumn clinging to his skin and hair.

'Good evening Mizz Buchanan.' Logan greeted Elspeth with deliberate courtesy, shaking her hand and giving her a charming smile. 'It seems only yesterday when you chased me off your jetty with your broom. Hope I'm safe tonight, ma'am?'

'He's sassy, no mistake,' Elspeth grinned over at the judge. 'Wonder who he gets that from?'

Logan walked over to his grandfather and hugged him, taking care not to bowl him over.

'You know India, of course,' his grandfather gestured towards her.

'Of course.'

Their glances met in the window and India burned under his blistering regard. If she'd forgotten how he could turn her blood and bones to water with a glance, she was reminded of it. How easy it would be to forget there was bad blood between them. To imagine that all she had to do was turn towards him and run into his arms then all the misunderstandings and the hurtful things they'd said and done would be forgotten.

She felt like one of those girls who, on Halloween, conjured up the form of their future husband in a candle lit mirror. Suddenly, she was afraid to turn and face Logan in case he vanished, like a spectre.

Then he drew his eyes away and the spell was broken.

'Do I have time to shower and change?' He acted as if India was beneath his notice, beyond his contempt.

'Yes,' his grandfather replied, clearly displeased by his grandson's brusqueness. 'We were going to wait dinner for you anyway, son.'

'Good.' Logan smiled fondly at the old man and Elspeth, making it plain that his quarrel was with India, alone. 'I'll be as quick as I can. Excuse me, ma'am.' Picking up his leather grip, he left the room.

Over by the window, India was struck by the hopelessness of her situation.

'Is there a bathroom I could use?' Keeping the quiver out of her voice, she turned to face him and Elspeth. 'I - I need to fix my make up.'

'Sure.'

Glad to get the awkward moment out of the way, John pointed his cane at a door across the hall and India made her escape.

Once inside the cloakroom she removed the ring, rummaged in her bag and found the blue leather box it normally resided in. Unthreading the ring from the ribbon, she placed it in the box and closed the lid. Cramming the box into her handbag she turned her attention to her make up. Not that it needed touching up, it was perfect as it was: understated, simple and suited to her new life in the country.

But MacFarlane had just declared war. She needed to respond in kind. Standing in front of the mirror she skilfully applied the painted mask of a high achiever who worked in

New York, weekended in Martha's Vineyard and holidayed in the West Indies. She accented eyes with smudgy shadow and eyeliner, defined cheek bones with an upward sweep of blusher, and outlined lips with a garnet red pencil. She'd been wearing Chanel 19, but that now seemed far too soft, too feminine. Rooting in her bag she searched for a perfume more fitting to the role she was about to play this evening, a slim phial of Dior's *'POISON'*.

She drenched herself in that, coughing as it caught the back of her throat. Her hair was styled in a collar-length long bob - however, that was far too ingenuous a look for this evening. Retrieving combs and brush, she pulled two wings of hair away from her face and pinned them on the crown of her head. Then she drew two heavy lines along her eyebrows, giving her the look of a heart breaker.

Or should that be . . . ball breaker?

A hard-headed business woman stared back and India smiled at her with grim satisfaction. Smoothing down her little black dress, she tucked her bag under her arm and returned to the sitting room. Elspeth and John were drinking martinis and laughing over a shared memory regarding someone they'd known back in the day.

'I always suspected he was sweet on you, Ellie. I shoulda punched him on the nose when I had a chance, back in high school.'

Elspeth laughed, openly pleased that John hadn't forgotten she'd been sought after, the belle of the ball. Then she turned her attention to her great-niece. 'Landsakes, India!'

Ignoring Elspeth's reaction, India walked over to the drinks trolley and fixed herself a large Martini, knocking it back in one. Her eyes widened at its potency; better slow down, she needed her wits about her if she was to survive the evening.

Half an hour later MacFarlane joined them wearing a dinner jacket which fitted like a second skin. An evocative combination of subtle aftershave and newly washed hair reached India as he walked past her and sat down in one of the armchairs. Again, without giving her a second glance.

'Fix yourself a drink, Logan. Wanna whiskey?'

'Sure.' Pushing himself out of the armchair, Logan poured himself a neat whiskey.

'I'm sure India would like another Martini, fix her one, will you?'

An indifferent shrug met this request, but he did as his grandfather requested. His hand unsteady as he passed India a Martini in a long-stemmed cocktail glass, giving her a critical once over. India responded with a hard, challenging look, and a smile which didn't quite reach her eyes. Taking the glass, she turned her back on him. Two could play that game.

She walked over to her great-aunt.

'Are you warm enough Elspeth? Shall I fetch your wrap from the hall?' Although her voice was steady, she spilled some of the cocktail as she stirred the olive around in her glass. Her great-aunt assured her that she was fine and looked as if she wanted to say more. However, at that moment, Martha announced, somewhat testily, that dinner was served.

Going over to a side table the judge picked up two cellophane boxes. He gave one to MacFarlane.

'Gardenias.' His voice was gruff, full of emotion. 'Over sixty years ago Elspeth and I stood in this room. We were going to dinner in Sister Bay, and I had a corsage waiting for her in the ice box. Then we quarrelled, and - well, the rest is history. Tonight, I'm going to pin this gardenia to your dress Elspeth, and I wish to God it was as easy to turn the clock back. Have it to do over.'

Leaning heavily on her stick Elspeth walked over to John MacFarlane. With clumsy, rheumatic hands, he pinned the gardenia to her dress, and then kissed her on the lips.

'It took you sixty years to admit you were wrong, John MacFarlane,' Elspeth said forthrightly, hiding her emotion. 'But it was worth the wait.'

The judge extended his arm and escorted her into dinner.

A lump formed in India's throat at the parallel between their situation and hers and MacFarlane's. Would she have to wait sixty years before MacFarlane finally admitted he'd acted rashly that day and made an error of judgement? Judging by his inimical look, an apology - let alone any positive outcome this evening - wasn't on the cards.

'Logan, pin India's corsage to her dress and then come on through to dinner,' the judge threw over his shoulder. 'Before Martha tenders her resignation.'

Then they were alone.

MacFarlane viewed the gardenia as if it was poisoned ivy. Sensing his reluctance to touch her, India informed him: 'I'm quite capable of pinning it on myself, thank you, MacFarlane.'

'Lady, you're capable of a lot more than *that*.' He gave her hair and makeup an unflattering, second appraisal.

'Really?'

'You bet.'

Their eyes locked - his cold, arctic green, hers sparking with anger. She wouldn't be the first to look away, she vowed; wouldn't give him the satisfaction of browbeating her. She raised her obstinate Buchanan chin a notch higher, treating him to a haughty look which made her opinion of him crystal clear, keeping her despondency hidden.

This wasn't how she'd imagined things turning out.

Okay, he was still smarting about what had happened over the house - and between himself and Harvey, she got that. She knew a reconciliation wasn't going to be easy. However, even in her worst nightmares she hadn't foreseen this icy implacability, or that achieving some kind of rapprochement would be this difficult, if not impossible.

'Give me the bloody gardenia, MacFarlane.' Her voice was clipped, very British. If he touched her whilst pinning on the corsage, he would feel her quiver, and know that things *weren't* over between them. She couldn't allow that to happen, couldn't lose the last shreds of her dignity and self-respect.

'Can't bear to be contaminated? That it?'

He took a step towards her, full of dark purpose, and she flinched before the force of his anger. However, before she had time to protest, he'd removed the corsage from the cellophane, slid cool fingers under the neckline of her dress and pinned the gardenia to her bodice. He carried out the task grim-faced, as though it gave him no pleasure to touch her. Nevertheless, his breath was warm on her collar bone and his fingers trailed along her skin, awakening old memories. India dare not look up into those dark fringed eyes, instead she focused on the crescent shaped scar on his upper lip, the place where he'd nicked himself shaving this evening, and freckles accentuated by the tropical sun.

Then she was released and her torment was over. MacFarlane drained his whiskey in one gulp, slamming the glass on top of the piano.

'Look,' he began, choosing his words carefully. 'I don't want to be here tonight. And judging by your expression, neither do you. No. Hear me out.' He raised his hand when India tried to speak. 'However - it's important to my grandfather and Elspeth that we *are* here. And that's good enough for me. I think we're both mature enough to sit through a Thanksgiving dinner without destroying their happiness. Don't you?'

India nodded.

There being nothing more to add, he held out his arm and, after a moment's hesitation, India placed her hand on it. With empty gallantry MacFarlane escorted her across the hall and into the dining room, guiding her to her place and pulling out her chair. Then he took his place opposite, they shook out their napkins and Martha was signalled to serve the soup.

Chapter Seventeen

Somehow, India and MacFarlane maintained polite conversation over the meal, avoiding all controversial topics: politics, religion, and the old MacFarlane homestead now *Buchanan's Bed and Breakfast*. Once they were back in the sitting room drinking coffee India snatched a surreptitious glance at her watch. Catching the slight twist of her head, MacFarlane raised his brandy glass in mocking tribute. As if to say: *don't worry, your ordeal is almost over.*

'Logan. We've told you our news. Come on, don't hold out on us. Tell us about your time in the Far East, your plans for the future.' The judge turned to Elspeth and India, proud of his grandson and his achievements.

'The position I was offered in the D.A.'s office has been kept open, but not indefinitely. I have to give them my final answer in the New Year. If I want to advance my career, I have to move to Washington, simple as that.' He glanced once, briefly, in India's direction. 'I've rented out my apartment, but if I decide to move to Washington permanently, I'll sell the lease and buy a house in Alexandria. It was voted one of America's Top Art Places recently, home to over eighty studios and galleries, including the Art League School and the Northern Virginia Fine Arts Association. Having reignited my passion for art, I'm reluctant to let go.'

'Sounds like a plan, Logan.'

'There's nothing to keep me here, now you're leaving.' The last remark was directed at India, and they all knew it.

'When do you leave?' Her great-aunt asked the question India couldn't bring herself to voice.

'End of next week.' He looked at India, as if expecting a comment. 'Martha will look after grandfather's house in our absence.' His expansive gesture took in the old house and the to-die-for lakeside view. 'Maybe I'll come back for the sailing in the summer. Maybe not.' He shrugged, as if it didn't matter to him, either way.

Ironic that, after years of litigation, the MacFarlanes were leaving the Landing without a backward glance. As though, in the end, India's house and their possession of it was no longer important.

The judge summed it up, neatly.

'Well I guess that's the end of a chapter. The practice will continue in Chicago and Sturgeon Bay; our partners are more than capable of running it without my interference. The only difference is I'll be in Palm Springs and Logan will, most likely, be in Washington once his odyssey is over. Guess that just leaves India to keep a lamp in the window for us to find our way home by.'

His words destroyed the last of India's composure. She

had to get away before anyone realised that MacFarlane's words and his indifference had shattered her heart into a thousand tiny pieces. It took a supreme effort for her to glance at her watch again, this time with the cool poise of a time-strapped business woman.

'I'm *really* busy with Thanksgiving Weekend looming. So . . . if no one minds . . .'

'Sure; you go along India. But Elspeth, you'll stay on a while, won't you? We've got things to discuss. My chauffeur'll take you home, whenever you want. You aren't tired are you, sweetheart?' The care and consideration evident in his tone was in direct contrast to his grandson's attitude towards India.

Elspeth looked as perky as ever. 'Who me? Why the night's just beginning. You go home India. I'll see you tomorrow, I'll need some help with my packing.' She looked as excited as a young bride about to set out on her honeymoon.

'Of course. I think Lotte will help, too, if necessary. Good night.' India picked up her bag.

'Logan. Fetch India's coat, will you?' India kissed the old people good night and allowed MacFarlane to help her into her coat. She didn't want to burden them with her problems. They were on the brink of a new life together and she wanted them to enjoy every moment of it.

'Thanks,' she replied gracelessly when he opened the front door, and she was sure they couldn't be overheard.

'You're welcome, ma'am,' he responded in equal measure, standing to one side so she could walk out onto the porch.

Thank God she'd had the presence of mind to come in her own car. To have waited for the judge's chauffeur, to have spent another minute in MacFarlane's company was more than she could bear.

The Buick was waiting on the drive, a thin film of frost riming its curved windscreen. Summer was finally over, she acknowledged dispiritedly as she touched the frost flowers with her fingers. She could no more stem the tide of the seasons than she could change what lay between her and MacFarlane. And, after his open hostility, she was no longer sure that she wanted to.

With a heavy sigh she climbed into the car, glad of the cover afforded by the dark interior and frosted windscreen. Here in the friendly darkness she no longer had to pretend. Overwhelmed by despondency, her body slumped. She'd been living in a fool's paradise to imagine for a moment that she could straighten things out between them. Now she knew where she stood and could get on with her life. Squaring her shoulders, she turned the engine over. It gave a protesting shudder and then died.

'No-ooh. Don't let me down now, please.' Bowing her head over her hands India expelled a long breath, this was last straw - a fitting end to a perfectly bloody evening.

Instinctively, she glanced towards the rectangle of light streaming out from the house. MacFarlane was standing in the doorway, impatient for her to leave - if his body language was anything to judge by. Every tender feeling she possessed had suffered at his hands this evening and now - damn him

- he stood there watching her futile attempts to start the car. Covering her face with her hands she waited, giving the old car a chance to recover from repeated turning of the key in the ignition. A rush of cold air startled her as MacFarlane yanked opened the door and stuck his head inside the Buick.

'Need any help, ma'am?' It was the same mocking gallantry he had directed towards her all night. They both knew she'd rather crawl home on her hands and knees over broken glass than ask him for help. Then, seemingly noticing her dejected look, the droop to her mouth, his expression altered. A fleeting shadow of emotion, and his face softened, his tone became gentle. 'You look frozen. Go back into the house. I'll bring my hire car round and take you home.'

'That won't be necessary, thank you. Phone the break down truck. I'll wait here till they arrive.' She clutched the steering wheel as if it were a lifeline. Any sympathy MacFarlane might have felt for her predicament vanished along with his patience.

'Are you crazy? The temperature's dropping. Do you want to freeze your stubborn . . .?' She quelled him with a haughty look before he could utter the final word.

'I'm quite happy where I am. Now, are you going to phone the breakdown service, or not?' She stared straight ahead, through the iced-over windscreen, holding back the tears she wouldn't let him see.

At that his forbearance snapped.

'Get out of the goddam car, India.' Catching her by the arm, he half-dragged/helped her out and slammed the door. Losing balance in her high-heeled shoes India bounced off his chest, and then fell against the car, cold metal biting through the thin stuff of her coat. Grim-faced, MacFarlane steadied her by grabbing onto her coat's lapels, anything rather than touch her. India pulled away, brushing down her coat with exaggerated care, as if contaminated by his touch.

'Allow me, princess.' He ground out, angrier than she'd ever seen him.

He straightened her collar where it had rucked up, and as he did so, fingers grazed the sensitive hair on the nape of her neck. India drew back in blind panic as warm fingers came into contact with cold skin. Simultaneously, MacFarlane took a step away from her, in case the contagion entered his blood stream, too.

They stood facing each other like prize fighters, cold breaths mingling as the temperature dropped.

Then, miraculously, his anger slipped away and was replaced by something deeper, elemental and infinitely more dangerous. India read the desire in his eyes and knew it demanded an answering response. Their breathing became more rapid and she burned with a heat she recognised only too well. The sexual alchemy between them was as strong as ever, how could she have doubted it? The one constant in their ever-changing relationship. But, desire without love wasn't what she wanted, or needed.

Shaking her head, she denied her heart.

'Logan; no. I . . . can't.'

At that, something fundamental changed in MacFarlane.

He imprisoned her against the car, an arm on either side of her shoulders, as though he'd never let her go.

'India . . . God; yes,' he exhaled on a shaky breath.

His voice had a rough edge, as if the words were torn from him. That standing close to her was a torment, and the last thing he wanted or needed. He wrestled with his emotions, seemingly remembering pledges he'd made concerning her. Never to touch her. Never to speak to her. However, when she looked into his eyes, she saw the misery and emptiness mirrored in her own heart. Bending his head, he moved closer. A soft moan escaped India, admitting that the fight was over and no longer caring that he knew. Turning bright eyes on him, she invited and anticipated his kiss.

And they were lost.

His mouth came down on hers. For several seconds it seemed her heart had stopped beating and she had fainted clean away, only remaining upright because her coat had snagged on the Buick's door handle. Then his lips were on her throat, making the blood beat thickly in her veins. His hands slipped under her coat, found the small of her back and pulled her into him. His arousal was unmistakable and India's heart sang a wild, exultant song, knowing he wasn't indifferent to her, after all.

She twisted her fingers in his thick hair and his hand curved around her breast. Tongues touched and ignited the flame of desire they had been at such pains to deny. MacFarlane became desperate to touch her skin, so silky smooth beneath the rough wool of her coat. His hand reached questingly for the heart shaped neckline of her dress and caught on the pin fastening the gardenia there.

'Damn,' he swore softly. The pin drew blood, smearing India's neckline as he drew away. The injury provided a timely distraction, reminding them of the folly they were about to commit. Her face flushed, her lips swollen from his kisses, India leaned back against the car in an attitude of complete abandonment. MacFarlane looked at the wound and then back at India and, with a supreme effort, put her from him.

Sensing his withdrawal, India whispered: 'MacFarlane, please . . .'

'I - I'm sorry India, I can't; I should've known better than to let that happen.' For several seconds he appeared disorientated, as if his senses were befuddled. Then, gaining mastery over himself, was in control again. 'Pop the hood and I'll check the engine,' he said, concentrating on safer, more practical matters.

India was too stunned to move, then after a few moments the world righted itself. She became aware of biting wind off the lake, the light streaming from the house, and the fact that his warm body was no longer shielding her from the elements. She started to shiver uncontrollably and pulled her coat around her as, like an automaton, she got into the car and popped the hood.

'Turn the engine over,' he called.

With nerveless hands she turned the key and the treacherous engine sparked to life. She gunned the throttle a couple of times and then let it idle. Closing the hood,

MacFarlane wiped his hands on a handkerchief, entered the car and sat in the passenger seat.

'It was a loose connection. It'll be okay.'

'Good,' she said, tonelessly.

'Kill the engine, India. You and I have to talk.'

With sinking heart, she did as commanded. In the ensuing silence, they both stared out into the darkness beyond the windscreen. Across the lake, the light at the end of the jetty on MacFarlane's Landing blinked, rhythmically, it was soothing somehow to count the seconds between each flash. It helped centre them.

'It's time you and I made our peace, India. I'm going away and I don't want to think of this *thing* between us, burning away for years to come. Like John and Elspeth.'

'I see.' She bowed her head and gripped the steering wheel.

'God, this is hard . . .' Turning in the confined space, he looked at her for what seemed forever and then shook his head. 'I'd hoped that - what we'd shared in Chicago, would have developed into something more than sexual attraction.' She stirred restlessly and was about to speak but he put a finger on her lip. 'No, hear me out. Please?' She nodded and he removed his finger. 'The past, the house, mutual mistrust and prejudice destroyed our relationship even before it got started.' A mirthless little laugh mocked his own shortcomings. 'God knows I can't be in the same room as you without wanting you. But in the end that wouldn't be enough, for either of us.'

303

'Logan . . .' If she stopped him now, told him that she loved him, perhaps . . . But she wasn't given the chance, he ploughed on with his little speech as if he'd rehearsed it on his long flight over from Penang.

'I underestimated you India. Your determination. Your grit. Your sheer cussedness. But I should never have doubted your integrity. I was a fool to lose my head that day when we got back from Chicago.' He gave a shadow of the quirky smile that had first captured her heart. Her love beat out in waves towards him, surely, he could feel it? However, he carried on with what he had to say. As if it'd been on his mind and he was glad to be free of it, at last.

'I should have told you the truth Logan.' India cut in, then added helplessly. 'But I was so unsure of where I stood. I was afraid of losing you.'

'We were both afraid, *and* blind. I was getting in too deep - too fast, India. I'd never gotten so involved with any woman. I couldn't think straight. Couldn't get you out of my head. I wasn't prepared for how quickly you'd become an indispensable part of my life.' He looked at her, a shadow crossing his face as he remembered. 'I suppose, in a way, I used Harvey as an excuse to back off.' He shook his head regretfully. 'I didn't think straight that day. I was madder than hell because I thought you'd taken me for a ride. It was like every row I'd witnessed between my Mom and Dad come back to haunt me.'

'Ah, Logan,' She turned away, but he tilted her face round to him, as though what he said next was important.

'You should've trusted me. Told me about the house; about Harvey.'

'I was about to tell you when he rang the doorbell.' This was her chance, he had to believe her. 'I know that sounds lame, but it's the truth.' Her eyes were lambent with tears. Logan nodded - but didn't allow himself to be deflected from his purpose.

'I should have trusted *you*. You should have trusted *me*.'

'I know that. I . . . I'm so sorry, Logan.'

'So am I.'

India swallowed her pride. 'Can't we start over?'

He shook his head. 'Our lives are leading us down different paths. Neither of us is ready for serious commitment.' He traced a circle on her cheek with his finger, with a tenderness which cut India to the quick. For the sake of her self-esteem she nodded, pretending to agree. If that's how he felt, then . . . He gave her a rueful smile. 'You have your business now, you've realised your dream. I'm still trying to figure out what mine *is*. Bumming around the Far East painting was great, but it felt unreal. And, to tell you the truth, I'd never felt lonelier. I kept remembering our time in my apartment.'

That gave her hope. She wanted to ask why they couldn't have it all: Washington, *Buchanan's*. Each other. But MacFarlane continued, practical to the last painful detail.

'I . . .'

'Please, India, hear me out, I acted like a real bastard tonight, and I'm sorry. I guess your great-aunt was right,

MacFarlanes are sore losers.' India pressed her cheek miserably against the side window of the Buick as he continued almost abstractedly, exorcising the anguish of the last few months. 'Despite all that had happened between us, I hoped that you'd be pleased to see me tonight. I guess it was too much to hope for. When you stood with your back towards me, I read you loud and clear.

'I didn't mean . . .'

'That's okay, I'm not sore at you, India.' He gave her a faint smile and then changed the subject. 'You still got the ring?'

'Yes, it's in my bag.' Her voice was husky but surprisingly even, given the emotionally charged atmosphere. She fetched the blue leather box out of her handbag and gave it to him. He opened the box and looked at the ring then, seemingly reaching a decision, closed the box and returned it to her.

'It's a family piece but I want you to keep it. Have something of the MacFarlanes in your home; in our old home. I couldn't give it to another woman.' A sombre mood fell on them, the chilling cold of the night striking India to her very core and leaving her numb. Trembling, she pulled her coat more tightly around her for warmth and comfort. 'I hoped that you'd be wearing it tonight. When you weren't, I took it as a sign things couldn't be put right.' Why had they left it until now to open up to each other? Unable to stop herself, India let out a groan of despair. MacFarlane, taking it that she was growing tired of the conversation, gave a self-depreciatory smile. 'I'd planned that, when we got back to MacFarlane's Landing, after Chicago, I'd put it on your finger. Then, if things'd worked out - well, I kinda hoped that I'd replace it with a wedding ring.'

'Don't say that!' India broke in, thinking of all they'd thrown away.

MacFarlane misread her a second time.

'Guess that *was* expecting too much.' He turned away, leaving her crushed by the hopelessness of their situation. It would be futile now to confess her love for him, because never once had MacFarlane mentioned loving *her*.

Desire . . . Passion . . . Ambition . . . Mistrust. Words he'd used to catalogue their relationship; but never love. India believed that, only through love, would they be able to revisit their past mistakes, put things right and have a chance of a future together. Without love everything was pointless. MacFarlane was right; best to cut their losses, part as friends, and go their separate ways.

'This is goodbye then, MacFarlane.' Hiding her pain behind a façade of briskness, India turned in her seat and extended her hand. He took it, held it briefly in both of his and started to say something else, but India stopped him. 'No long goodbyes.' She swallowed hard, freeing the circle of pain tightening her throat and chest, and blinked away tears obscuring her view of the house.

'Sure. No long goodbyes.' He leaned towards her and kissed her gently on the lips. 'Good luck, India.'

She turned away, not because the kiss was unwelcome but to hide the anguish written all too clearly on her face.

'Thanks.' She busied herself fumbling for the ignition in the darkness and turned the car over. This time it started immediately and she sat staring out into the darkness, hands on the wheel, implying she was impatient to leave. The car rocked on its suspension briefly and the door closed. A great tearing sob escaped India, followed by another, then another. She wouldn't turn and look at him standing on the porch watching her drive away. She had *some* pride left.

Instead she gunned the car down the long drive and filtered onto the coast road.

Pulling over at the first opportunity, she switched off the engine, bowed her head over the steering wheel and cried as though her heart was breaking. At least here, in the darkness no-one could hear, or tell her that she'd been a fool.

Chapter Eighteen

India confirmed her flight to London and replaced the phone.

Next week she'd be staying at Granny Meredith's before travelling onto Paris via the Eurostar. Upon arrival at Gare du Nord, she'd be collected by a car bearing Corps Diplomatique number plates and taken to her parents' apartment in the 16th Arrondissement. Predictably, the accommodation allocated to her father as *senior foreign service officer* assigned to the US embassy, had not met with Daphne Buchanan's approval. Instead, they'd chosen to rent a four-bedroom apartment - complete with swimming pool and terrace garden with a view of the Eiffel Tower and were keen to show it to their daughter. Her mother had plans for a mammoth shopping expedition at Galleries Lafayette and her father wanted to tour the galleries and museums, pointing out favourite paintings and sculptures.

India rubbed a weary hand over her eyes. She really didn't have time for this 'vacation' but felt that she couldn't disappoint either her parents or Granny Meredith. She already had the beginnings of a headache knowing exactly how the visit would pan out.

Her mother would expound at length over how much trouble they'd taken to prepare the apartment for her arrival, and emphasise - no pressure, natch - that she'd be expected to visit for at least *some* (if not all) of the national holidays - American, British *and* French. Paris was her father's last post before retirement and her parents planned to make it a memorable one. In turn, she would explain she couldn't afford to take time away from *Buchanan's*. Whereupon, her mother would roll her eyes, and make a not-so-veiled reference to her daughter playing 'landlady' to any Tom, Dick or Harry who could afford to stay at the bed and breakfast.

Landlady? Not quite how India saw herself, but no matter – best let her mother have her say, as she always did.

India had thought of crying off the proposed visit but decided she couldn't be that mean. In their own way her parents loved her, and once they'd accepted that she couldn't be swayed from her chosen path (or encouraged to marry Tom Harvey), they'd accepted the inevitable with good grace. Even writing a cheque to cover the last of *Buchanan's* renovations. By Easter - when a grand re-opening was planned, kicking off with an Easter Egg hunt for the local children - extra guest accommodation would be available. India was confident that, come the summer, *Buchanan's* would be well on its way to becoming a success.

Only the memory of her emotional leave taking from MacFarlane cast a cloud over her happiness. However, she'd promised herself she wouldn't think about MacFarlane today; or any other day for that matter. That way lay madness. Once she was on the plane to Heathrow she could step sideways in time and pretend the last few months were a bad dream that'd happened to someone else. It would be comforting to be with people who knew nothing of her involvement with Logan.

Raising her head from her desk, she glanced out of the window towards the jetty where volunteers were putting last minute touches to the annual MacFarlane's Landing Ski Run. She'd considered *not* allowing the race to go ahead; the trip to Europe, overseeing further renovations to her property, *and* a proposed visit to Elspeth and Judge MacFarlane providing the perfect excuse.

However, she couldn't be that selfish. As far back as anyone could remember, the race had started at Judge MacFarlane's house, crossed onto her land and finished at the jetty. It'd be shabby to refuse permission and disappoint the locals who'd been one hundred and ten percent behind her business. Her great-aunt had understood the significance of the race and hadn't allowed her poor state of health to stop the event going ahead. Although, India suspected that Elspeth used the race as a way of keeping in touch with Judge John MacFarlane, without actually meeting him.

India's reasons for not wanting to hold the race were more complex. She didn't want to rake over old ashes by discussing arrangements with MacFarlane. Besides which, an email she'd received from him over a month ago requesting that the ski race took place had cut her to the core. She slipped the email out from under her desk blotter and then, as she had done every day since the message had arrived in her in-box, re-read it - searching for some personal message which would indicate how he felt about her; about them.

The email was succinct and to the point.

Hi, I hope you are well. My grandfather and I would like permission to finish the annual ski race at your jetty. If this meets with your approval, please let the race committee know at your earliest convenience. Regards, Logan MacFarlane.

If she'd held some secret hope that they could forget the past and, at the very least remain friends, the impersonal email had knocked that notion on the head. Evidently, she didn't even warrant a 'Dear India', merely 'Hi'. MacFarlane had made his point. He'd moved on and it was time she did, too.

In the end, it was Lotte who'd persuaded her to change her mind, seeing the race as a chance to remind people about the history of MacFarlane's Landing, India's place in the local community, and the perfect opportunity to hand out flyers about the Easter Egg Hunt. Friends of Door County Lighthouses Trust had also applied gentle pressure, not willing to pass up on the possibility of charging a small entrance fee to anyone who entered the race, to go towards funds.

India could refuse neither party. Lotte, because she'd become a great friend over the last months, and the Trust because they'd given her a small grant to cover vital repairs to the original, nineteenth century Fresnel lenses in the lighthouse. The prisms were in a bad state and timely repairs would ensure that the lights were working in time for the race - the lighthouse with its steady beam being the landmark that competitors skied towards.

Recalling the judge's comment at the Thanksgiving Dinner: *'Guess that just leaves India to keep a lamp in the window for us to find our way home by,'* India gave another heavy sigh and pushed the email under the blotter. Then, mentally berated herself. What had she promised earlier? To stop thinking about Logan MacFarlane?

May as well tell the world to stop turning and hold back the seasons.

So - everything was decided. She'd head for Europe and return as soon as possible to supervise the next phase of renovations. Would she be stretching herself too far to fly home from Paris and visit Judge John and Elspeth in Palm Springs? She smiled for the first time that morning – *home* – isn't this exactly what she'd always wanted?

A place to put down roots, somewhere to call her own?

Further introspection was put on hold when Lotte entered the room carrying a large flat box on which she'd balanced two mugs and a packet of Oreos.

'Coffee?'

'Thanks, Lotte. What do you think?' India held up rough sketches for the Easter Egg Hunt.

'I think you work too hard.' Lotte placed the improvised tray on India's desk and the coffee mugs wobbled dangerously. 'Now, don't change the subject, have you booked your flight to London?'

'I have.'

'*And* Paris?'

'Yes, Ma'am,' India saluted.

'Good. Now, drink your coffee and eat your *biscuit* - see what I did there? They laughed at Lotte's substitution of *biscuit* for *cookie,* taking their mugs over to sit by the roaring fire. 'I can even say, *chocky bickie*. Does that mean I'm fluent in two languages?'

'I'd say so. Or, at the very least, two versions of the same one.' They smiled at each other and then India sobered. 'You're my right-hand woman, Lotte. I wouldn't have achieved half of this,' her gesture took in the whole of the house, 'without you. I want you to know that.'

'Indie, you rescued me from child-care-hell. I told Eddie, when I fell pregnant with number four, that it'd be different this time round. He'd have to do *more;* pay for a nursery place, take time off work when the baby's sick, give me some time to myself now the other three are in full time education. I don't want to turn around when they've left for college and wonder where the years went. Or realise that I've achieved nothing, for *me.*'

'Wow.' It was the longest speech Lotte had ever made.

'Thanks to you, I've re-discovered a talent for organisation I'd kinda forgotten I had. You know?'

'I do, my lovely friend.' Getting up from the armchair, India walked over and gave Lotte a hug.

'Although,' Lotte gave her a sheepish grin once she'd sat down again.

'Go on . . .'

'I've screwed up.'

'You have?" India was surprised to hear that. Raising four kids, keeping Eddie on track and helping with the family business had made Lotte the person she was. Cool, unflappable, practical. It was unlike her to make mistakes.

'Big time.'

'How big?'

'I took a booking via email and forgot all about it. When I re-read it, I realised that I'd booked a family into the room next to yours, on the day of the ski race. Want me to cancel?'

'How many are we talking about?'

'Two adults and a child. I'll see to everything. You concentrate on putting the final touches to the ski race, the Easter Egg Hunt flyers and packing for Europe.'

'Europe,' India mused. 'It seems like a foreign country.'

'Which it is, to *me*. I've never been farther than Chicago, I'd love to go to London and Paris and . . . but first, I need to get a passport. Right?'

'Right.' India recalled reading that only forty-six percent of US citizens held a valid passport. Looked as if Lotte was one of them. 'When you do, and when you're ready, I'll take you over to England. We can stay with Granny Meredith and then go on to France to my parents' apartment in the 16th Arrondissement.' She affected an exaggerated French accent. 'All you'll need is spending money, I'll take care of the rest.'

'Spending money? Now *that's* a new one.' Laughing, Lotte leaned forward and they clinked their mugs together.

'Which translates, roughly, into: *don't forget your credit card.*'

'Cool.'

The Oreos were passed round and both women turned slightly in their armchairs and pointed their feet towards the log fire. More snow was forecast and conditions for the ski race in two days' time should be perfect.

*****

Later that day, Indie remembered the FedEx parcel Lotte had used as a tray. She'd become expert at online shopping since leaving New York but couldn't remember ordering anything this size and shape. Retrieving a pair of scissors, she carefully cut around the protective packing, in case she had to return it via the local courier. The parcel was surprisingly large and heavy and when she removed the contents from its protective layer of bubble wrap, her legs buckled. Crashing down at her desk she peeled back more layers, until MacFarlane's watercolour of her great-aunt's house. Correction, *her* house, was fully revealed.

Why had he sent it? What did it mean?

Placing the painting carefully to one side, she felt around inside the box, feeling for a letter, a note, *anything* which would explain his motives. Eventually, she found a screwed-up sheet of A4 paper bearing the embossed heading: *MacFarlane, MacFarlane and Levison.* Her blood ran cold, it was as if she'd been left a bequest in someone's will and the lawyers had sent it on to her.

Had something happened to him and no one had

informed her? Unlikely. She counselled herself to get a grip. Her darkest fears put aside, she read the scribbled note, picturing him dashing it off in a hurry and then giving the watercolour and the message to some underling to Fed-Ex over to her.

'*I thought this would look better on your wall than languishing in storage. Logan.*'

Concise and to the point, as if he didn't want there to be any ambiguity or doubt. India read the note again and could only reach one depressing conclusion. The MacFarlanes had moved on and had no need for the painting. He'd moved on and there was no space for her in his life. The note, the watercolour and the terse email served to underline the fact.

India walked over to the large window to examine the watercolour more closely, remembering the day MacFarlane had shown her his studio and shared his dream of becoming an artist. Then she propped the watercolour up on the mantelpiece, holding it in place with two heavy brass candlesticks to prevent it slipping and crashing onto the hearth. Zoning out, she was lost in dreams again, until the heat from the log fire penetrated the thick wool of her tights and brought her back to reality.

She rubbed her thighs where they'd been scorched by the fire and then, turning her back on watercolours, cursory notes and abrupt emails, went upstairs to finish packing for her trip to Europe.

317

Chapter Nineteen

Two days later, with suitcases at the foot of her bed, India looked down on the wintery scene below. Multi-coloured lights were strung around the landing and pier and volunteers were erecting awnings to shelter spectators from the elements, should the weather worsen. An avenue of torches, designed to guide skiers home on the last stage of the race, stretched away towards a field in the near distance. The Friends of Door County Lighthouses had also been hard at work, ensuring newly installed lenses were working - sending a beam of light all the way across the bay to Judge MacFarlane's house.

India hadn't gone back there since the Thanksgiving dinner. It saddened her to imagine everything draped in dustsheets, apart from Martha the housekeeper's quarters. John and Elspeth were having a great time in Florida and would probably never return to MacFarlane's Landing. They planned to wed in early summer, just as soon as India could find a space in her diary to fly down and take part in a simple ceremony. Would Logan attend, India wondered? She didn't know and after the arrival of his dismissive notes and the watercolour, she didn't really care.

She got it. Move on. Enough already. There were more important things to concentrate on this evening.

Lotte was below, supervising the setting up of trestle tables whilst keeping an eye on her energetic children who kept wandering too close to the freezing lake. She'd set them the task of plunging bottles of beer and soft drinks into the snow while she got on with seeing to the hot beverages. Eddie was in charge of the BBQ and had chili dogs and burgers ready to slip into buns and rolls, once the race was over. Nearby, volunteer officials, wearing high-vis jackets and crash helmets were revving up snow mobiles, before setting off for the start of the race at Judge MacFarlane's house. They would accompany the skiers and be on hand to administer first aid or call for help should anyone be injured.

Although India had had lots of help getting the race ready, it'd been a bit of a headache checking that all necessary documents were up to date: Health and Safety compliance, Food Hygiene, Liquor licence. Not to mention shutting off the lighthouse to the public until she had the funds to devote to further repairs. Giving herself a metaphorical shake, she told herself to lighten up. These days she seemed preoccupied by all the hard work involved in setting up her business and hadn't dedicated nearly enough time to congratulating herself on how far she'd come.

Time to enjoy the moment. And the ski race was just the event to help her do that.

Walking over to the dressing table, she picked up a battered silver cup bearing the legend: *MacFarlane's Run*, and read the winning names engraved on tiny shields around the base. One Logan MacFarlane seemed to have won more times than was good for him. She smiled wryly, recalling overhearing several volunteers declaring they were glad he wasn't competing this year, as it would give someone else a chance to win. She breathed on the cup and polished it with the sleeve of her jumper. The wool snagged on a blank shield, waiting to be engraved after the race. Tucking the cup under her arm she left the bedroom, giving her cases at the foot of the bed one last glance.

A bubble of excitement rose in her chest at the thought of all the hugs and kisses she'd soon be receiving from Granny Meredith and her English cousins, and the idea of exploring Paris with her father. The trip round Galleries Lafayette? Not so much!

Good things were on the horizon, she *had* to keep reminding herself of that.

Hearing the front door open, she left the bedroom ready to hand the silver cup over to the race marshals. According to tradition it was carried with some ceremony to the start line, a visual reminder of what the competitors could win - a battered trophy, kudos, but, sadly, no prize money. Maybe she could rectify that next year? A dinner for two at the Inn and Cedar crossing? An English Afternoon Tea at *Buchanan's*?

Leaning over the banister she called down: 'I'm coming.' Unfamiliar footsteps crossed wooden floorboards.

'Lotte?'

'No. Not Lotte.'

It was as if someone had tipped a bucket of ice cold water over her head. Chilly fingers trailed along her nerve endings while her stomach flipped over. Looking over the bannister and down into the hall with commendable calm, she discovered MacFarlane.

'Can I come up, India?'

She opened her mouth to speak, but no words came. Vocal cords seized, her mouth was dry as the Sahara, cleaving her tongue to her palate. Logan waited, one hand on the newel post, one foot on the first tread of the stairs, plainly unsure of his reception. India nodded assent and he took the first step towards her. In her heightened state, it seemed as if he was on an escalator which, instead of bringing him closer, took him further away, the distance between them never seeming to diminish.

He must have skied cross country to get here, she thought inconsequentially, noticing his ski gear. He'd left his boots on the porch and his stockinged feet made no sound as he climbed the staircase, adding to India's feeling of unreality. Then he reached the top tread and was just feet away from her. Blood stopped pounding in her ears and her pulse slowed to a regular beat as her brain kicked up a gear, dismissing trivial details such as what he was wearing, and reminding her instead of everything she'd missed about him.

Tall and full of good health, bringing with him an aura of potent male sexuality even a maiden aunt couldn't fail to notice. His cheeks were stung by the freezing temperature, dark hair ruffled by wind off the lake, and his eyes were bright and inquiring. Plainly, he'd expected more by way of a welcome than this silence. Then he was level with her, stripping off gloves, unzipping his jacket, putting the ski mask on a nearby console table.

He broke the silence. 'How come you never wrote, India?'

'I---I never wrote, because I didn't think your email warranted, or *deserved*, a personal reply. I handed it over to the race committee and I suppose they filed it away.'

Her voice was surprisingly steady, not wanting him to know how hurt she'd been by that impersonal email. She'd *die* before admitting hiding it under her blotter and re-reading it a dozen times every day, just in case she'd missed some nuance, or hint that he sometimes thought about their time together. 'The committee answered for me. Wasn't that enough?'

'No. It wasn't.' They exchanged a burning look which suggested unfinished business between them. Why couldn't he just let her be? What was to be gained from re-opening old wounds?

Sudden anger sublimated all other emotions. Anger for giving him the power to hurt her; anger at herself for being fool enough to love him, and laying herself open to this anguish. But mostly, anger at her own weakness, for she knew he only had to stretch out his hand and all the resolutions she'd made concerning him would count for nothing.

Evidently sensing some of this, MacFarlane chose his words carefully. 'I guess I should have written to you, personally.'

'I guess you should.'

Realisation dawned on him that he was only making things worse by raking over old ashes and his shoulders slumped. He glanced down into the hall, fleetingly, as if remembering the last time they'd stood there. How it had been before Tom Harvey's arrival. The seconds stretched out, each lost in their own thoughts - and then he turned back to her. It was clear from his expression that he regretted the impulse to ski over to *Buchanan's*. It was also plain that something else was on his mind and he wasn't about to leave with it unsaid.

'India,' he broke the silence. 'I've written emails, postcards, long letters, all stamped and ready to go. But I never mailed them because I messed things up the night of the Thanksgiving dinner. I'd driven like a madman from Green Bay, desperate to see you. Yet despising myself for still wanting you, needing you, because of all that had transpired between us.'

'MacFarlane . . . we've been over this,' she shook her head, wearily.

'Let me finish. I'd made a fool of myself over Harvey, then compounded it that evening in the car, after dinner. Pride made me tell you half-truths. Forced me to drive another wedge between us, when all I wanted to do was take you into my arms.'

'Life isn't always that simple.' Deep inside India a flame of hope flickered.

'Don't I know it?' He gave one of his quirky smiles and then, as if realising now was not the time for humour, immediately sobered. Shaking his head, he answered her question. 'I figured that if I sent the letters, your opinion of me being what it was, you'd either file them under *Spam*. Or return them unopened.'

'I see.' The flame burned brighter.

'With the email, I reckoned that once I clicked SEND, it couldn't be called back. I hoped that maybe you'd read between the lines . . . see that I was trying to build a bridge between us. And if the email was short and to the point, then I'm sorry. That's not what I'd intended.' His look scorched the air between them. 'Not what I intended at all. I figured that if you answered my email,' he now continued more confidently, 'perhaps I'd be able to say all the things I was too proud to say that night in the car. All the things I held back.'

'Like what?' Wild hope surged through her, but she kept it in check. She had to be sure this time, *really* sure before declaring her love for him.

'Like, how miserable I've been. How lonely. How much I've wanted you,' he continued, catching her expression before she had time to school her features. He registered the half step she took towards him and his carefully rehearsed speech was forgotten as a flame leapt between them. 'God help me, India, I . . .'

'Go on,' she demanded sternly, giving no quarter, though her heart sang at the passion in his voice, the light in his eyes.

'You're the only woman I want, India. Have ever wanted,' he declared ardently. 'I've been a fool, and like all fools, have paid the price. Can you? *Will* you give me another chance?'

It was some time before India spoke. 'None of that matters, not anymore. There are things I want to say to you. But . . .' with some reluctance, she drew her gaze away and she glanced towards the front door. 'I'm expecting guests.'

'I checked with Lotte. We've got the house to ourselves - for now, at least.' The thought hung in the air between them, tantalising in its implications.

'So, there's no rush?'

'No rush,' MacFarlane agreed. 'I want to take this slow and easy; I don't want to screw things up this time, India.' The words *slow and easy* reminded India of their love-making in his wide bed. Bright colour stung her cheeks and she suddenly felt over heated.

However, with commendable calm she managed to say: 'Always supposing there's going to be a next time.'

'Do you doubt it?'

But she wasn't going to let him win that easily. 'Maybe I need convincing that you and me would be a good idea.'

'I could convince you.' He took a step towards her, but India held up a hand.

'I'm sure that you could, that part has never been in doubt. It's the rest of it; my career, your ambitions, Washington versus Door County, this house, our dreams and aspirations.' She encompassed it all with one gesture, taking in shadowy landing, hallway, the two of them.

'Can't we start over, India?' He sent a look of such

feeling that the last of her beleaguered defences crumbled and her heart was breached. He leaned against the bannister, clearly trying to read what was going on in her mind while she pretended to give the idea more consideration. But MacFarlane was beyond the point of deliberation and game-playing. 'God, India; don't tease.'

Reaching out he caught her by the wrists and pulled her into his arms, imprisoning her between his thighs and bending his head towards her.

'MacFarlane, really, I . . .'

India opened her mouth to protest, but his mouth closed over hers and when his tongue found the sensitive skin of her inner lip, she knew it was time to stop pretending. She loved him and this time she'd be sure to tell him. And, as they kissed, memories flooded back thick and strong; and she remembered how it had been between them, to be held in his arms, touched by him. She gave a small purr of pleasure and kissed him back, knowing the fusion between them was complete when she tasted the salt of his blood on her lips.

In the distance a bell rang.

It took several long seconds before she realised it was the phone. Dazedly, she pulled back from the madness that threatened to overwhelm, even as it made her blood sing and her heart beat, fit to burst.

'Phone,' she managed to say against his lips.

'Let the machine pick up.'

They kissed on but couldn't block out the taxi company's message confirming her booking to Green Bay airport.

Releasing her, MacFarlane leaned back against the bannister rail and folded his arms, as if that was the only way he could keep his hands off her.

'Lotte said you're going to London, then Paris. I was kinda hoping I could persuade you to change your mind.' Taking her hand, he led her into her bedroom and sat her on the edge of the bed, next to her suitcases. He shrugged off his jacket, tossing it on the bed before slipping his shoulders out of the braces holding up his salopettes and rolling them down to his trim waist. 'Don't know why but I feel kind of hot all of a sudden.' A boyish grin. 'Come here India.' Raising her to her feet, he treated her to a lengthy scrutiny before drawling, 'Something's missing.'

'It is?'

Instead of answering, he glanced round the room until his eyes lit on a blue leather box in pride of place on India's dressing table. Retrieving the box, he opened it. The gold and garnet ring was exactly where it had lain since the night of the Thanksgiving dinner, tucked up in its white velvet bed. 'Gimme your hand, India,' he commanded, taking the ring from the box. 'Now, I know how you like to argue, but this time I'm doing the talking and you're doing the listening. Capisce?'

'Capisce! Now, wait a minute . . .'

'No more minutes, no more waiting or second-guessing. I'm gonna say my piece and then it's up to you. So here goes. All my other messages: the email, the painting and the note accompanying it have been misconstrued, misinterpreted because I was too dumb to say what I really felt. I've let you slip through my fingers twice; I'm not going to make that mistake a third time.'

'How did you know . . .'

'That you kept the ring there? Lotte told me. In fact, she's been keeping me up to date on your life, telling me about all the guys clamouring at your door, wanting to take you to dinner. That, if I didn't soon get my rear into gear you'd be snapped up and that'd be it.'

India kept a straight face. *Guys clamouring at her door?* Carpenters, painters and decorators, maybe, but no love-sick swains or fit guys demanding that she go out on a hot date. Perhaps she should put Lotte in charge of *Buchanan's* publicity, she seemed to have a talent for bigging things up!

'Lotte had no right doing that.' India feigned an anger which convinced neither of them. 'I don't want you thinking, that . . .' The sentence was left unfinished as MacFarlane slipped the ring over her wedding finger and enclosed her hand in both of his.

'Forget Lotte, forget everything. Concentrate on this moment and listen to what I have to say. That ring belongs on your finger. If I hadn't been such a goddam fool I would have given it to you in Chicago before we left. But my nerve deserted me, I hesitated and - well, I guess we both know what happened next.' He was suddenly serious, although his eyes were full of light and love. 'There are things I want to say to you, India. Things you and I have to straighten out. But not right now. I want you to think about us: marriage -

kids - a future together, the whole nine yards. If you're there at the finishing line tomorrow, I'll know your answer.'

'Is that an ultimatum, MacFarlane?'

'Yes. I guess you could call it that.' He was unrepentant.

'Well, maybe I don't care for ultimatums.' India declared, spoiling the effect by blurting out as he pulled up the top half of his salopettes, 'You're not going, are you?'

'Lady,' he stopped dressing and gave her a considering look which sent her heart soaring in expectation, 'you send out some very mixed messages, know that? But I'll leave you with something to be thinking about until tomorrow.' He pushed her down onto the bed and kissed her hard and long, both drawing the kiss to a conclusion with some difficulty. Propping himself up on one elbow he looked down and traced the outline of her lips with his forefinger. 'I love you India Buchanan. Guess I have done since the moment I saw you painting your aunt's fence and you made it clear you had a very low opinion of me. Reckon I've been trying to change your mind ever since. And *you* love *me*; don't bother denying it.'

'Know that for a fact, do ya, mister?' India demanded, although her soul was singing.

'No,' he replied succinctly, 'just guessin' and hopin' I'm right, ma'am.' Getting to his feet, he pulled on his skiing jacket. 'Don't look at me like that or I'll never leave and we'll spend the rest of the day making love. And, pleasurable though that might be, it wouldn't solve anything. In fact,' he paused to give his words greater effect, 'I find my faculty for reasoned thinking becomes suspended when I'm near you. I'd tell you that you drive me crazy, but it'd only swell your head.'

'Think so?' India had trouble breathing, speaking.

'Know so.' MacFarlane was clearly enjoying the lovers' banter. After that, India said nothing but curled her left hand into a fist and held the ring close to her heart. 'Be there at the finishing line tomorrow and I'll have my answer.'

With that he left, closing the door softly behind him.

*****

'Here they come!'

While gathered spectators looked across the darkening fields, wavering lights could be seen as skiers made their way towards them through the avenue of blazing torches.

Soon, MacFarlane would cross the finishing line. India, standing at the front of the crowd, shivered with a mixture of cold and nervousness and drew the collar of her red woollen coat up around her ears for warmth. She felt completely wrung out, having spent a sleepless night going over and over things in her mind.

Declarations of love were one thing – but, how *could* it work out between herself and MacFarlane? Unless things changed, he wanted to work in Washington; she wanted to live in Door County. Make a home where her children could grow up with a set of values which owed nothing to cities, money, power. Could she risk all she'd achieved, all that she hoped to accomplish in the future for the chance of a life with MacFarlane?

She knew that she loved him. Now she was certain of

his love for her. That was the one constant in their ever-changing relationship. Whenever he held her in his arms all the thousand-and-one doubts which beset her, vanished. It was when she was alone that fears and uncertainties crowded in.

The skiers were now coming into view. Time she made up her mind. Torch flares dipped and danced, shimmering like fireflies as competitors skied towards them. Her stomach felt as if it was a cement mixer and bricks were going round and round in it.

Lotte gripped her arm excitedly. 'Look, India. Logan's in the lead.'

'He's going like a rocket,' one spectator said.

'That's MacFarlane all right. Always plays to win,' another observed sourly at India's elbow.

Yes, he does, and that was part of the problem, India mused. They'd finish up being rivals in the end; their respective careers, different values and ambitions pulling them in opposite directions, tearing them apart. Her introspection was cut short as the skiers rushed towards them, down the avenue of torches, the swoosh of their skis quite audible as they came closer. Logan was still in the lead by several yards and now she could make out his face, his determination was clear to see.

'Logan. Logan.' she shouted. And her heart added: *I love you.* No matter what happens, that will always be true. Now he was fifty yards from her, twenty, ten, almost at the finishing line. He looked up; saw her, registered her uncertainty, the downward turn to her mouth. His concentration slipped and the steady rhythm he'd used to plough across the fields was broken as his skis crunched together. He was jostled out of the way by another skier. And, a yard from the finishing line, executed a perfect cartwheel - all arms, legs and ski sticks.

A collective 'Ooh' of shock and disappointment rose up from the crowd. Then the other skiers crossed the finishing line and MacFarlane was forgotten.

Except by India.

'Logan! 'she cried and pushed through the crowd to reach him, not caring that it was her job to give the trophy to the winner. Grim faced, Logan gathered himself together and brushed the powdery snow off his clothes. He gave her one long look, and then concentrated on releasing his boots from his skis. He stood up, but his legs refused to support him.

'Damn it!' he cursed.

'Have you broken anything?' India asked, rushing to his side.

'No. I think it's only a pulled muscle.' He shook off her gentle hands and concern. Pulling his sticks towards him he used them to lever himself up. 'Let me alone, India. I've lost the race, and I've lost you. I could see it in your face as I neared the finishing line. You don't trust me enough to take a risk with our relationship, or our future. You've never trusted me and that's what really hurts.'

'That's not true, Logan,' she protested.

'Isn't it?' he asked, openly willing her to contradict him. The banked down hope in his eyes showing that, like her, he needed to be convinced it would work out for them. That he'd spent a sleepless night beset by doubts. The difference between them was that he was prepared to take a risk - for their love, their future together, while she wanted certainties, guarantees.

Then, in a moment of epiphany, India realised that love didn't come with a 30-day money back guarantee or cooling off period. It was a leap of faith; a question of trust. Perhaps . . . if they both entered into this relationship aware of the pitfalls, the dangers, it could work out. With a resolution born of love for him she pushed away her fears.

'I do trust you Logan. I give you all of my love and all of me. Forever, if you'll have me.' She started tentatively and then, gaining greater assurance, rushed on. 'Nobody knows for certain how their life is going to turn out. But I'd rather spend my life with you than with any other man.'

She put her arm round his waist, helping him to his feet.

Her simple declaration affected Logan profoundly. He let out a long, shuddering breath and gathered her into his arms. Balancing awkwardly on his uninjured ankle, he tilted her face towards him in the torch-lit darkness.

'Do you mean it, India? Just now, at the finishing line, I thought . . .'

'I'm sure.' Her love beat out towards him in the snowy darkness and he pulled her into his arms and they stood, drawing comfort from each other.

'I love you, India Buchanan.' Her heart gave a kick of excitement as she experienced a rush of emotion on hearing those words.

Riding high on that tide of feeling she responded unfalteringly, 'And I love you, too, Logan MacFarlane.' Then she looked up at him and spoke from the heart. 'Don't you see? If we love each other we can talk through our problems. Sort out our differences; together we can help and support each other.' She felt strong enough for both of them – and never more certain of anything in her whole life.

'I don't want to wait sixty years, like grandfather and Elspeth,' MacFarlane declared. 'We'll get married just as soon as we can. I'm not giving you time to change your mind,' he went on gravely.

'I won't change my mind. Not now. Not ever. As far as I'm concerned, tomorrow starts right here, with you and me. We'll put the past behind us . . . It'll be a risk. But, then, what's life without a little risk?' She took a shuddering breath and the final barrier was gone. 'I'd risk everything for you, Logan.'

This time they both knew that it was true.

'India.' His words were drowned out as the firework display began and fire crackers exploded around them. But the look they shared in the green and yellow phosphorescent light was eloquent enough.

Logan drew India into his arms and kissed her as pyrotechnics lit up house, landing jetty and fields beyond. The very possessions they had fought over, providing a backdrop for their love. And, as the kiss drew to a conclusion and they both looked towards the brilliantly lit house, it seemed to stretch out loving arms beckoning them forwards.

They exchanged a smile. A lover's smile, full of promise and hope. Then, wordlessly, they turned their backs on the darkening fields and walked towards the floodlit house and their future together.

THE END

Acknowledgements

In order to produce a typo-free manuscript, I had help from proof readers Sharyn Farnaby and Nina Kenchington. My novel, both paperback and kindle version, has been formatted by Sarah Houldcroft of Goldcrest Books. Special mention is also due to sounding boards/beta readers and all round wonderful 'critical' friends, Isabella Tartaruga (La Diva), Jane Little, and Ms A Wrafter. Thanks to Anni Paulsen (BA) who found time to read Take Me, I'm Yours whilst studying for an additional degree in optometrics, pointing out any inconsistencies I might have missed. Big high five to Mark and Ann Jinkins for buying a download (each!) of my novels, and for Tara and Erik Arness who answered my queries about winter in Wisconsin. Finally, to sisters Lotte Sutton and Alice Twaite, thank you for your friendship and support, now you have both appeared as characters in my novels.

Mega thanks also to my co-conspirators and best writing buddies, June Kearns, Adrienne Vaughan, and Mags Cullingford (New Romantics Press) who have travelled on this journey with me, and are never more than a phone call away.

In case anyone is wondering if I have abandoned Scotland in favour of Chicago and Door County, I've already plotted out three future novels featuring lochs, lairds, castles, plucky heroines, and hot men in kilts. Otherwise, how can I justify spending the summer touring Scotland and the autumn and winter months researching kilt suppliers on-line?

A sad footnote

Our parrot Jasper passed away just as I was finishing this novel. He'd been our baby for 22 years and has left a gaping hole in our lives and hearts. He was best mates with Bert the parrot Philips, who went to heaven just weeks earlier, and is missed by Katie, Mike, Lee and Naomi. I like to think that Jasper and Bert are together - happy, healthy and flying free.

A personal message from Lizzie to her readers

First of all, thank you for buying *Take Me, I'm Yours* and an extra big thanks to those readers who've journeyed alongside me since I published *Tall, Dark and Kilted* in 2012. You guys rock.

I've always wanted to be a writer but had to put that ambition on hold while I concentrated on being a primary school teacher. It wasn't until I left the profession that I was able to give my writing the attention it deserved. I joined the Romantic Novelists' Association and formed the New Romantics Press with three other members of the RNA's New Writers' Scheme and – deciding time and tide wait for no writer – went down the self-publishing route.

Between 2012 and 2018 I've published five novels; *Tall, Dark and Kilted, Boot Camp Bride, Scotch on the Rocks, Girl in the Castle* which have all been well received - and now, *Take Me, I'm Yours*. I'm currently working on a rough draft of number six which will be a 'road trip' from Cornwall to Cape Wrath, north west Scotland with lots of fireworks between the hero and heroine.

I'm often asked where I get my inspiration, drive and determination from and my answer is, all around me. Just look, it's there.

If you'd like to read more about me and my path to publication, check out my website at www.lizzielamb.co.uk.

Lizzie
X

I'd love to hear from you so do get in touch

email: lizzielambwriter@gmail.com
website: www.lizzielamb.co.uk
twitter.com/@lizzie_lamb
www.facebook.com/LizzieLambwriter
New Romantics4 blog: www.newromanticspress.com
www.facebook.com/NewRomanticsPress
twitter.com/@newromanticspress

GIRL IN THE CASTLE

by Lizzie Lamb

A heart-warming romance set in the Highlands of Scotland

Her academic career in tatters, Dr Henriette Bruar needs somewhere to lay low, plan her comeback and restore her tarnished reputation.

Fate takes her to a remote Scottish castle to auction the contents of an ancient library to pay the laird's mounting debts. The family are in deep mourning over a tragedy which happened years before, resulting in a toxic relationship between the laird and his son, Keir MacKenzie. Cue a phantom piper, a lost Jacobite treasure, and a cast of characters who - with Henri's help, encourage the MacKenzies to confront the past and move on.

However - will the Girl in the Castle be able to return to university once her task is completed, and leave gorgeous, sexy Keir MacKenzie behind?

Some reviews for Girl in the Castle

"It was the first paragraph that did it. A ghostly lament, images of an ancient Scottish castle above a loch, swirling mists and - yes - the word Sassenachs. Hey, I'm a huge fan of Outlander. How could I resist?"

"Lizzie must have done hours of research to get the facts right and they fit into the book beautifully. There's also a bit of paranormal activity too, buried treasure and of course, lots of her trademark humour."

"One of Lizzie Lamb's big strengths is her descriptive settings; the history and Gaelic references she includes add such sparkle and authenticity to the story."

"I was totally hooked from the moment the heroine, Henriette, stepped off the train & walked into the swirling mists & the great adventure awaiting her."

"I wonder how many people are inspired to visit Scotland after reading one of Lizzie Lamb's books? I bet quite a few ..."

"Girl in the Castle is a lovely, escapist romantic read which is expertly executed by this talented writer."

SCOTCH ON THE ROCKS

by Lizzie Lamb

Family secrets, love and romance in the Highlands of Scotland

ISHABEL STUART is at the crossroads of her life. Her wealthy industrialist father has died unexpectedly, leaving her a half-share in a ruined whisky distillery and the task of scattering his ashes on a Munro. After discovering her fiancé playing away from home, she cancels their lavish Christmas wedding at St Giles Cathedral, Edinburgh and heads for the only place she feels safe - Eilean na Sgairbh, a windswept island on Scotland's west coast -where the cormorants outnumber the inhabitants, ten to one.

When she arrives at her family home - now a bed and breakfast managed by her left-wing, firebrand Aunt Esme, she finds a guest in situ - BRODIE. Issy longs for peace and the chance to lick her wounds, but gorgeous, sexy American, Brodie, turns her world upside down.

In spite of her vow to steer clear of men, she grows to rely on Brodie. However, she suspects him of having an ulterior motive for staying at her aunt's B&B on remote Cormorant Island. Having been let down twice by the men in her life, will it be third time lucky for Issy? Is it wise to trust a man she knows nothing about - a man who presents her with more questions than answers?

As for Aunt Esme, she has secrets of her own.

Some reviews for Scotch on the Rocks

"A cracking book that stays with you long after you have finished"

"I like the way she weaves 'older characters' into the story; how love isn't just for the young"

"Lots of romance, humour, quirky secondary characters and a mad parrot. I was kept engaged, right up to the last page"

"A five star romance from a five star romantic novelist"

TALL DARK AND KILTED

by Lizzie Lamb

A contemporary romance set in the highlands of Scotland

Fliss Bagshawe longs for a passport out of Pimlico where she works as a holistic therapist. After attending a party in Notting Hill she loses her job and with it the dream of being her own boss. She's offered the chance to take over a failing therapy centre, but there's a catch. The centre lies five hundred miles north in Wester Ross, Scotland.

Fliss's romantic view of the highlands populated by Men in Kilts is shattered when she has an upclose and personal encounter with the Laird of Kinloch Mara, Ruairi Urquhart. He's determined to pull the plug on the business, bring his eccentric family to heel and eject undesirables from his estate - starting with Fliss.

Facing the dole queue once more Fliss resolves to make sexy, infuriating Ruairi revise his unflattering opinion of her, turn the therapy centre around and sort out his dysfunctional family. Can Fliss tame the Monarch of the Glen and find the happiness she deserves?

Some reviews for Tall, Dark and Kilted

"This story is full of romantic Scottish themes; Kilts, bagpipes, scenery, Gaelic whisperings, Clan Urquhart tartans and Strathspey reels. Definitely an enjoyable read."

"I really couldn't put it down. Makes me want to buy my hubby a kilt."

"No complications just a relaxing story that drags you in to the end. Quite sad to finish it."

"You won't be disappointed ladies and men, you could learn a thing or two."

"I truly enjoyed this book. I stumbled across it on Twitter. I was looking for a light read. However, I had trouble putting this one down."

BOOT CAMP BRIDE

by Lizzie Lamb

Romance and Intrigue on the Norfolk marshes

Take an up-for-anything rookie reporter. Add a world-weary photo-journalist. Put them together . . . light the blue touch paper and stand well back! Posing as a bride-to-be, Charlee Montague goes undercover at a boot camp for brides in Norfolk to photograph supermodel Anastasia Markova looking less than perfect. At Charlee's side and posing as her fiancé, is Rafael Ffinch award winning photographer and survivor of a kidnap attempt in Colombia. He's in no mood to cut inexperienced Charlee any slack and has made it plain that once the investigation is over, their partnership - and fake engagement - will be terminated, too.

Soon Charlee has more questions than answers. What's the real reason behind Ffinch's interest in the boot camp? How is it connected to his kidnap in Colombia? In setting out to uncover the truth, Charlee puts herself in danger . . .

As the investigation draws to a close, she wonders if she'll be able to hand back the engagement ring and walk away from Rafa without a backward glance.

Some reviews for Boot Camp Bride

"Loved it"

"Another sparkling read, full of passion and laughter, but with a sinister undertone that keeps you turning the pages."

"A definitely great read, as was Lizzie's Debut book, Tall Dark & Kilted... roll on book 3!"

"That good I read it twice!"

"The dialogue between the two main characters, rookie journalist Charlee Montague, and world-weary photographer, Rafael Ffinch is brilliant and full of repartee."

Before you go . . .

Please Tweet/ Share that you have finished
Take Me, I'm Yours

Rate this book ★★★★★

Novels published by New Romantics Press

Lizzie Lamb

Tall, Dark and Kilted

Boot Camp Bride

Scotch on the Rocks

Girl in the Castle

Take Me, I'm Yours!

June Kearns

An English Woman's Guide to the Cowboy

The Twenties Girl, a Ghost and All That Jazz